THE POCKET INSTRUCTOR

WRITING

THE POCKET INSTRUCTOR

Diana Fuss and William A. Gleason, Series Editors

The Pocket Instructor series presents practical teaching guides for the college classroom featuring hands-on exercises for new and veteran teachers alike. They offer creative, interactive, user-friendly classroom activities with clear step-by-step instructions followed by helpful tips and reflections on the exercise in action. Adaptable to different class sizes and course levels, these favorite in-class activities are designed to get students talking, thinking, questioning, innovating, and learning. Gathering together in one place a range of the best teaching exercises in the field, The Pocket Instructor guides offer handy go-to activities for whenever you or your students may need them.

THE POCKET INSTRUCTOR

WRITING

50 EXERCISES FOR THE COLLEGE CLASSROOM

EDITED BY
AMANDA IRWIN WILKINS
AND KEITH SHAW

PRINCETON UNIVERSITY PRESS
PRINCETON AND OXFORD

Published by Princeton University Press
41 William Street, Princeton, New Jersey 08540
99 Banbury Road, Oxford OX2 6JX

press.princeton.edu

ISBN 9780691173955
ISBN (pbk.) 9780691173962
ISBN (e-book) 9780691256566

British Library Cataloging-in-Publication Data is available

Editorial: Anne Savarese and James Collier
Production Editorial: Jaden Young
Text Design: Carmina Alvarez
Jacket/Cover Design: Heather Hansen
Production: Erin Suydam
Publicity: William Pagdatoon and Elizabeth Blazejewski
Copyeditor: Lachlan Brooks

This book has been composed in Sabon Next LT Pro and Futura Std

Printed on acid-free paper. ∞

Printed in the United States of America

1 3 5 7 9 10 8 6 4 2

For the teachers in our families and our family of teachers.

CONTENTS

ACKNOWLEDGEMENTS

No one writes alone. That core lesson we've spent decades teaching our students has turned out to be radically true in the course of editing this volume. The debts we have accumulated surpass what we can faithfully cite here, an irony not lost on teachers of careful source use. We are grateful to Bill Gleason and Diana Fuss for entrusting us with the mission of continuing the Pocket Instructor series. For us, Bill and Diana are the models of faculty who use writing to teach their field; we hope this book can make some small contribution to showing the next generation of teacher-scholars how to do the same. Thanks also to Anne Savarese and everyone at Princeton University Press. They have been gracious shepherds of the project through the myriad stages required from concept to manuscript to printed books. The admin team of the Princeton Writing Program routinely fielded the roughest of rough drafts from the outset, offered invaluable feedback on our revision of the "Lexicon," and allowed us to treat "coeditor" as a part-time job.

No one should teach alone either. *The Pocket Instructor: Writing* is infused with shared wisdom from a far-flung, multigenerational network of writing teachers, some of whom we've been lucky to have as mentors and colleagues, but many of whom we've never met. They all bore with us patiently through many, many rounds of revision as the volume took shape. Working with our contributors underscored the value of being part of a community of inspired teachers who continually surprise with new and fun ways to teach a skill set we expect students will find daunting—or boring. We hope this book gives a welcome taste of the range of intellectual and artistic creativity that faculty can bring to the teaching of writing.

We were both lucky to experience career turning points via stewardship of Princeton's Writing Center. Many years and three directors later, we remain grateful for, and amazed by, the kindness, rigor, and sheer volume of helpful near-peer feedback provided by students to students there. We're especially thankful to our student Head Fellows (Jedi Councils) who, too many moons ago, helped us find our sea legs and taught a whole generation of Princeton students to "Be the Tortoise." Having accumulated more than forty-five years of classroom teaching between us, the number of students we wish we could acknowledge far exceeds the space available. We're grateful for their collective willingness to enthusiastically follow our lead, make class a friendly and kinetic intellectual refuge, and humor our various misfires.

It was also our shared good fortune to have Kerry Walk as our mentor while she directed the Princeton Writing Program (2001–2009). With her, we learned to practice the pedagogy of open-ended questions with many possible answers. We have always appreciated her standing exception to that rule: the correct response to "What do you like best about teaching?" is always "The students." Our longtime colleague Judy Swan has brought her superpower of asking "Why?" and "What are we hoping to accomplish here?" to countless enlightening conversations over the years. She has tirelessly demonstrated that writing across the disciplines, including in the natural sciences and engineering, relies on building blocks of motivated argument held in common by scholarly writers.

Lillipies Bakery served as the welcoming bunker where much of the early work on this volume got done, fueled by hot drinks, fresh bread, and the staff's warm welcome. As a former teacher herself, Marie's encouraging and no-nonsense humor got us through many a rough morning of drafting and revising.

Finally, but also first of all, thank you to our families, who have made supporting us through The Book a part of their own lives for longer than any of us quite imagined at the outset. It would not be finished in your hands today without their understanding and encouragement: Tim Wilkins, Fran and Will Irwin; Jenn Hall, Bill and Sharon Shaw.

INTRODUCTION

Quick: think about a piece of academic writing that really mattered for your own intellectual growth. For Amanda, it's Allyson Booth's *Postcards from the Trenches*. For Keith, it's Judith Shklar's "The Liberalism of Fear."[1] Why is it important to you? Did it change the way you think about a question you're invested in? Did you begin the piece as a skeptic, but ultimately find yourself persuaded by its counterintuitive claim? Did it model for you how you want your own writing to look or sound or feel? Why *does* it succeed in the way it does? Now, having considered why it's good, ask yourself how it got to be that way. How *did* the author(s) produce it? How can *we* learn to produce writing of that quality? How can we *teach* it to others?

The potentially unpleasant truth of such works is that they took a lot more effort than is evident on the page. Strong writing may have an air of deceptive ease as it places itself in conversation with both future readers and past authors, offering nuanced explorations of challenging ideas and complex evidence—and ultimately new ways of looking at the world. Its finished clarity and elegance hide the labor that went into its production.

In teaching academic writing to undergraduates, we often appeal to the familiar iceberg metaphor. What looms above the waterline, the salient argument that has the potential to make such a lasting impression on those who encounter it, is supported by a much larger volume of intellectual engagement—researching, reading, brainstorming, drafting, revising—that lurks below, unseen by the readers of the finished piece. The 10 percent of an iceberg that's above water would seem to be wildly out of balance with the 90 percent underwater. Yet that is the usual ratio for an iceberg in a state of isostasy—floating in perfect equilibrium.

Novice writers usually focus on the visible part. We often hear students say on the first day of class that they're hoping to become "faster" and "more efficient" writers, for example. But successful writing instruction entails convincing them to properly attend to the hidden 90 percent. When they do, they experience their own fabulously dangerous icebergs emerging from the depths. When they don't, their arguments sink below the waves, unsupported by the necessary invisible work that constitutes the vast majority of successful scholarship. The books students check out of the library but never cite in the end, the data collection that doesn't go the way they anticipate, the pages that get cut from the draft, the troubling counterargument from a skeptical reader, the false starts and wrong turns all *feel* like stalled progress. It can be cold and frustrating to navigate underwater. But the work and time students may fear is wasted never really is.

To teach academic writing is to teach thinking—that is to say, every step that goes into creating an insightful, rigorously argued essay. Success lies in teaching students not simply to answer questions but to ask their own, to follow their curiosity and question their assumptions. It lies in helping them cultivate a tolerance for suspense and uncertainty—for not knowing in advance where their research will lead them, what evidence they will uncover, what discoveries they will make, or what their argument will be. That intellectual openness extends to engaging with texts that are curated for them, sources they might at first find opaque, boring, or irrelevant, but upon further analysis speak to them in a way they did not anticipate and come to be valued for providing just that surprise. And finally, success lies in convincing students to take their time, to decouple fast writing from good writing and harness the power of radical revision. We teach our students to "Be the Tortoise," reminding them of that ancient race in Aesop's fable: the tortoise took it slow and steady and won, while the hare napped and sprinted and lost.

The Pocket Instructor: Writing offers fifty exercises for the college classroom to help student tortoises embrace the structured chaos of argument-driven writing, persevering through the iterative process that will yield their best work. Like its predecessor, *The Pocket Instructor: Literature*, edited by Diana Fuss and William A. Gleason, this is a practical book for instructors that transforms the abstract principles of active learning into concrete classroom activities.[2] We hope it will help answer perennial questions like, "How can I teach my students to build beyond summary and do their own analysis?" or more simply, "When I get into the classroom, what do I *do*?" In collecting these exercises, our goal is to share what we've inherited from the loud mob of teaching geniuses who came before us, and what we're learning from the brilliant new generation of instructors coming up with us now.

Contributors come from a range of institutions: small and large, public and private, in the United States and abroad. Many teach in dedicated writing programs while others regularly integrate writing exercises into their disciplinary (and cross-disciplinary) teaching. Some emerged from the extended pedagogical family tree of which the Princeton Writing Program is a part, while others provide exciting and innovative contributions wholly independent of it. This volume is for anyone, in any field, department, or discipline, who cares about the teaching of writing or writing as a mode of thinking. While the volume's focus on argument in a college context naturally privileges the academic essay, many of the exercises could nevertheless be adapted for writing in other contexts, including journalistic, creative, or technical, even though they are not featured here.

The exercises in *The Pocket Instructor: Writing* focus on "The Big Things"—thesis and motive, evidence and analysis, method and structure, and so on—as opposed to the construction of grammatically sound sentences and other matters of linguistic proficiency, for which there is already a superabundance of resources. Mechanics do matter, of course, and we find that inviting students to participate in real, evolving, meaningful debates creates a useful incentive: they learn the details when they realize that's the price of admission to play with the big ideas—and have theirs taken seriously. Teaching this way involves treating students as junior scholars, which in turn means embracing two principles that are in clear but productive tension: 1) meeting students where they are, and 2) asking them to do ambitious things that they've never been asked to do before. Navigating this tension means encouraging students to stretch as far as they can in the context of a supportive classroom community; your own active instruction should model the target they're aiming for.

Some of the exercises in this book were originally developed for the writing or composition classroom. We are particularly indebted to our colleagues in rhetoric and composition for the practitioner research, rhetorical awareness, and teaching expertise that underwrites much of the pedagogy of the writing-centered classroom. But *Pocket Instructor: Writing* is not the product of any one discipline. Many of its exercises are sourced from faculty across the humanities, social sciences, and STEM using writing to teach their field. Here's why you shouldn't hesitate to browse omnivorously within this diversity: academic writing both is and is not the same across the disciplines. There is common ground (a good argument needs a good question) alongside variation (what counts as a good question in literary studies will differ from what counts as a good question in physics or sociology). Within a discipline, too, there is usually both common ground and notable variation. We see this particularly in fields that employ multidisciplinary methods, such as American studies, or cross the divisional boundaries between the humanities and social sciences (like history), or between the social and natural sciences (like psychology). Just as we push our students to transfer what they learn in one context and apply it in another, we ourselves learn from practicing that work of transfer as teachers. So we hope, for example, that you'll take the "Stages of Historical Analysis" on a fieldtrip from its obvious disciplinary home and apply it to, say, philosophy or economics or, perhaps, civil engineering. Likewise, we hope you'll experiment with "Charting Your Contribution" beyond the mathematical and scientific context for which it was originally developed and give it a try in your literature or anthropology or sociology class. For our colleagues in rhetoric and composition, for whom writing and its practice are themselves the objects of study, we hope the genre and disciplinary range on offer here provide fertile ground.

THE WRITING CLASSROOM

Here's the secret: every classroom can be a writing classroom, and it's possible to travel light to get there. If nothing else, pack 1) a shared set of terms for talking about writing, and 2) the draft workshop as a core practice. You'll find both in

The Pocket Instructor: Writing as foundations to start from and as undergirding for the fifty exercises.

Teaching writing works best when you start with a shared vocabulary, so we open the volume by sharing ours: "A Writing Lexicon." "Ours" is an especially complicated term when it comes to this particular list. "A Writing Lexicon" traces a clear genealogical line from Gordon Harvey's "The Elements of the Academic Essay," a writing pedagogy classic by virtue of encouraging teachers to do a simple, necessary, revolutionary thing: name what we're trying to teach. By isolating and labeling individual components of successful academic writing, Harvey made it far easier to see for ourselves, and therefore teach our students, how these parts can merge into a clear and persuasive whole. His list of terms, which has gone through substantial revision and some replacement, was introduced to Princeton by Kerry Walk in 2001 and has been influenced by the insights of myriad students and colleagues since. In particular, Judy Swan brought the perspective of scientific writing, Kristin Dombek inspired the inclusion of "ethos," and Raphael Allison came up with the nickname to capture its adaptability: the "Flexicon."

It's in the "Flexicon" spirit that the volume's first section introduces its core set of terms: motive, thesis, analysis, evidence, sources, key terms, method, structure, conventions, orienting, mechanics, style, ethos. Though calibrated for scholarly, thesis-driven writing, the Lexicon's terms are not just adaptable across academic disciplines but valuable for other contexts and genres where the motive of a given project or its audience is quite different. We illustrate some examples of its versatility in the volume's final section on "Transferring."

Along with "A Writing Lexicon," the second essential document to carry forward through the semester is "The Draft Workshop." At the heart of the draft workshop is a radical belief in readers and in revision. All too often, the assigning, writing, reading, and grading of a paper unfolds as a silent transaction between student and teacher. At best, any discussion of a draft happens privately outside the classroom. The instructor is the only reader, the writing process itself isn't a topic of conversation in class, and frequently there is just one deadline that is also the final deadline. Draft workshops undo all of that. Student writers gain the opportunity to hear feedback from multiple readers, discuss revision strategies as an integral part of their classroom work, and then rethink their arguments in time for a second deadline. Not only do they learn how to benefit from extensive—and sometimes conflicting—feedback on their own writing, but they also learn to be careful and considerate readers as they offer feedback to others.

The essence of the draft workshop technique—identify and discuss strengths, identify and discuss weaknesses, chart a plan for revision—is almost infinitely versatile. It can be used at almost any stage of the process, from early pre-draft materials to finished drafts, and it can be used for anything from fully developed arguments to paper titles, openers, introductions, conclusions, body paragraphs, figures, charts, works cited lists, transition sentences, or thesis statements. You'll find a thorough guide to draft workshop basics to start off the section on "Revising." Also included are fifteen brief variations on the traditional draft workshop, as well as two more extended variations in the form of exercises: "Speedback" and "The Editorial Board."

THE CLASSROOM EXERCISES

The Pocket Instructor: Writing is organized into six sections. After "A Writing Lexicon," the next three sections follow the arc of the writing process: "Starting," "Drafting," and "Revising." The "Transferring" section then offers a sampling of exercises that empower students to take what they've learned about writing in one context and make the challenging but all-important move of applying it in another context. The volume concludes with two brief bonus sections, "Preventing Plagiarism" and "Lightning Strikes." The former addresses the issue of plagiarism by spinning a topic that typically relies on scare tactics as an invitation to scholarship, and the latter offers instructors quick interventions in the writing classroom when they only have fifteen minutes or less to spare.

The exercises themselves consist of step-by-step directions followed by reflections, in which the author provides a peek inside the classroom—glimpses of how their own students have engaged with the activity, more detail on what you might expect if you try it yourself, and suggestions for troubleshooting. Reflections frequently include variations on the exercise steps that can help you adjust for time constraints, disciplinary focus, or follow-up activities.

At the very beginning of each exercise, just under the title, you'll find a tagline that succinctly signals the primary goal of each exercise. For example: "Students jumpstart the writing process by using voice recordings to brainstorm new ideas" (from "Copy That!"). Or "Students appreciate the value of key terms by losing track of them first" (from "Losing Your Keys").

Following the tagline are a handful of navigational keys to help you quickly gauge whether the exercise is right for the purpose and circumstances you have in mind:

Writing Focus: *motive, thesis, analysis, evidence, sources, key terms, method, structure, conventions, orienting, mechanics, style, ethos*
Teacher Preparation: *low, medium, high*
Student Preparation: *none, low, medium, high*
Estimated Time: *number of minutes*
General Disciplines: *humanities, social sciences, sciences*

The first three keys identify the main lexicon elements the exercise emphasizes, along with a sense of how much preparation is necessary on both the teacher and student side for the exercise to work, making it easier to plan ahead. An exercise with low teacher prep (or zero student prep) could be taught on the same day you first encounter it—we happily field-tested this scenario. (For science.) Conversely, students should get significant advance warning about the work they'll need to do for an exercise with high student prep.

The estimated time key does not include time students might spend on homework (reading, note-taking, researching, outlining, writing) but instead designates classroom time only. Class size, course level, even semester timing can influence how long it takes to execute an exercise successfully. Still, when first trying an exercise, it can be helpful to have a sense of how long it might take. You'll likely notice that most of the exercises in this volume congregate around the fifty-minute or eighty-minute range, reasonably common class periods for college writing courses. All of the exercises may easily be accordioned up or down, and many of them include explicit options for doing so.

Before you get to the step-by-step classroom directions, you will also find a more detailed account of the prep work specifying the materials—physical or electronic—that you and your students need to have on hand. For example, many exercises launch with students reading a short text the instructor has carefully curated for that purpose. Often, another text may substitute perfectly well, and contributors offer alternative suggestions or the logic for selecting a text oneself. Since time is at a premium, the ideal text multitasks: it shows off something we want students to do (or not do!), it injects new ideas or arguments into discussion that matter for the course, and it may serve as a primary text for students to analyze in their own writing. But don't overthink it. As instructors, it's possible to overvalue the selection of a text that cleanly falls into our course's substantive playground, when the most important thing is that the text exemplifies the intellectual moves being modeled—for better or for worse. As you'll see in exercises to come, we have a certain pedagogical appreciation for the Declaration of Independence because it shows the rhetorical limits of a listing structure, the dangers of claiming a principle is self-evident, and a number of other things that remain true in a class that has nothing to do with American political thought.

Because timing and pacing can be among the harder skills for any teacher to manage, we have included, at the end of the volume, five cross-indexes to help instructors plan ahead. The cross-indexes will help you quickly locate writing exercises that work particularly well early in the term, others that are suitable for the end of term, and still others that can be repeated throughout. You will also find cross-indexes for exercises that require writing before class, reading before class, or both. Finally, the volume's general index, which includes related key terms or concepts not highlighted in the lexicon or in the opening keys but that are nonetheless critical features of writing—such as brainstorming, researching, or formulating a question—will provide an additional resource for navigating your way through the volume.

Though originally designed for small or medium-sized classes, most of the exercises are flexible enough to be adapted to larger scales if needed. In fact, integrating collaborative group activities and draft workshops offers valuable practical advantages if you are teaching writing to a big class. Modeling tasks, circulating among small groups to answer questions, and reconvening to help students stick the landing allows you to leverage their engagement productively. And the opportunities for iterative feedback increase dramatically beyond what you would be able to provide on your own.

The exercises in this volume were designed for in-person teaching, but the COVID-19 pandemic forced an extended experiment in their application to a remote environment. We were glad to find that they translated quite well. We also learned we had to allow extra time for each exercise, since establishing the active learning paradigm on which they rely goes more slowly online. As a general guide, convert a fifty-minute exercise into an eighty-minute exercise, and plan an eighty-minute exercise to require two hours—and therefore probably two class sessions—unless you proactively trim the exercise or keep general discussions short. The technology for online teaching will continue to evolve, but as of this writing, there are myriad ways to get everyone on the same page even when they aren't in the same place for draft workshops and brainstorming sessions. Virtual breakout rooms have the virtue of providing quiet space for small group activities, even if you miss the energizing buzz generated by having all the students working in the same physical classroom. The chat feature works nicely for the distribution of handouts, as well as being a substitute blackboard for running notes on key discussion insights. It also invites contributions from students who may be hesitant to participate in other ways.

In short, the active learning pedagogy that makes such a difference for student engagement in three dimensions still works in two, but it takes a little more work to establish. If you find yourself teaching writing remotely, we think you'll find it possible, and worth the investment, to adjust the following exercises to the virtual environment. For specialized guidance in doing so with thoughtfulness and intention, we highly recommend *Small Teaching Online: Applying Learning Science in Online Classes* (2019), by Flower Darby with James M. Lang.[3]

WHY THIS BOOK?

Given the quantity and quality of guides on writing and teaching writing that are currently available, you may reasonably ask what justifies one more. We view *The Pocket Instructor: Writing* as complementing rather than superseding these works, precisely because of how much we have learned from them and the extent to which they have shaped our classrooms and helped our students. That said: *The Pocket Instructor: Writing* is teacher-facing (a user-friendly guide for instructors) and not student-facing (a writing resource for undergraduates), which already distinguishes it from a broad swath of print and online resources about writing.

Among our perennial go-to resources for students, *The Craft of Research* (4th edition, 2016), by Wayne C. Booth, Gregory G. Columb, Joseph M. Williams, Joseph Bizup, and William T. Fitzgerald and *The Imaginative Argument: A Practical Manifesto for Writers* (2nd edition, 2017) by Frank Cioffi are both incisive guides to argument formation and the research process. Gerald Graff and Cathy Birkenstein's *They Say, I Say: The Moves that Matter in Academic Writing* (2021), now in its 7th edition, lucidly articulates common ground across the disciplines and empowers students to practice the work of scholarship through a series of short templates.[4]

We often assign snippets from Peter Elbow, whose classic books *Writing with Power* (2nd edition, 1998) and *Writing Without Teachers* (2nd edition, 1998) have encouraged generations of students to engage writing as a process that helps them find their voice and be heard. More recently, Richard E. Miller and Ann Jurecic's invaluable *Habits of the Creative Mind: A Guide to Reading, Writing, and Thinking* (2nd edition, 2019) helps students discover and practice the curiosity that makes it meaningful to write. Perhaps our all-time favorite is Anne Lamott's *Bird by Bird: Some Instructions on Writing and Life* (2nd edition, 2019). Lamott's book isn't specific to academic argument, but the relief on students' faces when we read together her "Shitty First Drafts" as they're trying to get started on a paper is priceless.[5]

John C. Bean and Dan Melzer's *Engaging Ideas* (3rd edition, 2021) is one of the most comprehensive guides available when it comes to teaching writing as thinking. The latest edition is an essential resource for everything from assignment design to grading and offering feedback, and its guidance on tasks that promote active learning provides a useful complement to the detailed exercises offered in this volume. Another valuable complement can be found in *Small Teaching: Everyday Lessons from the Science of Learning* (2nd edition, 2021), by James M. Lang (who also cowrote *Small Teaching Online*, mentioned above). This handy book identifies targeted interventions that make a big difference in the classroom, no matter what kind of course you teach.[6] One fabulous article that we've used over the years to teach students and faculty about scholarly motive is Mark Gaipa's "Breaking into the Conversation: How Students Can Acquire Authority for Their Writing."[7]

Finally, books on teaching writing designed for high school instructors abound, and frequently include creative, detailed lesson plans. Those for an advanced high school writing curriculum can be very valuable for college instructors, in some cases because the same techniques may transfer well to your classroom and in other cases because simply understanding more about what your students may have experienced as high school writers provides you with crucial context. As two excellent examples in this category, we recommend *Lesson Plans for Teaching Writing* (2007), edited by Chris Jennings Dixon, and *Teaching Arguments: Rhetorical Comprehension, Critique, and Response* (2015), by Jennifer Fletcher.[8]

Within college and university writing programs, many instructors enthusiastically exchange plans on an ad hoc basis. It's rare, though, to find writing exercises formalized and made broadly accessible, either for writing program instructors or indeed for faculty elsewhere in the university who may be new to using writing as a tool for teaching their discipline. We hope you'll find *The Pocket Instructor: Writing* a useful addition to your library as you embark with students on their iceberg adventures.

NOTES

1. Allyson Booth, *Postcards from the Trenches: Negotiating the Space Between Modernism and the First World War* (New York: Oxford University Press, 1996); Judith N. Shklar, "The Liberalism of Fear," in *Liberalism and the Moral Life*, edited by Nancy L. Rosenblum (Cambridge, MA: Harvard University Press, 1989).

2. Diana Fuss and William A. Gleason, *The Pocket Instructor: Literature; 101 Exercises for the College Classroom* (Princeton, NJ: Princeton University Press, 2016).
3. Flower Darby, *Small Teaching Online: Applying Learning Science in Online Classes*, with James M. Lang (San Francisco: Jossey-Bass, 2019).
4. Wayne C. Booth, Gregory G. Columb, Joseph M. Williams, Joseph Bizup, and William T. Fitzgerald, *The Craft of Research*, 4th ed. (Chicago: Chicago University Press, 2016); Frank L. Cioffi, *The Imaginative Argument: A Practical Manifesto for Writers*, 2nd ed. (Princeton, NJ: Princeton University Press, 2017); Gerald Graff and Cathy Birkenstein, *They Say, I Say: The Moves That Matter in Academic Writing*, 7th ed. (New York: Norton, 2021).
5. Peter Elbow, *Writing With Power: Techniques for Mastering the Writing Process*, 2nd ed. (New York: Oxford University Press, 1998); Peter Elbow, *Writing Without Teachers*, 2nd ed. (New York, Oxford University Press, 1998); Richard E. Miller and Ann Jurecic, *Habits of the Creative Mind: A Guide to Reading, Writing, and Thinking*, 2nd ed. (Boston: Bedford, 2020; Anne Lamott, *Bird by Bird: Some Instructions on Writing and Life*, 25th Anniversary Edition (New York: Anchor Books, 2019).
6. John C. Bean and Dan Melzer, *Engaging Ideas: The Professor's Guide to Integrating Writing, Critical Thinking, and Active Learning in the Classroom*, 3rd ed. (San Francisco: Jossey-Bass, 2021); James M. Lang, *Small Teaching: Everyday Lessons from the Science of Learning*, 2nd ed. (San Francisco: Jossey Bass, 2021).
7. Mark Gaipa, "Breaking into the Conversation: How Students Can Acquire Authority for Their Writing," in *Pedagogy*, Volume 4, Issue 3, Fall 2004, 419–437.
8. Chris Jennings Dixon, ed., *Lesson Plans for Teaching Writing* (Champaign, IL: National Council of Teachers of English, 2007); Jennifer Fletcher, *Teaching Arguments: Rhetorical Comprehension, Critique, and Response* (Portland, ME: Stenhouse, 2015).

A WRITING LEXICON

Read that title closely, we encourage students. It's not "*The* Writing Lexicon." It's "*A* Writing Lexicon," affectionately known as the "Flexicon." Motive, thesis, analysis, evidence, sources, key terms, method, structure, conventions, orienting, mechanics, style, ethos—these lexicon terms aren't by any means the only ones you can use to talk about writing. Nor are they intended as a set of definitional constraints. Instead, they are a generative way to identify the constituent parts and qualities of writing that travel well across the academic landscape and help navigate its deep disciplinary diversity. To help you select, sequence, or mix and match lessons, a "Writing Focus" key calibrated to the lexicon accompanies each exercise. "Project Falcon," for example, prioritizes motive and thesis, while "Wrecking a Sentence" is a valuable tool for teaching style, mechanics, and conventions. Following "A Writing Lexicon" itself, you'll find two exercises that are well suited to introducing it at the start of the semester ("Declaring Your Independence" and "A Small Green Turtle"), as well as one that's especially helpful for students who have some experience working with it already ("Student, Grade Thyself"). Any lexicon will work best when actively revised to suit your teaching needs—especially over time, based on what you learn from your own students and colleagues. We've done that ourselves here, updating the lexicon we inherited to reflect the way we've come to teach different writing concepts and the close relationships between them. But there's nothing sacred about these terms or definitions. We encourage you to tinker away!

A WRITING LEXICON

A Writing Lexicon

These terms help break down and identify key component parts, functions, or qualities, of academic writing.

Motive: The compelling question, problem, or puzzle to which the essay's **thesis** responds. It is the writer's responsibility to ground their motive in a fair assessment of the **evidence**, and to demonstrate why a persuasive answer matters. A strong motive specifies why the reader should care about the **thesis**, identifies where there is room for fresh insight in an ongoing scholarly conversation, and lays the groundwork for a valuable contribution. The major **structural** goal of an essay's introduction is to set up the motive (and **thesis**), though motive should reemerge, in layered and complex ways, throughout an essay, especially in its conclusion. These layers of motive are distinct from a writer's personal motivation for choosing a topic or making an argument, but personal motivation can be a powerful source of energy for an essay. Different fields have different **conventions** for whether and to what extent traces of personal motivation appear in a scholarly work.

Thesis: The central argument that drives an essay. A successful thesis clearly and persuasively advances a position or offers an interpretation that fills the niche opened by the essay's **motive**. The thesis should not be obviously or self-evidently true, but rather builds its case through rigorous **analysis** of appropriate **evidence**. The needs of the thesis determine the essay's **structure**; each paragraph should be logically connected to the thesis, and sequenced so that readers can best understand and evaluate the overall argument. Along with **motive**, articulating the thesis is the primary objective of an essay's introduction.

Analysis: The work of interpreting **evidence** to develop an essay's **thesis**. Just as a strong thesis goes beyond pointing out the obvious or self-evidently true, so strong analysis goes beyond surface observation or summary. The particular **method**(s) chosen for analysis varies by discipline and by the nature of the **motivating** question being asked, but typically entails breaking **evidence** down into component parts, combining it in new ways, evaluating it according to a given metric, placing it in fresh context, and/or drawing insight through comparison.

Evidence: All material curated from **sources** for **analysis** in an essay to advance its **thesis**. Evidence—whether text, data, image, or anything else—should be chosen carefully and never cherry-picked, providing a fair representation of the object of study. A writer's **motive** emerges from the evidence, which in turn suggests further **source** material that should be consulted for an essay project. Evidence is never *self*-evident; writers must **analyze** it to develop their arguments.

Sources: Any material from which **evidence** is derived. While often texts, sources can also consist of data sets, artistic representations, physical artifacts, or nearly anything else. Sources provide the primary object of **analysis**, and they also play other roles—for example, giving **orienting** contextual information or defining a **key term**. Sources are the foundation from which multiple layers of **motive** emerge: they may generate your central question and provide scholarly interlocutors whose work your essay responds to. Sources may be *quoted*, *paraphrased*, *summarized*, or *referenced*, but regardless of how they appear, they must *always* be cited in academic writing. Careful source use and citation practices establish trust with your readers. You show the receipts for your **evidence**, making explicit *how* you know what you know, allowing your readers to track down your sources, analyze them independently, and make sense of the various scholarly voices you have brought together. The citation style employed (e.g., MLA, APA, CMS, CSE) depends on the discipline.

Key Terms: The most important concepts for an essay's **analysis**. A key term can be any particular idea that a writer applies to gain leverage on the topic or **evidence**. They might be everyday concepts like fairness, melancholy, or resistance. But they also might derive from scholarship: a philosophical idea (i.e., the marketplace of ideas), a statistical tendency (reversion to the mean), a social science principle (Goodhart's law), a scientific theory (punctuated equilibrium), or a physical law (centrifugal force). Key terms must be defined and used consistently to avoid confusion. They usually appear together in an essay's **thesis** with their relationship clearly articulated. Key terms are most often borrowed, with citation, from other **sources**, though authors may usefully invent their own key terms, and sometimes the invention and defense of a key term itself becomes a **thesis** (as with Darwin and natural selection).

Method: The procedure for performing **analysis** on **evidence** to arrive at the **thesis**. Writers must select the method appropriate for their **motivating** question. Methods usually derive from, and often define, disciplinary practice; historians are known for their archival research, literary scholars for close reading, and anthropologists for ethnography. Most scholarly fields employ multiple methods, and fields tend to share methods among them (both sociologists and political scientists, for example, analyze survey research). The term "method" can refer to multiple layers of practice: an overall philosophy of problem solving (e.g., the scientific method), intermediate steps in the process (e.g., forming a hypothesis, making observations in the field or lab, testing measurements for accuracy and precision, analyzing data), or a particular technique used in a given subfield (e.g., isochron dating for a geochronologist). Progressing through a field means cultivating methodological expertise, and the difference between experts and novices in a field can often be measured by their ability to employ its methods rigorously and creatively. The inability to apply an appropriate method, perhaps because the writer hasn't yet learned it, or lacks the time or resources to use it, sometimes constrains an otherwise promising writing project.

Structure: The organization and sequence of an argument. **Thesis** should determine structure, not the other way around (as in the five-paragraph essay formula, where *any* **thesis** is forcibly squeezed into: introduction, three **analytical** paragraphs, and conclusion). A good structure, therefore, is any sequence that conveys the relevant **analysis** and **evidence** clearly and persuasively. However, field-specific **conventions** and reader expectations condition structural choices in important ways.

Conventions: The **structural** and **stylistic** practices and etiquette of professional writing in a given genre or discipline. For example, the **structure** of many science and empirical social science papers is standardized: abstract, introduction, methods, results, and discussion. In the humanities, by contrast, the **structural** conventions are less transparent, which provides writers with greater freedom but also makes the expectations more difficult to learn. **Stylistically**, the prose in a lab report reads differently from a historical narrative of the Partition of India, which reads differently from a philosophical interpretation of Confucius's *Analects*. Failing to observe conventions doesn't make one a bad writer, but such writing may be perceived as unprofessional or unsophisticated by experts. Majoring in a field tends to expose students to its conventions, but they aren't always explicitly taught.

Orienting: Information that a reader needs to know in order to follow and evaluate the argument. Early in an essay, orienting must establish the context for **motive** and **thesis** without distracting from them. Orienting tends to emerge on a smaller scale throughout a paper—for example, introducing new **sources**. Writers must consider the expertise of their audience when deciding what type of orienting information, and how much of it, to include. Too little produces confusion; too much risks shortchanging one's argument in favor of unnecessary description.

Mechanics: The nuts-and-bolts rules that make communication fundamentally possible between a writer and reader sharing a language (e.g., grammar, punctuation, and spelling). Solid sentence-level mechanics are less an end in themselves and instead an essential tool for executing all the other components of the lexicon.

Style: The distinctive voice writers craft through their sentence-level prose; the aggregate set of choices they make about syntax, vocabulary, and tone. A poor command of **mechanics** detracts from style, and writers are typically expected to attend to the stylistic **conventions** of their field.

Ethos: The credibility and character of the writer as reflected throughout an essay. For example, ethos will appear in **motive** (in particular its good-faith stance toward its topic and central question), **style**, faithful engagement with **sources**, readiness to acknowledge counterargument, fidelity to **convention**, and conscientious attention to the needs of the reader. Writers should normally attempt to establish the ethos of a trustworthy, even-handed, transparent, and rigorous guide through their argument. Ethos varies across genres: op-ed writers may present as intentionally provocative firestarters, whereas book reviewers may become sympathetic critics, praising another writer's high-level aims while poking logical and empirical holes where the **source** material warrants. College-level writers are engaged in the long game of cultivating writerly ethos, even if it manifests itself in different ways with different writing tasks and evolves, sometimes in unexpected ways, with time and experience.

Declaring Your Independence

Keith Shaw and Kerry Walk

Set the stage for students to develop a writing lexicon on their own with an active reading exercise.

Writing Focus: *key terms*
Teacher Preparation: *low*
Student Preparation: *none*
Estimated Time: *50 minutes*
General Disciplines: *humanities, social sciences, sciences*

EXERCISE

Prep Work: The instructor should prepare three handouts: 1) the Declaration of Independence (or an alternative document); 2) "Active Reading Questions" (see sample below); and 3) "A Writing Lexicon."

Step One: (15 minutes) Distribute the Declaration and "Active Reading Questions" handouts. Divide students into small groups and ask them to read the document and begin answering the active reading questions with their group members. It's worth explicitly saying that you're not collecting their responses, so they don't think you're quizzing them (especially if this is used on the first day).

Since it will be quiet while students are reading, it's possible that they will be anxious about breaking that silence to start discussion. After they've been reading for five minutes, prompt them to start talking to each other. Wander between the groups to listen, and lightly intervene if necessary.

Step Two: (20 minutes) Lead a discussion based on their observations of the text. There's no need to proceed in the exact order of the questions, though starting with number one gets them to the *thesis* right away. As you hit on lexicon terms, collect them on the board (using either the "proper" terms from "A Writing Lexicon" or the terms the students develop, it doesn't matter). You'll probably get *thesis*, *structure*, *evidence*, and *key terms*, or their close equivalents. If you're lucky, you'll get *analysis*, *sources*, and *orienting*. It's not likely that you'll get *motive* per se, but they *are* likely to mention audience or purpose and you can spin that toward the idea. It's crucial that you spend time on motive (or its component parts), because it's the high-order concept likely to be most mysterious. If the students don't get there on their own, you can prompt them by asking something like: "What are some clues that Jefferson cared about his argument? How did he make his various audiences care? Has he made *you* care? How?"

Step Three: (10 minutes) As the discussion develops, encourage students to draw links between the various sections of the Declaration, and then generalize to similar relationships between lexicon elements. Track these relationships on the board. For example, students will likely connect Jefferson's long list of grievances against George III with the basic claim that the colonists should secede. This is an opportunity for you to link evidence to thesis via analysis.

Step Four: (5 minutes) Now that your students have named half or more of its terms, pass out "A Writing Lexicon" (and perhaps assign it for the next class). If you have time, ask them to scan it quickly now, and see if they can find any of the elements absent in your discussion from steps two and three in the text of the Declaration.

Step Five: (~3 seconds) Quietly congratulate yourself. Your class now has a working vocabulary to describe academic writing.

REFLECTIONS

We use this exercise the first day of academic writing courses. It provides the context for students to develop important principles for themselves, in the hopes that inductive discovery proves stickier than listening to deductive lecturing. The "Active Reading Questions" lead them to identify and assess the key writing functions they'll work with all semester. They might not volunteer the exact terms in the "Lexicon," but that's less important than their ability to identify the functions those terms represent. You could easily hand out the "Lexicon" first and ask students to find the different terms operating in the Declaration. It would certainly save time. But the discussions that result from *not* having the terms are the whole point of the exercise.

This plan is easily adapted to any type of course. It hinges on finding a short text, or self-contained excerpt of a longer one, that is substantively useful for your class and reasonably understandable to your students before you've taught them anything. For bonus points, choose a text that is both familiar and "authoritative," so that it will not have occurred to your students to subject it to critical scrutiny. The Declaration is a fun selection in part because of what happens when students discover they are allowed to criticize Thomas Jefferson. The license to do so introduces students to their role as active scholars and critics rather than passive recipients of others' ideas. Examples of alternative texts include Descartes's "First Meditation," sections 25–27 of Locke's *Second Treatise of Government*, and excerpts from chapter 14 of Darwin's *On the Origin of Species* or Malcolm X's "The Ballot or the Bullet."

The Declaration is a fairly easy read, but a modified version of the "Active Reading Questions" (using the "real" lexicon terms) can be used to help students break down and make sense of more difficult texts. Once, one of us (Keith; Kerry is innocent) made the dubious decision to assign William James's "What Pragmatism Means" in his writing seminar. When students failed to make much headway and politely suggested that he might be insane, an impromptu version of this exercise came to the rescue. It helped them better imagine what James was trying to convey and, more importantly, ask stronger analytical questions of the text.

HANDOUT

Active Reading Questions

Instructions: Read the Declaration of Independence. In your small group, work with the text to answer the following questions in as much detail as possible:

1. Distill Jefferson's words into three sentences or less. At its core, what does the Declaration *say?*
2. Mark the major transitions in the Declaration by dividing it into sections. How many major sections do you think there are?
3. What led you to divide the sections in the way you did? What distinguishes each one from the next?
4. Look again at each section you've marked off. What is the relationship between that section and your answer to Q1? What does each section *do?*
5. Circle up to five words or phrases that seem particularly significant to Jefferson's argument. Why do they matter?
6. Underline your favorite sentence and explain why it's your favorite.
7. Where do you find yourself especially persuaded or impressed by Jefferson's writing? What makes you feel that way?
8. Where do you find yourself resistant to or skeptical of Jefferson's writing? What makes you feel that way?

A Small Green Turtle

Ardon Z. Shorr

Motivate the writing lexicon as a tool that surfaces what we already know.

Writing Focus: *key terms, mechanics*
Teacher Preparation: *low*
Student Preparation: *none*
Estimated time: *50 minutes*
General Disciplines: *humanities, social sciences, sciences*

EXERCISE

Prep Work: Bring copies of a strong writing sample about your course topic that is short, interesting, and contains motive. In my class on conspiracies, I use a two-page excerpt (roughly a thousand words) from *The United States of Paranoia* by Jesse Walker. You'll also need copies of "A Writing Lexicon."

Step One: (5 minutes) Put two sentences on the board and ask a volunteer to read them:

I have a small green turtle

I have a green small turtle

Poll the class: Which one feels correct? (The first one). Why? Let students guess, ideally struggling a bit. Sometimes they'll have no idea, sometimes they'll find creative justifications to explain their intuition, and occasionally someone will happen to know that there is an English grammar rule that adjectives should be sequenced in a particular order. (I've never had a student who actually *knows* the order.) Any and all of these responses are useful; let them spend some time pitching ideas. The point is: there are some things we know and don't know at the same time. We know them unconsciously, but we can't name them consciously.

Step Two: (10 minutes) In groups of three, give students eight Post-it Notes consisting of seven adjectives and one noun in a randomized order. Their job is to assemble them in the order that feels right. The goal is to experience some difficulty in the task, and possibilities for silliness abound. Once they have decided on the sequencing that seems right to them, reveal the "grammatically correct" order: Subjective opinion, observable property, age, color, provenance, material, purpose, noun. (The seven adjectives you've given them, of course, should each fit one of these categories.) Ask students to read out their sentences and report on how well they did.

Some examples from my class include:

- A silly little brand-new orange Iranian silk ballroom gown
- A valuable heavy modern baby-blue French metal whittling knife
- A gorgeous rusted ancient crimson Romanian wooden decorative gate
- A dangerous small young green American bejazzled snapping turtle

Of course, we don't *really* care about the formal grammar rules surrounding adjectival sequence in Standard English, and you might take a moment to make sure everyone knows that's not the point—we care far more about their ideas. This will also help keep this step from turning into an unintended debate about what constitutes "proper" English. Explain to the students that the purpose of this exercise is not to enforce linguistic uniformity (or the social hierarchies such uniformity can maintain); nor is it to suggest there is only one authoritative version of English. Rather, you are introducing these rules as a metaphor to help foreground the difference between intuitive and articulated knowledge. Playing with adjectives reveals that intuition can fail us when the sentence gets too long. It's only by naming what we already know that we can level up to build something with a higher degree of complexity.

Step Three: (15 minutes) Now pivot to naming intuitions around writing. Put students back into small groups, distribute the sample, and invite them to articulate what they find effective about it. To help keep their focus on the experience of reading, offer three low-stakes (but very productive) questions: What do you like? What do you find interesting? What makes this persuasive?

Step Four: (10 minutes) Collect answers on the board, using their words. Students may or may not land on precise lexicon terms, but it doesn't matter so long as they get to the function. The concept of *motive* is often newest to them, and may require prompting along the lines of: "How do you know this matters? Why was this written?" Ideally, a motive-rich writing example will generate responses like, "It opens up new questions," "It feels relevant to modern events," or even, "The author disagrees with other people."

Step Five: (10 minutes) Distribute "A Writing Lexicon" and congratulate your students for already knowing what good writing is! Like adjective order, the lexicon names what they already know intuitively about effective writing. Though the actual terms don't matter—they're nearly as arbitrary as the adjective sequence—having a shared language around writing provides a powerful diagnostic tool.

Then return to the list of things the students like about the writing sample and invite them to begin mapping the lexicon's terms to their terms. This not only familiarizes them with the lexicon, but it can also help clarify misunderstandings. For example, students sometimes use "motive" to mean "goal"—as in, "the author's motive is to show that X is true"—when they are actually describing thesis. Or they commonly use "mechanics" to mean "the specific steps the author took to generate the evidence" when they are actually describing method. It's helpful to catch these early on and affirm that, while those are totally legitimate readings, in the context of writing, these words have specialized meanings.

Finally, ask students why a shared language around writing matters, and use their responses to draw links between the lexicon's terms. We care about *method*, for instance, because it informs the strength of the *evidence*. *Analysis* connects *evidence* to the *thesis*. (And so on.) Conclude by emphasizing that they'll be making similar links in their own writing projects.

REFLECTIONS

I introduce this activity on the first day of class, and it works well online and in person. My students have been surprised at the strength of their preference for "small green turtle" over "green small turtle," so much so that one time a student struggled to even read the second sentence out loud. When there are only two adjectives, they find their intuition gives them a strong signal.

But when sentences get more complex, relying on intuition alone becomes a problem. A hypothetical choice between a "small green dangerous turtle" or a "dangerous small green turtle" leaves them suddenly unsure. Escalating in step two to *seven* adjectives on Post-it Notes makes intuition alone insufficient to find the "right" answer. They disagree with each other, or comment that their sentence "feels weird," but they struggle with diagnosing *why* it feels weird.

The order of adjectives is sufficiently trivial that students seem to have fun even when they get it "wrong." My favorite moment is when students realize they have a specific preference but can't say why. Sometimes they make new connections ("I just realized Chinese does this too!") or generate testable hypotheses ("Maybe because most turtles are green?"). It's a form of safe failure that invites students to put aside their fear of being wrong in order to explore a wider landscape of ideas in the classroom. Moreover, the physicality of arranging the Post-its, or their digital equivalents online, invites a sense of play.

Of course, knowing the proper order of adjectives in Standard English might not feel life-changing outside of the Post-it exercise. But having the lexicon will. I tell my students that instead of banging your head against the wall, knowing that something is wrong but not quite being able to put your finger on it, the lexicon focuses your attention from all the edits you *could* make to the few revisions that make the most difference. Instead of doing some of these moves, some of the time, by intuition, you can do *all* of them, *all* of the time, *on purpose*—unlocking your power to bring your ideas into the world.

Since I first started running this exercise, adjective order in English has become more widely known as a fun factoid. That's ok—students haven't memorized the order, and struggle with the (unrealistic) seven-adjective example. Once, online, a student dropped a link into the chat explaining the adjective order. I simply asked them to see how far they could get with their intuition alone before we looked at the link together. (One such reference is Mark Forsyth's *The Elements of Eloquence: How to Turn the Perfect English Phrase*, which highlights adjective order as implicit knowledge.) Another time a student told me he explicitly learned this grammar rule when studying English. I asked him what that was like, and it turned into an opportunity to discuss the differences between learning a language as a native speaker versus through formal coursework.

When teaching this exercise, I always slip "dangerous" into the discussion of the small green turtle to set up what students call a "mic drop" ending: at its core, the work of writing in the liberal arts is about persuasion. Persuasion is about the power of ideas, not the position of the speaker, and therefore has the capacity to upset social hierarchies. That makes persuasion dangerous. I'm here to make you more dangerous.

Student, Grade Thyself

Keith Shaw

Trick your students into generating their own grading standards, which just happen to be your grading standards. (Sadly, this is not a workshop in which students actually *do* your grading.)

Writing Focus: *key terms, ethos*
Teacher Preparation: *low*
Student Preparation: *none*
Estimated Time: *30 minutes*
General Disciplines: *humanities, social sciences, sciences*

EXERCISE

Prep Work: Bring copies of "A Writing Lexicon." Time this exercise for when students are either about to turn in an essay or have recently done so. Ideally, students should already have some working familiarity with the lexicon.

Step One: (10 minutes) Place students in small groups, have them take out "A Writing Lexicon," and ask them to discuss how important each element is to a successful academic argument. How much, for example, does analysis "count" when weighed against thesis or mechanics? Under no circumstances should you explain why you're making them do this. Give them about five minutes to talk, and then ask each group to go to the board and represent their conversation by ranking the elements in three to five tiers. In other words, students don't need an ordinal ranking of each element, but they need to gauge the elements' relative worth: elements in tier one are roughly equivalent, and they are all significantly more important than those in tier two, which are significantly more important than those in tier three. Anyone who has participated in a fantasy football draft will immediately understand the procedure. Students will produce charts that have a ton of overlap despite some differences (see the sample charts in the "Reflections" section).

Step Two: (15 minutes) Talk through the (usually mild) disagreements on the student charts, while noting how the high degree of overlap suggests that we intuitively share priorities, and only disagree around the margins. Some disagreements are predictable and are signaled in the "Reflections." You'll likely find that this step unearths some latent confusions about what some of the terms mean and why they matter. That's useful! Give the discussion some breathing room, and your students might correct their peers without much input from you.

Step Three: (5 minutes) Allow groups a few minutes to revise their tiers, as the discussion should change their thinking. This will almost certainly move in the direction of greater conformity, though sometimes groups will double down on odd claims. Let it go if it's something minor, but it would be worth intervening if students insist, for example, that "thesis" is tier three. Be sure to reemphasize the near consensus about the relative significance of the different elements.

Now the big reveal: tell your students that they have replicated the standards by which you'll grade their essays. What they've done won't be identical to the language about grading on your syllabus, but they should see the strong intellectual affinity.

Close the session by sharing that you're doing this not just for transparency's sake, but also to demonstrate that we all agree on what the standards are, even if we didn't explicitly articulate them. Emphasize the importance you place on fairness and transparency in your grading. The shared criteria matter precisely to show that while grading writing always has an element of the *subjective*, it doesn't follow that subjectivity makes grading *arbitrary*.

REFLECTIONS

Teaching writing courses has given me a deep appreciation both for the creativity of student mythologizing around grading, and also for the damage that the mythologizing can inflict in the absence of a reality check. Despite many attempts over the years to communicate in my syllabus what I take to be fair and transparent grading criteria, to apply that criteria in my feedback on student papers, and to offer to meet with students to discuss the reasons behind their grades, I'm always surprised by the deep misconceptions that students retain around the evaluation of written work. But this *shouldn't* be a surprise, especially in a higher education environment that increasingly fetishizes quantitative measurement. Writing quality *is* harder to evaluate than, say, a problem set or multiple-choice exam.

That doesn't mean we can't evaluate academic writing fairly, but we must admit that it's complicated. And if we're not careful, that complexity can make the process appear arcane and opaque, or even arbitrary and unfair. The confusion surrounding different grading standards suggests we have an obligation to our students to show them how we grade, and in particular how grading is downstream from articulating what we value in academic writing. The good news is that sharing your process is also highly effective at building trust in the classroom. I now teach this exercise the class after my students turn in their first graded essay, and it consistently helps me build a community grounded in shared intellectual values. That they love the reveal that their charts are their grading standards, and are excited to get a peek behind the curtain of how teaching works, also makes this one of the more fun classes of the semester.

When you use this exercise for the first time, you'll just have to trust me that, so long as your students have been using the "Lexicon" with some regularity,

Table 1 ("Student, Grade Thyself")

Group A	Group B	Group C
Thesis/Motive/Analysis/ Ethos	Thesis	Thesis/Motive/ Sources
Evidence/Structure/Sources/ Key Terms	Motive	Analysis/ Evidence/Ethos/ Method
Mechanics/Method/ Orienting/Conventions/ Style	Analysis/Evidence/ Key Terms/Method	Structure/ Orienting/ Key Terms
	Structure/Sources	Conventions/ Mechanics/Style
	Orienting/Conventions/ Mechanics/Ethos/Style	

your small groups in step one will produce similar charts. A sample from a recent class produced the results shown in Table 1.

The groups' similarities clearly outweighed their differences. These students roughly agreed that thesis and motive matter most, and that some mix of analysis, evidence, sources, and key terms have elevated but perhaps not primary importance. They differed both in how many tiers they should have, and in how the remaining elements ought to be ranked. These disagreements are predictable and useful.

The placement of sources can be surprisingly volatile, as students often fixate on the citation component of that term. Some students are inclined to view citation practices almost as a category of conventions, thinking it means the citation format (which they view as unimportant), rather than the weightier ethical considerations. Others, fearing Honor Code Jail (see this volume's concluding section on "Preventing Plagiarism"), put sources in the top tier. This is a productive tension to talk through, but don't let it obscure that the lexicon term "sources" includes much more than citation. Be sure to discuss how source selection provides evidence and establishes scholarly motive (which usually leads students to revise sources' importance upward).

Ethos is also volatile, because, alongside motive, it's the most difficult element to teach. Some students tie the credibility component to thesis—"If they don't trust *me,* they won't trust the *argument*"—and thereby rank ethos quite high. Others tend to conflate it with style and underestimate its significance. In conversation I push toward a middle ground, as in Group C above. In contrast, almost everyone will put thesis in the top tier, but it's interesting to hear students walk through their arguments for why it should either stand alone or stand alongside other high-order priorities, like motive and analysis. Beginning students are likely to underestimate motive and key terms. You may need to make the case for why motive enhances thesis and analysis, and key terms enhance analysis and structure.

While you can argue around the margins, it's important to emphasize that there *is* a roughly correct hierarchy; otherwise, you undermine your own claim that these are the grading criteria. Usually, by the time students complete their step-three revisions, they arrive at enough of a consensus that I don't feel the need to share my own ranking. But when I do, it looks like this:

Tier 1: thesis, motive
Tier 2: analysis, evidence, sources, key terms, ethos
Tier 3: structure, method
Tier 4: orienting, style
Tier 5: conventions, mechanics

While I have never had a class respond unfavorably to this lesson, I have found it strikes home most with students who are used to being graded according to a highly detailed rubric. Once a typically reserved, composed student veteran who recently transferred from a community college stopped me in the middle of class just to confirm what he was hearing: "Wait, you mean you *don't* start by giving us a hundred points, and then take off points every time we do something wrong?" Since he had gone to a school that replicated this rubric across *all* his classes, it simply didn't occur to him that teachers had other ways to evaluate his writing. None of this is to reject rubrics as a valid evaluation tool; the point is simply to narrow the chasm between what we do and what even our most engaged students might *think* we do when we read and grade their writing. They deserve to know; sharing your process with them inspires a trust that pays off in myriad ways down the line.

STARTING

Get students started writing before they even realize that's what they're doing. Students often think of writing as the thing they do *after* the work of figuring out what they want to say. But understanding assignments, scrutinizing models, brainstorming ideas, curating sources, asking questions, learning methods, analyzing evidence, developing arguments, and responding to objections are all part of the writing process, not separate intellectual activities preceding it. This argument is an easier sell in some disciplines than others. Practitioners of the empirical social sciences, natural sciences, and engineering are more likely to view writing as a final reporting activity ("writing it up") separate from doing the work of the field. Scholars in the humanities and qualitative social sciences, by contrast, may more naturally define their work as indistinguishable from their writing. Regardless of discipline, though, the individual components of intellectual labor that precede drafting make for rewarding investments of class time. Cultivating expertise in a field requires showing students the virtues of a well-regarded journal article or book chapter as a target to aim for. It also involves breaking down and naming the steps that lead to the completion of that final product, showing how they fit together and build on each other to strike a path across the empty page. This section focuses on those early steps, featuring exercises in which students learn how to move beyond the classic five-paragraph essay, discover their personal motive for writing, decode an essay prompt, improvise a thesis, and other strategies for establishing an ethos and launching a project.

ESTABLISHING AN ETHOS

A Storytelling Game

Rock Your Classroom

Down with the Campus Food Monopoly!

Mapping Personal and Scholarly Motive

A Storytelling Game

Leah Klement

Students learn strategies for close reading by first imagining how they would tell their own story.

Writing Focus: *analysis, style, ethos*
Teacher Preparation: *low*
Student Preparation: *none*
Estimated Time: *45 minutes*
General Disciplines: *humanities, social sciences*

EXERCISE

Prep Work: Typically none. Inspired by Geoffrey Chaucer's *Canterbury Tales*, in which a group of pilgrims, strangers to each other, keep themselves entertained on their journey to Canterbury by trading stories, this exercise similarly invites students to play storyteller. If the *Canterbury Tales* are germane to your course topic, then you could pair this exercise with Chaucer's General Prologue or a tale or two. But if not, introducing the basic premise of the storytelling game works fine, and no prep work is involved. It's ideal for early in the term.

Step One: (8 minutes) Tell your students that you will be starting class that day with a game: you are all about to embark on the journey of the quarter/semester together, and each student will be asked to tell one story to introduce themselves to the group. It could be a story about something that happened to them, but it could also be a story that they have heard and found interesting, or that represents an idea they feel passionately about. Emphasize that the story need not be personal nor disclose sensitive information. It should simply tell the class something—whatever they wish, however big or small—about who they are. Give them some time to plan their story out. (Some students may ask for more guidance on structuring their story; you can politely decline. The success of the exercise rests on them considering, and weighing, their own narrative decisions.)

Step Two: (7 minutes) Have students partner up and begin telling their stories to each other. Prompt them to switch storytellers after about three minutes. They may not have finished their stories—this is okay.

Step Three: (10 minutes) Pause the class and announce that you won't be asking students to share their stories with the whole group, unless they particularly wish to do so. (This generally provokes a collective sigh of relief, though some students may be eager to share.) Instead, ask them to reflect on the questions and decisions that went through their minds as they figured out what they wanted to say. Ask students to talk to their partner about the storytelling experience, and to write down, together, as many of those decisions and questions as they can remember. How did they choose their topic? How did they figure out where to start? What tone were they aiming for and how did that affect their choice of wording or the form of their story? Did they change their storytelling based on their partner's reaction? What did the listener notice most in the story, and what decision-making process went into creating that element for the speaker?

While the students are working with their partners, draw a chart on the board with two columns. At the top of the first column, write: "Questions that went through our minds." Don't title the second column yet.

Step Four: (20 minutes) Now bring the students back together to compare their results. You might invite a couple of groups to share their responses to get the discussion started, writing the questions that they generated in the first column on the chart. Add new questions as the other groups report, and lead the class in a discussion of their findings. What kinds of questions did they need to answer in order to prepare their story? Why?

After 7 or 8 minutes, shift the students' attention to the second column on the chart, to which you can now add this title: "Questions to ask about textual narratives." For the rest of the exercise, help students translate the questions they felt they had to answer before they could turn their own stories into questions that they can ask when doing a close reading. This discussion is the real meat of the exercise, so spend plenty of time here.

At the end of the exercise, students should have a list of essential questions for analyzing texts. By reflecting on their own experience as storytellers, students learn what categories of things to pay attention to when they're analyzing narratives. That kind of analysis is a foundational skill for scholarly writing.

REFLECTIONS

This exercise works particularly well in one of the first few course meetings, both because its performative element creates energy and because it asks students to generate analytical questions rooted in their own experience, rather than a prepared text. Announcing that they will be telling each other stories provokes a murmur and some excitement about the upcoming performance. A little bit of anxiety can help engage students in the narrative planning that is critical to this activity. I want students to start thinking about the choice of story, and how to tell it, with the slight pressure of their peers' reception in their minds. At the same time, however, it is important that the exercise not cause students undue stress, and so I always emphasize that their stories need not include any information they don't want to share. I've used this exercise in writing courses, an introduction to literary analysis, and an English literature survey course, but it can be used in any course with an element of narrative analysis.

Many novice writers struggle to adopt a critical approach to analyzing textual narratives. Written texts can look like a sea of details, each one potentially as significant as another. Frustrated students sometimes conclude that textual analysis is therefore "arbitrary." I have found this exercise helpful in flipping the script for students. Casting them temporarily in the role of author and performer—and helping them reflect on their own practice as social beings and storytellers—make them more sensitive to the many decisions and possible alternatives that go into composition. Some students will disclose that they really couldn't decide between stories and were panicking. Lean into these comments! They help students acknowledge the complexity of trying to communicate through the written word and start to notice the elements of writing that are "behind the scenes." I also like to point out that even if students feel like novices in textual interpretation, they have demonstrated through this exercise that they already possess valuable expertise about major factors that shape the writing and reading of texts. If they can bring the active frame of mind that they had while considering their story to their analysis of other narrative texts, they will be off to a great start.

Though it looks like a simple storytelling game, the exercise quietly leads students to reflect on their own narrative process in order to develop a set of analytical questions to guide close reading. Sometimes, when students are working with their partners in step three, they will focus only on their choice of story, and not fully notice all the other decisions they made during and after that big decision. In these cases, you may need to prompt them to get more granular in their thought process and send them back to their partners for some further reflection. Usually, however, I find that as a group, students are able to generate many useful critical questions that they can then carry over to their analysis of narratives written by others.

Questions that come up with some regularity in my classroom in the first part of step four include:

- What story should I tell? Why?
- Do I tell a story about myself or one that I heard?
- Where do I start it? Where do I end?
- How long should it be? What level of detail? Isn't it going to be embarrassing if my listeners are bored?
- What kind of language should I use? Do I want to be funny, formal, serious? Do I want to imitate a recognizable writer or storyteller, or go my own way?
- What will my first sentence/word be?
- How do I show my audience the connection between the story and what I want them to know about me?
- What is my audience expecting? Who is my audience? What will they think of my story, and how do I anticipate that?
- What parts of the story are really important?
- How do I get the meaning of the story across?
- How do I make a good story out of this material (how do I make a narrative)? What is a "good" story in this context?

These questions touch on major elements to consider in engaging in any form of narrative or rhetorical analysis, including tone, point of view, audience, style, structure, context, and so on. Table 2 shows some examples of how you might help students translate them into a guide for close reading. If your field has specific questions toward which you would like to guide your students, you can of course adjust accordingly.

Table 2 ("A Storytelling Game")

Questions that went through our minds:	Questions to ask about textual narratives:
What do I want my audience to know about me? What do I want to hold back?	What is the focus of this text? Equally, what is (perhaps conspicuously) absent?
Where do I start and where do I end?	How is this narrative framed?
Whose story should I tell? Mine or someone else's?	From what point of view is this story being told?
How should I tell it?	What style is this text written in? What kind of language does it use?
How are my classmates going to interpret this story?	Who is the audience for this narrative? How might that affect its rhetorical features?
Should my story be funny, or serious, or clever, or suspenseful?	What genre does this text belong to?
How do I get my audience interested in the story?	What is particularly striking (resonant, suggestive, unusual, intriguing) about this text?
What level of detail do I need to include?	What does this text presume its readers already know? What cultural cues or historical (or literary) references, if any, does it include? How do these details help define the text's audience—both who is included and who is excluded?
Where do I go next in the story?	How is this narrative structured?
Eek! How do I do this in only five minutes?	What other constraints or context might have influenced this text?

Rock Your Classroom

Patrick Thomas Morgan

Juxtapose two disciplinary methods of analysis to teach students to fearlessly rethink and revise their writing, pushing the boundaries of textual interpretation and scholarly creativity.

Writing Focus: *analysis, method, sources*
Teacher Preparation: *medium*
Student Preparation: *low*
Estimated Time: *50 minutes*
General Disciplines: *humanities, sciences*

EXERCISE

Prep Work: Choose a poem and a sedimentary rock. Create two "Analytic Paraphrase" revision worksheets like the handouts provided below.

Step One: (5 minutes) It's the beginning of class. As students file in, hand out a poem, such as Emily Dickinson's "I Died for Beauty," instructing students to work in pairs to paraphrase the poem as succinctly as possible, condensing its lyric center into a pithy one-sentence description. When they're done, have them write their sentences on the board, being sure they leave room for a subsequent revision.

Step Two: (5 minutes) Now that students think this is a straightforward activity about describing a lyric poem, it's time to give the class a turn of the screw. Hold up a rock hand-sample, perhaps a light brown parallel-bedded sandstone (any rock will do, though a local specimen will give added resonance to the lesson). Ask the pairs to approach the rock in a similar fashion, encouraging them to be as adventuresome in their attempts to capture the rock as they'd like. Have them write their sentences about the rock underneath their sentences about the poem, again being sure to leave room for a subsequent revision.

Step Three: (7 minutes) Reconvene and ask students to read through all the sentences on the board, comparing their descriptions. Ask the students how they approached the two objects of study and in what ways they were differently challenging. Students will describe the poem, more often than not, in one of three ways: some will describe the plot ("The writer died for beauty, then is joined by someone who died for truth, and a conversation ensues, ending with moss silencing them"); others will use more generalized thematic language ("This is a poem about Truth and Beauty being united"); and a few students might use abstracted formal language ("This poem is composed of alternating lines of tetrameter and trimeter, with an ABCB rhyme scheme"). They'll describe the rock in even more reductive terms, usually fixating on color (like "brown").

Step Four: (8 minutes) After students have exhausted their critical vocabularies, distribute the two worksheets detailing three steps toward building an "Analytic Paraphrase"—one for poems, and one for rocks. The poetic paraphrase is a reading technique I learned from poetry critic Helen Vendler, while the rock paraphrase—a standard practice for describing sedimentary rock lithology—I learned from stratigrapher D. Jeffrey Over. The poetic paraphrase involves defining the poem's content (a one- or two-word summary of the poem's main mission, such as elegy, death poem, occasional poem), the sequence of major addresses (this is a listing of speech acts, like self-presentation, narration, lament), and the poem's form (meter, rhythm, stanza shape). The analytic paraphrase for rock lithology involves defining the rock's color (using a rock-color chart, with phrases and color samples like "pale yellowish brown," "dusky yellow green," and "moderate orange pink"), the rock's sedimentary structure (observing how the grains of the rock are arranged in a pattern, such as bedding, bioturbation, or imbrication), and the rock's compositional name (such as pure quartz arenite, arkose, sandstone).

After you have walked students through the worksheets, you can frame the activity by acknowledging that they likely won't know how to apply all these terms. These are tools experts in the field—literature scholars and geologists, respectively—use among themselves. Explain that while they might need further disciplinary training to deploy the terms fully and accurately, the next step of the exercise offers them an early opportunity to try out their analytic skills.

Step Five: (8 minutes) With the new vocabulary in hand ask the pairs to rewrite their earlier descriptions, this time in the form of the "Analytic Paraphrase." (Depending on your appraisal of what your students know, it might be smart just to give them the right term for one or more of the entries. For example, if the rock is pure quartz arenite and students can't possibly know that, just tell them that's what it is and ask them to use the other categories to complete their Analytic Paraphrase.) When they're finished, have them add their new sentences below their originals on the board.

Step Six: (7 minutes) Reconvene again and invite the pairs to reflect on how their analytic paraphrases differ from their first attempts at description. To guide discussion, ask: What insights into poems and rocks do these analytic paraphrases allow that were unavailable in the earlier descriptions? What kinds of connections are there between the way we analyzed the poem and the way we analyzed the rock? What was distinct about the approaches? How did the seemingly unpredictable pairing of rock and poem make you think about each object differently?

Step Seven: (10 minutes) To bring things to a close, broaden the discussion by asking: How might we envision the relationship between literature and science? One way to visualize this question is to draw a dotted vertical line—denoting a porous boundary—on the blackboard, with "science" on one side and "literature" on the other. Every time students articulate a relationship between these two disciplines, plot it on this diagram.

The aim of the wrap-up discussion is to have students recognize that disciplines may approach different objects of study with distinct analytical tools, including their own specialized vocabularies. At the same time, disciplines are artificial constructions without clearly fixed boundaries, and overlap in sometimes surprising ways—even in fields as seemingly different as English and geology. This comparative approach can be a recurring motif in a literature-and-science course, as each text and critic places science and literature into different configurations, articulating the porousness of that dotted line to varying degrees.

REFLECTIONS

I've found this exercise especially valuable because it challenges students' conceptions of a "text," broadening the horizon of what qualifies as a primary object of study. It also allows them to see the dramatic differences in depth between their first attempt at descriptions and their subsequent revisions employing disciplinary terms as analytic tools. In a sense, it does a discipline-specific version of what "A Writing Lexicon" does for writing pedagogy more generally.

I use the exercise in a science and literature course, but it is highly adaptable since every discipline has its objects and modes of description. In an art history class, for example, you could juxtapose a painting and a rock; in a law course, you could focus on a case study; in a performing arts course, you could describe a dance show on campus. For its part, in a geology classroom, you could use analytic paraphrase to expand students' views of what constitutes "data." Or you can encourage your science students to select their words as carefully and with as much exactitude as a poet.

This exercise also allows students to think about a crucial foundation of argument: the analysis of a primary source. By witnessing common intellectual moves across seemingly disparate fields, students can begin to appreciate how that foundation is constructed differently according to the particular discipline and object of study. Although disciplines have distinct goals and objects, they can often share intellectual practices—such as primary text analysis. And students can become more powerful and precise writers by attending to both the common rhetorical practices across disciplines and the particular vocabularies and modes of attention within disciplines.

For instance, we may assume that the sciences tend to orient themselves toward things and the humanities toward people. Once, a student mentioned how the poem is "produced," while the rock was "received." This led to a discussion of intention and allowed us to unearth fundamental assumptions students were making about the land. Students often presume, for example, that you can say more about a poem than you can about a rock, as if the earth is not worth as much analysis or doesn't contain as much ambiguity. It's as if, for students, rocks demand less from their readers than poems do, being apparently outside the realms of emotion, value, and moral judgment.

In the end, students don't leave the class with their questions answered but with their sense of possibilities deepened. "Culture" versus "nature," people versus things, pointing-to-the-self versus outside-the-self, temporal medium versus spatial medium, different senses of "form"—there are many possible basic observations that tend to emerge in discussion, including the question over how exactly we might align the two descriptions. If the rock is "out there," and the life event the poem describes is also "out there," then does that mean the rock description and the poem itself are on similar discursive levels, and that the description of the poem is on a level of abstraction all its own? If Dickinson's "I Died for Beauty" implicitly asks us to inhabit the private thoughts of a mute, dead body, does this mean the rock asks us to inhabit a paleoenvironment, as is the case with a specimen of the Wingate Sandstone formation, a sand dune environment from two hundred million years ago? By seriously considering sedimentary rocks as texts, we can illuminate central issues regarding interpretation, such as intention and how we read "the human" versus "the nonhuman." Ultimately, I want students to walk away with a larger sense of the kinds of things poems say, the kinds of things rocks say, and the ability to radically reimagine the way they look at a text.

HANDOUTS

How to Create an Analytic Paraphrase for Rock Lithology

(Combine Parts 1, 2, & 3 into a single statement)

1. ***Color***: use a rock-color chart to summarize the rock's main color.

Common Colors

light brown	pale reddish brown	dark yellowish orange	pale yellowish brown
moderate reddish orange	grayish green	dusky yellow green	dusky blue
moderate orange pink	greenish black	light gray	grayish black

2. ***Sedimentary Structure***: describe how the rock grains are arranged in a pattern.

Major Sedimentary Structures

cross-bedding	mud cracks	lamination	parallel bedding (bedded)
graded bedding	bedding (bedded)	asymmetrical ripple marks	massive
imbrication	bioturbation	raindrop impressions	symmetrical ripple marks

3. ***Rock Name***: classify based on physical characteristics (e.g., percentage of quartz/feldspar/rock fragments, etc.).

Frequently Used Sedimentary Rock Names

shale	pure quartz arenite	sandy shale	arkose
siltstone	silty sandstone	conglomerate	bafflestone
sandstone	silty shale	breccia	wackestone

How to Create an Analytic Paraphrase for Poems

(Combine Parts 1, 2 & 3 into a single statement)

1. ***Content***: briefly summarize the poem's main mission or type.

Major Poetic Types

landscape poem	travel poem	aubade	love poem
friendship poem	death poem	occasional poem	war poem
autobiographical poem	elegy	spring/winter/ summer/fall poem	

2. ***Address***: assign each thought-unit to a rhetorical utterance.

Common Addresses

command	exclamation	question	declaration
apology	narration	conversation	instruction
lament	supposition	plea	request
description	rhetorical question	boast	self-presentation

3. ***Form***: name (choose at least two) the rhythm, rhyme, meter, stanza shape, and (if applicable) formal genre.

Frequently Used Forms

rising rhythm	falling rhythm	iambic	trochaic
tetrameter	pentameter	sonnet	quatrain
terza rima	prose poem	free verse	blank verse
common measure	ballad stanza	couplet	triplet

Down with the Campus Food Monopoly!

Megan Brankley Abbas

Deconstruct the classic five-paragraph essay and show the value of a more complex argument structure.

Writing Focus: *structure, thesis, analysis*
Teacher Preparation: *low*
Student Preparation: *none*
Estimated Time: *80 minutes*
General Disciplines: *humanities, social sciences, sciences*

EXERCISE

Step One: (10 minutes) Begin by inviting students to take two minutes to jot down one thing that they would change about their college or university. They can proffer any type of change, no matter how large, small, realistic, or fantastical. Offer an idiosyncratic example, like "Prohibiting all courses from starting before 10 a.m. because I am definitely *not* a morning person." Examples tend to lighten the mood, encouraging students to enjoy themselves. Next, have students share their responses. Ideally, these responses will produce a lot of chatter (they may get excited about their ideas and complaints so nudge them to keep their answers brief). Make sure to jot down their ideas on the board (they will be useful in the next step).

Step Two: (5 minutes) Once your students' proposals are on the board, poll the class on which ideas sound the most promising. You can facilitate this quick conversation as a full class or in small groups, depending on how outgoing the students are. Use student comments to narrow down the proposals to two options and then conduct an informal vote. In my classes, two memorable winners were: "Improve the dining hall food" and "Install outdoor escalators on campus to alleviate the need to climb the awfully steep hills."

Step Three: (20 minutes) Now the real work begins. Explain to students that the class has been offered the great opportunity to write a persuasive letter to the College President about their proposed change. As successful high school graduates, they have, of course, decided to construct their letter as a classic five-paragraph essay. Their task is to build an outline for that five-paragraph essay together as a class.

Encourage students to guide you through the process of writing a five-paragraph essay. What does the introduction typically look like? What is the ideal opening sentence, and how does the paragraph develop? Invariably, one student will explain the need to start broad, really broad, and then gradually narrow the paragraph down to the specific thesis statement. Apply the student advice to the class's chosen proposal/thesis by drafting with them, on the board, the introduction (which is likely to be brief). Let them call out words or sentences as you go. You can intentionally exaggerate the scope of the opening sentence in particular, so that students later can consider more specific ways to orient readers to their essay.

Next, encourage students to explain how the three internal paragraphs work in a five-paragraph essay. What is each body paragraph supposed to accomplish? How do you come up with the major claims for each? Students will stress that you need exactly three claims to support your thesis and that you should use them as your topic sentences. Ask students to brainstorm a quick list of potential topic sentences for each of the three body paragraphs. Poll the class on their favorites and then insert them into an essay outline on the board.

Walk through the same process with the conclusion that you did with the introduction. What does a conclusion typically look like in the five-paragraph essay? What is an ideal final sentence? You can write out the whole conclusion, as you did with the introduction, or, if pressed for time, just concentrate on a final sentence. And voila! The class now has a classic five-paragraph essay at its disposal.

Step Four: (10 minutes) Take a step back from your collective hard work and ask students to assess the persuasiveness of the essay outline. What are the strengths of this essay? What are its weaknesses? Do they think the essay in its current form will convince their audience? These reflections are a crucial part of the exercise. Most students will quickly agree that their five-paragraph essay form is not particularly convincing, but they might need some prodding to identify specific reasons for why it falls short. Use this as an opening to reflect on what might make a more compelling structure. For example, you might ask them: If that unconnected set of body paragraphs fails to be convincing, what structure might work better? And how might a different structure better anticipate or accommodate some of their audience's likely concerns about their proposal?

Step Five: (25 minutes) Guide students through the process of using the mounting criticisms to produce a revised version of the essay. This step requires some creative, quick, and collaborative thinking. You may wish to continue focusing on causation and counterargument, two common elements in shaping an essay's structure. Ask students to consider ways of tying together those unconnected body paragraphs. Does one of the claims cause another? Does one serve as the foundational problem from which a series of branch issues sprout? How is their audience likely to respond? What are the potential counterarguments, and how can they best be addressed? This step will take longer than generating the five-paragraph essay, precisely because the relationship between the different analytical claims is richer and more complex. You'll likely have to foreclose some lines of argument to keep the thesis focused.

Step Six: (10 minutes) Ask the students to do a side-by-side analysis of the two outlines they have produced. What are their comparative strengths and weaknesses? Which is likely to be more persuasive and why? Students will see why the second essay is stronger, but it's also important to entertain what is useful and powerful, if limiting, about the five-paragraph structure. Then zoom out from the two outlines to reflect on what this experience suggests about essay structuring more generally. Rather than dropping a thesis into a predetermined structure, college-level essay writing requires the structure to be determined by the analytical needs of the thesis.

REFLECTIONS

For most college freshmen, the five-paragraph essay is simply *the way* to write an argument-driven essay. After all, its rules are straightforward and adaptable for any subject, and it served them well throughout high school. Most, therefore, are understandably reluctant to let it go. I like this exercise because it meets freshmen and other inexperienced college writers where they are. It recognizes their expertise in the five-paragraph essay form and then encourages them to reflect on its limitations. Many students will jump on this opportunity to criticize the five-paragraph essay, calling it "boring" and "restrictive." These comments represent an ideal opening for introducing more sophisticated approaches to structure because the criticisms are coming directly from the students. Indeed, rather than merely telling students that the five-paragraph essay is not appropriate at the college level, this exercise enables them both to articulate its weaknesses and brainstorm ways to improve it for themselves. It can therefore help sidestep two common student frustrations: that the rules for good writing keep changing on them, and that teachers seem to have arbitrary or idiosyncratic grading standards for essays.

This exercise is especially effective early in the semester when it can also be used as an icebreaker. After I give students time to ponder what they would like to see changed about their school, I have them introduce themselves to the class as they provide their answers. Icebreakers help students both get to know one another and feel comfortable speaking early and often in the classroom. This particular icebreaker of course has a larger pedagogical purpose: it's a brainstorm for the day's exercise on structure.

The exercise also establishes a shared reference point for later in the semester when students are struggling with structuring their own essays. It especially helps to depersonalize major structural criticisms of draft essays. Students often become defensive or discouraged when they receive critical feedback on their drafts, particularly if the feedback asks them to rethink the entire structure of their essay. An activity like this one can demonstrate that structure is a shared challenge and that, with a bit of creative thinking, five-paragraph essays can be transformed into more sophisticated forms of writing.

Complaints about campus food are a popular issue with students. At a prior institution, my students' collective essay introduction, in its initial five-paragraph essay structure, looked like this: *"Since the dawn of history, human beings have had to eat food to survive. Generally, they like food that is well cooked and well spiced. Our college currently lacks this human essential. Therefore, we argue that the cafeteria food needs to be improved."* In the conversation that followed, as we began to discuss the importance of causation in structuring an essay, one student suggested that we could blame the low quality of campus food on the college's decision to hire only one company to supply all dining halls and snack bars. In other words, there was a food monopoly on campus! Other students saw the wisdom in this remark and decided that the first paragraph must point out the existence of this unfortunate food monopoly to the president.

But was that all there was to be said about causation? I asked students to reflect on this food monopoly's impacts and they produced a list of important consequences: low quality food, lack of selection, and low wages for student employees, all due to the lack of competition. Were any of these consequences causing further problems? One student offered that the general low quality of food encouraged students to avoid the entrées and eat more fried foods and snacks, which was having a negative impact on the health of the student body. Within about twenty minutes, my students transformed a lackluster five-paragraph essay into an insightful and well-structured persuasive paper. They even revised the thesis statement into a stronger and more specific argument.

Students also did a great job identifying potential counterarguments. They suggested that the president might be concerned that food costs would rise if the college did not offer noncompetitive five-year contracts. They recognized this argument as a legitimate concern that could derail their entire proposal, but where should the essay address this issue? We discussed different options, but most students agreed that it would be best to locate this paragraph toward the end of the essay, after the president had already been convinced about the benefits of the proposal. Here are the essay's outlines before and after:

Five-Paragraph Essay	Revised Essay
Thesis: We need to improve the food in the dining halls.	Thesis: The food monopoly on campus is causing a number of problems and needs to end.
Paragraph 1: There is very little selection in the dining halls.	Paragraph 1: There is a food monopoly on campus, which has thrived due to the noncompete, five-year contract, the required meal plans, and the geographic location of the college.

Paragraph 2: The meals, especially the entrées, are gross.	Paragraph 2: This monopoly has enabled the dining halls to reduce selection and quality without losing customers.
Paragraph 3: The nearest grocery store is too far away and freshman and sophomores are required to have meal plans, so students don't have other viable options.	Paragraph 3: Because the entrées are particularly low quality, students eat more fried foods and deserts, causing health problems.
	Paragraph 4: In addition to the food and health problems, the monopoly has produced poor labor conditions for both student and full-time, nonstudent employees. Salaries are low, and schedules are unfair.
	Paragraph 5: The college might lose money initially because companies offer low bids to get that noncompete contract. However, more competition will eventually persuade companies to become more efficient, and better food will attract more upperclassmen to eat on campus.
Conclusion: For these three reasons, we need to improve the food.	Conclusion: Ending the food monopoly and encouraging more competition would make the campus a healthier and happier place.

Don't assume that all your students are already familiar with the five-paragraph form. It's an especially risky assumption to make about international students, who often encounter very different styles of writing instruction before college. Take a moment early in the class to acknowledge that not everyone may know the five-paragraph essay and to suggest that perhaps this "lack of background" will work to their advantage. This point becomes even clearer when the exercise turns to criticizing the form. Students without knowledge of this model can certainly contribute during the criticism and revision steps of the exercise. In fact, they are often the most vocal participants in the revision stages, drawing on their own training and experience.

Mapping Personal and Scholarly Motive

Amanda Irwin Wilkins

Students discover how their personal motivation for researching a topic relates to the intellectual context they establish for their scholarly audience.

Writing Focus: *motive, ethos, conventions*
Teacher Preparation: *low*
Student Preparation: *none*
Estimated Time: *50 minutes*
General Disciplines: *humanities, social sciences, sciences*

EXERCISE

Prep Work: Prepare two handouts: 1) Gordon Harvey's definition of motive; and 2) an excerpt of professional writing that includes traces of both personal and scholarly motive. The length of the excerpt you choose might vary from a few paragraphs to several pages, depending on how efficiently the text articulates the two elements of motive—and on how much time students will have to read and discuss.

Step One: (5 minutes) Begin with a careful reading, together as a class, of Gordon Harvey's definition of motive (handout 1). For the purposes of this exercise, it's helpful to pay particular attention to sorting out the key terms at play in the definition (intellectual context, audience, motive, personal motivation, private, idiosyncratic) and focus on the distinction that Harvey offers midway through: "Your motive should be aimed at your audience: it won't necessarily be the reason you first got interested in the topic (which could be private and idiosyncratic) or the personal motivation behind your engagement with the topic."

Step Two: (15 minutes) To delve more deeply into the discussion, ask students to skim the brief excerpt of professional writing that has traces of personal motivation along with scholarly motive (handout 2). Explain that the goal is to analyze the decision the author has made about integrating the autobiographical into their scholarly work. As they read, ask students to keep track—on a separate sheet of paper—of moments in the text where they see the scholarly motive articulated (in one column) and moments in the text where they see traces of personal motivation appearing (in a second column). These notes can serve as a useful springboard into discussion of questions like: How does the author implicitly or explicitly make the link between personal motivation and scholarly motive? How commonly in their experience as readers have they seen personal motivation made visible in different kinds of texts? What might be the arguments for including it? For excluding it? The takeaway here: there is no one-size-fits-all answer. It depends on discipline, genre, and—within those constraints—an author's preference.

Step Three: (15 minutes) Next, transition to the relevance of the discussion for their own work as writers, suggesting that regardless of how visible the personal motivation ends up being in the final argument for their intended audience, it can be useful to reflect on it during the writing process. Ask students to take a fresh sheet of paper, draw a line across the middle of the page, and respond to the following prompt: "Above the line, articulate the scholarly motive—the intellectual context—for your own project. Below the line, articulate the personal motivation, perhaps grounded in your own experiences." They're welcome to start either above the line or below the line, whichever feels more comfortable.

After about four or five minutes, ask for a volunteer to share what he or she has written, and facilitate a discussion about the connections between the two kinds of motive for the particular project; how the purely personal might be translated into a more generally accessible, scholarly issue; and how much, if any, of the personal motivation to make visible in the final document for a given audience. Generalize from the discussion to offer a clear sense of the parameters appropriate for the assignment at hand.

Step Four: (15 minutes) Have students work in pairs to give each other feedback according to the conversation modeled as a full group. The student who has volunteered can join another pair as a third voice.

REFLECTIONS

For me as a writer and as a teacher, there has been no more transformative concept than "motive," which I learned first in Gordon Harvey's definition. That definition forms the basis for the exercise because its very insistence on the distinction between a personal motivation and the motive articulated for an audience raises important questions for us as writers: If they're not the same thing, why is that? Why is it important to know the difference? What *is* the relationship between them, and what influences it? Those tensions and ambiguities animate the early work of the exercise before students practice mapping personal and scholarly motives for their own projects.

A few sample texts that I've found serve well as excerpts for discussion in step two: *The Great War and Modern Memory*, by literary scholar Paul Fussell (dedication and afterword); *Nature's Metropolis*, by historian William Cronon (opening five pages and final two pages of the prologue); and *Whistling Vivaldi: How Stereotypes Affect Us and What We Can Do*, by social psychologist Claude M. Steele (the opening sections of chapters 1 and 2). One thing to keep in mind as you're choosing your excerpts and leading discussion of them is the frequency with which traces of personal motivation are cordoned off in a foreword, introduction, dedication, or afterword. The insistence with which these borders are often maintained raises a range of interesting questions about the extent to which academic argument limits the visibility of the autobiographical, personal dimensions of motive.

Motive depends mostly on audience, which means we have to ask ourselves both about our own individual tolerance for traces of personal experience in the scholarship we read and about the tolerance of our respective disciplines. In leading workshops with interdisciplinary groups of faculty about precisely this question, I've been struck by the range of views about the extent to which it's appropriate for traces of the personal to appear in academic work. From the medieval historian who said that signs of the personal in scholarship filled him with a sense of "epistemological despair" to the scholar of folklore who saw it as an ethical breach *not* to show oneself as a presence in the project, the vehement reactions have revealed deeply held disciplinary beliefs and assumptions about how we know what we know.

While a detailed exploration of disciplinary beliefs is beyond the scope of the exercise, even a brief discussion can be a valuable way to sensitize students to the issues at stake where the academic and the autobiographical intersect, equip them as readers to observe how different authors handle those issues, and equip them as writers to make thoughtful choices about the ethos they want to cultivate in relation to their own readers.

Ultimately, though, whether we have a high tolerance or zero tolerance for explicit traces of personal motivation and personal experience in academic argument, the premise of the exercise is that to reflect on the personal dimension influencing our choice of (or argument about) a topic is an invaluable part of the writing process. It can offer an entry point for writers struggling to invest in an assignment, or it can give writers the chance to take a fresh look at a topic they know about from a particular perspective. One of my students, for example, used her long-standing passion for Pokémon to energize an analysis of the game's potential to raise environmental awareness. Her use of Viktor Shklovsky's theory of defamiliarization to build her argument was particularly fitting given that she herself had managed to defamiliarize her relationship with Pokémon from fan to scholar.

I've also found the exercise can help me as a teacher understand the underlying source of confusingly emphatic or ambivalent elements in a draft, as was the case, for instance, with a student whose highly charged interpretation of a literary text turned out to be entangled with memories of his older brother enlisting in the Marines. This should not be, it's important to say, an occasion for intruding on what's private. Rather, it's an opportunity to frame your feedback on a piece of writing in a way that acknowledges personal experience while focusing on how to ground the argument persuasively in the shared textual evidence that both writer and reader have equal access to.

The exercise can also be useful when it comes to helping students discern which genre might work best for the topic they have in mind. A student who had selected his grandfather's grave as the memorial site for a research paper had a great deal to say about the topic personally but ran into difficulty framing a scholarly motive. While not impossible to imagine a version of the project that would use his particularly personal site of memory as a window into larger historical and cultural issues, the exercise ended up clarifying that the center of gravity for the student was so far on the side of personal motivation that a personal essay would likely be a better fit than a researched argument.

I have been reminded in teaching this exercise how important it is that the concept of personal motive remain flexible through the discussion. If its meaning gets closed down to one particular kind of experience or narrative, not everyone will be able to connect to it. On one occasion, for example, students were preparing to write graduate school application essays, and many in the group readily began to reflect on the links between their personal histories and the direction of their research. The pattern was logical and recognizable: having witnessed—or having themselves undergone—an experience of injustice, discrimination, illness, or alienation, they wanted to understand the issues better through the scrutiny of scholarship. The hope in the room seemed to hinge on the ideal that by gaining a combination of knowledge and stature they might be better positioned to help amend what needed amending in the world. After numerous similar accounts that tightly threaded personal history and social identity together with scholarly motive, one student spoke up in a combination of anxiety, frustration, and confusion, saying, in effect, "I guess I don't have a personal motive."

Our subsequent exchange (with apologies to my scientific readers) went something like this: "What do you study?" "Ice cores." "Why?" "So we can learn from them about the possible composition of other planets." "So cool! But why are you interested in other planets?" "Since I was a kid, I've always been obsessed with outer space." "Hmm. So, you study Earth because you've always been obsessed with space. What's so great about outer space?" "Well, for me it's the thing we all ultimately have in common. The common denominator, the place where all our differences get reduced down to nothing." Which sounded like a pretty amazing personal motive to me, and an invaluable reminder that they do not all come in the same form.

HANDOUT

Gordon Harvey's Definition of Motive

Motive: the intellectual context that you establish for your topic and thesis at the start of your essay, in order to suggest why someone, besides your instructor, might want to read an essay on this topic or need to hear your particular thesis argued—why your thesis isn't just obvious to all, why other people might hold *other* theses (that you think are wrong). Your motive should be aimed at your audience: it won't necessarily be the reason you first got interested in the topic (which could be private and idiosyncratic) or the personal motivation behind your engagement with the topic. Indeed it's where you suggest that your argument *isn't* idiosyncratic, but rather is generally interesting. The motive you set up should be genuine: a misapprehension or puzzle that an intelligent reader (not a straw dummy) would really have, a point that such a reader would really overlook. Defining motive should be the main business of your introductory paragraphs, where it is usually introduced by a form of the complicating word "But."

From Gordon Harvey's "Elements of the Academic Essay"

LAUNCHING A PROJECT

A Moveable Feast

Copy That!

The How and the Why

Great Expectations

The Scholarship of Strange Sources

Thesis Improv

A Moveable Feast

Briallen Hopper and Rebecca Rainof

Launch students into a new intellectual inquiry and let them play classroom detective by sifting through primary evidence.

Writing Focus: *evidence, key terms, analysis*
Teacher Preparation: *high*
Student Preparation: *none*
Estimated Time: *60 minutes*
General Disciplines: *humanities, social sciences, sciences*

EXERCISE

Prep Work: Bring in a surprise assortment of primary sources related to the theme of your course or next assignment. In our cotaught class on Writing About Family, we use a large stack of illustrated children's books and photography books. Courses in other fields might use musical instruments, anatomical diagrams, film posters, playbills, plant samples, maps, star charts, cookbooks, food items—whatever generates a curiosity directed toward your intended subject and themes. The aim is to select sources that are good conversation starters and can be visually analyzed on the spot without special disciplinary expertise. Distribute these sources around the classroom before class starts. As students get settled, they will have sources nearby to pick up and scrutinize.

Step One: (10 minutes) Invite students to circulate and consider the sources around the room. Encourage them to talk together about what they are seeing, but don't overdirect—the point is to let them follow whatever leads the sources inspire.

Step Two: (10 minutes) Form small groups, ensuring each group has at least three sources. Ask them to discuss the sources with a few guiding questions. For example, in Writing about Family, we ask students, "What common themes seem to emerge among the sources? What definitions of family do you see being represented? Which images resonate with you and which inspire pushback?" Don't overprescribe the questions; students should pursue their curiosity and not yours. After a few minutes, follow up with a more concrete prompt: have them choose three key terms that they think best reflect the important concepts that emerged in their conversation.

Step Three: (10 minutes) Now have each group select one source they want to study more deeply. What strikes them as surprising, puzzling, or leads them to want to know more? Drawing on their key terms from step two, what analytical questions can they ask of their source? What more specific key terms might be useful to help us talk about *this* source? Have them agree on three analytical questions and three *new* key terms.

Step Four: (20 minutes) Divide your board space into two sections. In the first, have each group write all six of their key terms—the broader terms from step two plus those specific to their single source that emerged in step three. In the second section of the board, have each group record their analytical questions. Reconvene and ask each group to present on their source, why they want answers to the questions they asked, and how their key terms help in asking and answering them. As students present, it's worth drawing attention to those key terms that keep recurring or seem to do especially heavy lifting.

Step Five: (10 minutes) After the groups are done, return to the chaotic list of key terms. End by leading a discussion asking students to identify which key terms seem especially useful for considering the patterns and contrasts they observed, as well as the implicit arguments, assumptions, and points of view they noticed across the different sources.

REFLECTIONS

This exercise gives students the opportunity to browse a moveable feast of children's books, photographs, advertisements, maps, or other objects, producing an active learning environment that sparks curiosity, pivots toward analysis, and helps students make important connections between the work of the class and their lives outside. Its writing goal is to show firsthand how key terms initially emerge from analysis of evidence, and then in turn become useful tools to help analyze that particular evidence (and often related sources) more deeply.

We originally developed this activity as a first-day exercise, since it also works well as an engaging icebreaker. From among the feast of sources around the room, one group in Writing about Family chose to focus on *The Little Brute Family* by Russell Hoban, a children's book about an imaginary family of nonhuman characters, scruffy monsters called "Brutes" who experience a conversion from misery to contentment after the "baby Brute" brings home "a happy feeling." This conversion registers on the level of appearance (the once untidy Brutes are shown suddenly coiffed, smiling, holding flowers) and behavior (rather than fighting and grumbling, they now commune at the kitchen table and express gratitude openly). Sample key terms that surfaced included "class," "manners," "hygiene," "poverty," "animalization." Another group chose an anthology of images from *Little Golden Books*, including illustrations of the Good Humor Man distributing ice cream to smiling, racially homogenous families, as well as images from *The Pokey Little Puppy*. Sample key terms from this group included "race," "homogenous," "nuclear family," "middle class." Other groups worked with sources like *The Family of Man*, a book of photographs based on the exhibit at MoMA from the 1950s curated by Edward Steichen, and *Love Makes a Family: Portraits of Lesbian, Gay, Bisexual and Transgendered Parents and their Families*.

Coming together as a class to review key terms and think about larger patterns, our conversation opened onto a debate about whether depicting families of animals and imaginary creatures sidestepped questions of class, race, and gender, or foregrounded them in interesting and (often) problematic ways. Students from different groups asked: how did representations of families through illustrated animals change between the 1950s and present-day examples of children's literature? The students also discussed how certain books seemed invested in consolidating and narrowing definitions of family, while others worked both through text and image to expand or challenge those definitions.

Briallen also uses this exercise in a course called Writing about Religion. Asking students to consider objects including a *Golden Girls* prayer candle, a dollar bill, a box of matzo ball mix, a colander (important in Pastafarianism), and a box of incense with a lotus on the label, she asks: "How is this a religious object? How is it *not* a religious object?" These questions invite students to reflect on their preexisting definitions of religion and to develop working definitions of religion for the purposes of class. Are we defining religion in relation to beliefs, communities, texts, practices, and/or traditions? Do the words "In God We Trust" make a piece of paper religious, regardless of how it is used? How is venerating Betty White different from venerating a saint (or is it)?

Using the exercise at the beginning of the term helps build a sense of cohesion among students, allowing them to circulate freely, form more intimate groupings on their own, and get comfortable. Creating a sense of open play is key. Since everyone is encountering the sources for the first time, everyone can engage freely regardless of their level of previous knowledge or preparation. The conversations can then serve as a touchstone through the semester. In Writing about Family, we've also used the exercise later in the term—for example, on the first day back in the classroom after spring break, when transitioning from a unit on portraits to a unit on place. In truth, "A Moveable Feast" is flexible enough to be useful at almost any time, particularly as a curveball that helps unsettle, reframe, or otherwise shake up the terms of discussion and reintroduce the sense of exploratory inquiry so key to the classroom dynamic.

Copy That!

Jacqueline Campbell

Students jumpstart the writing process by using voice recordings to brainstorm new ideas.

Writing Focus: *motive, key terms, evidence*
Teacher Preparation: *medium*
Student Preparation: *medium*
Estimated Time: *40 minutes*
General Disciplines: *humanities, social sciences, sciences*

EXERCISE

Prep Work: For homework, ask students to select an object of study: a specific text, entity, or concept they plan to analyze in an upcoming writing assignment. Provide a prompt with open-ended questions that encourages students to explore subjective experiences ("Why are you drawn to this object of study?" or "What makes this object intriguing, exciting, confusing, or strange?") as well as test out goals for the upcoming assignment ("What do you hope to accomplish in this essay?"). Here's the twist: instead of writing their responses, students should use a smartphone or laptop to create a three-minute audio recording. Offer to assist any students who might need to borrow equipment and instruct students to bring their recordings and a pair of headphones to class. Make sure to have a contingency plan in case students forget to bring their device (save files to the cloud for easy access) or headphones (hold the phone to their ear instead). Prepare for odd numbers or unexpected absences by making your own recording if you like and potentially pairing with a student.

When introducing this assignment, keep the stakes low. Assure students that their recordings won't be played aloud in class or shared with you in advance. No one needs to write a script or spend hours practicing. Let students know that it's okay to speak off the cuff, change their mind, or ramble if they get lost—as long as they make it to the three-minute mark. Make it clear that the goal of this exercise is not to achieve perfection, but to instead take the terror out of starting a paper by providing an opportunity to generate ideas informally and share them with a peer.

Step One: (5 minutes) Break the ice and get students comfortable talking about the writing process with a quick round of "fill in the blank." Ask the group to complete the following sentence: "Writing papers makes me . . ." Give students thirty seconds to jot down their responses, then go around the room for a rapid-fire share. Locate any common threads and discuss. You'll loop back to this discussion at the end of the exercise.

Step Two: (5 minutes) Separate students into pairs to begin this two-part active listening exercise. Ask students to listen to their partner's recording and jot down a quick bullet-point summary of the main ideas that stand out. Explain that this step is designed to move fast: they do not need to editorialize or ask questions just yet.

Step Three: (15 minutes) Students then listen to their partner's recording a second time, but with a different emphasis: They listen not only to *what* their partner says, but *how* they say it. On the board or on a handout, you might prompt them with questions like: What do they notice about their partner's tone of voice, volume, emotional register, or speed? Are there moments in the recording when the pace picks up or slows down? When do they hear boredom, intrigue, or an "aha" moment? What sounds like the most important moment in the recording? Ask pairs to swap notes and discuss. You might also invite students to listen to their own recordings again, noting what strikes them differently when they hear their ideas afresh.

Step Four: (15 minutes) Reconvene as a full group and guide students' reflection on the experience of making and sharing their recordings. Questions to facilitate discussion might include: What was it like working in this unfamiliar medium? Compared to freewriting, what was it like to say their ideas out loud? Was the recording process comfortable or uncomfortable, and why? What was it like to listen to their partner's recording? To listen again to their own recording? How would they describe the feedback they just received from their partner? Thinking back to the icebreaker ("Writing makes me______"), encourage students to consider which aspects of the exercise might prove particularly helpful in their own future writing process (the informal approach to getting started? the switch to a voice medium? the early opportunity for peer feedback?). If time allows, invite volunteers to share a nutshell summary of their work-in-progress with the full group and highlight the new insight they've gained.

REFLECTIONS

Even the most experienced writers struggle when faced with a blank page. This listening exercise gives students the freedom to brainstorm ideas without even taking out pen and paper (or opening a new file), producing an active learning environment that eases anxiety and fosters creative risk-taking at the start of a new writing project. By asking students to explore the responses sparked by their object of study—curiosity, confusion, fascination, obsession—this exercise invites students to unpack their motive for writing. Though students' motives might emerge as rough and idiosyncratic at first, these insights can develop and sharpen through collaboration with a partner.

In a literature course titled The Art of Loving, students' recordings varied in structure and style. Some students repeated the prompt verbatim and answered questions step-by-step. Others started with the prompt, then followed a winding tangent. Some made breakthroughs, while others encountered more questions. Most students, however, hit a stumbling block around the one-minute mark—listeners reported hearing a big "um."

The magic happens when students "drop the act" and talk more casually. After the first minute, one student started making wry parenthetical asides: The Cupid myth, they said, offers unfaithful lovers an all-too-convenient story to explain what "quote unquote makes them cheat." Another student began by defining the "self-crushing love" experienced by Janie, the protagonist in Zora Neale Hurston's novel *Their Eyes Were Watching God*—only to launch suddenly into an impassioned riff on what they love most about Janie ("how she had the tree of life basically inside her mind"). They wanted to try "writing a myth" based on Janie's character, even though they "hadn't experimented with it before." The strongest recordings made these kinds of unexpected jumps: moments when students stumbled across an idea, insight, or approach they hadn't considered before.

When guiding students through steps one, two, and three, foster an exploratory and open-minded atmosphere. Remind them that this is a brainstorming session and not a thesis workshop. During the opening icebreaker, you might also ask students to share some of their own experiences searching for writerly inspiration. Do they pace around their bedroom talking to themselves? Do they need to work through ideas with a friend (or a pet) before getting started?

Framed in this low-pressure way, the pairs' discussions tend to be lively, and students are quick to praise their peers' ideas with encouraging sentence-starters like "I really loved the way you . . ."

Step four is the moment when all the threads of the exercise come together. Take time to revisit the icebreaker when students describe how writing papers makes them feel (expect words like "stressed," "tired," "bored," and "overwhelmed," as well as more tangled blends of anxiety and curiosity, creativity and critical thinking). Now, however, students can go beyond bonding over the shared stress of writing and instead reflect on how the recording exercise both eases anxiety and aids the writing process. For example, my group appreciated the fact that partner work "made the conversation feel more personal" and allowed them to sort through messy ideas in a "relaxed" environment. They agreed among themselves that the three-minute requirement is a must: "It was challenging to get to three minutes, but it was helpful. One minute in, my brain started to wander and I got some new ideas." Most importantly, they left viewing their recording as a tool they could use to get their essay off the ground: "I'm happy I have something to come back to when I start to write my paper."

The exercise can help students formulate a question or identify a keyword to explore. It can even help students realize that their current idea just won't fly—a key insight in itself. Several students in The Art of Loving found that their object of study didn't yield as many ideas as they'd hoped, and they skillfully shifted their focus. Even in these cases, the recordings carried within them the seeds of related ideas or directions. For example, the student who initially planned to write an essay about the Cupid myth later wrote about the archetype of "the dreamer," finding the question of love as delusion more specific and compelling. The student who experimented with an inventive retelling of *Their Eyes Were Watching God* soon expanded and transformed the idea of "self-crushing love" into a clever pattern of recurring images: the "crush" of first love, trampled flowers, a meet-cute involving two colliding joggers, and a ponytail pulled too tight.

This exercise can work any time: to jumpstart the first assignment of the semester, offer a welcome change of pace when midterm fatigue sets in, shake up the brainstorming process for a final project, or even revise a previous essay. These steps can easily be adapted beyond the humanities classroom for projects in almost any field or discipline. Ultimately, "Copy That!" encourages all writers to push past anxiety and discover what's driving their intellectual interests.

The How and the Why

John Schulz

Decode the mysterious genre of the essay prompt and leverage the moment to practice asking generative questions.

Writing Focus: *motive, sources, key terms, thesis*
Teacher Preparation: *low*
Student Preparation: *none*
Estimated Time: *45 minutes*
General Disciplines: *humanities, social sciences*

EXERCISE

Prep Work: Curate three essay prompts related to your course topic (not necessarily authentic) or use the samples provided. On the first (maximalist) prompt only, highlight each of its structural components in a different color, but *do not* label them. The other two samples (minimalist and didactic) should not be highlighted or labeled. Make enough copies of all three for your students.

A *maximalist* prompt contains 1) a topic, 2) a task, 3) contextualizing information about the topic (possible examples, key terms, and hypotheses), and 4) some generative how-and-why questions that begin to analyze the topic and its contexts. Here, for example, is a maximalist prompt I wrote for a course on Irish Literature:

> [**blue highlight**:] Irish literature is haunted. [**yellow highlight**:] In James Joyce's *Ulysses* (1920), Stephen Dedalus proclaims that "history is a nightmare from which I am trying to awake." Across our syllabus, the past has a way of lingering on. If the *Accalam na Senórach* (c. 1200) marks the emergence of an Irish written tradition, it is also haunted by an earlier oral tradition. Asenath Nicholson's account of The Great Hunger depicts the starving as ghosts of their former selves. Then, in the drama of Patrick Pearse and Sean O'Casey, and, later, in Seamus Heaney's *North* (1975), the memory of the Irish Rebellion of 1798 resurfaces in evolving contexts of Irish independence. [**green highlight**:] Choose a text from our syllabus and make an argument about its meaning as haunted literature. [**magenta highlight**:] How does this haunting manifest itself and why? What, for instance, might your text's haunting(s) tell us about Irish history, the dream of independence, or how Irish writers imagine adversity? [**green highlight**:] Make sure your thesis has a motive and be sure to ground your

> argument in a close reading of evidence from the specific text you have chosen.

The *minimalist* prompt contains a topic and a task, but little else. For instance:

> Pick one poem from Heaney's *North*. Make an argument about surprising or puzzling imagery that Heaney uses to represent the Troubles in Northern Ireland.
>
> (In this example, "Heaney's *North*," "surprising or puzzling imagery," and "the Troubles" represent the topic. Everything else is the task.)

The *didactic* prompt, good for when you want to assess student's general retention of key course themes, offers a thesis as its topic, which it then invites students to engage:

> The Irish literary imagination cannot escape the Rebellion of 1798. Drawing on careful selections from our syllabus, argue how and why this is so.
>
> (In this version, the first sentence is the topic. The second sentence is the task.)

Step One: (5 minutes) Split your class into small groups and distribute copies of your highlighted maximalist prompt. Instruct them to close read the prompt and try to figure out why it is color-coded the way it is. What different purposes do the colored sections serve in guiding the writer?

Step Two: (15 minutes) Reconvene and ask each group to share their sense of what purpose each color-coded section serves. Students are likely to name some functions readily, like "topic" and "task," though they're also likely to use synonyms. In other cases, they may struggle to find a unifying term for a multitude of functions, like "examples," "key terms," or "evidence." Ultimately you want to steer conversation toward four primary functions: topic, task, context, and analytical (how/why) questions. It is likely that any reasonable student contribution will fall into one of these categories, and some contributions (key terms, evidence, etc.) may fall into more than one.

As you decode these features, be sure also to discuss what the prompt *requires* versus what it *suggests*. The maximalist prompt above, for example, requires students to write an essay about how and why Irish literature is haunted by the past, but it only suggests what texts they might discuss, and how or why they may be haunted. Ultimately, you'll want to arrive at the insight that engaging topic and task is essential for every prompt, while context and how/why questions are there to provide helpful guidance that the writer may or may not engage directly.

Step Three: (10 minutes) Put students back in groups, distribute the (unhighlighted, unlabeled) minimalist prompt, and ask them to decode again. What elements overlap with the maximalist prompt? What is absent that you need to provide yourself? Reconvene to discuss what they've noticed; students should see that topic and task remain, but context and analytical questions are missing.

Invite students to take a moment to practice generating their own how/why questions for the prompt and collect a few on the board. Emphasize that minimalist prompts rely on writers to take on the responsibility, and opportunity, of seeking out useful context and developing their own analytical questions to set the direction for their argument. Maximalist prompts, by contrast, do some of this work for the writer, but present the risk of confusing required tasks with suggested guidance.

Step Four: (15 minutes) Next, distribute the (unhighlighted, unlabeled) didactic sample, presenting it as another minimalist prompt but with an important difference. Ask students to return to their small groups and identify what's distinctive about the task this final prompt is setting. They should then discuss how their approach would need to change from that required by either of the earlier prompts.

Reconvene and reflect. Students should notice that there is an actual thesis—"The Irish literary imagination cannot escape the Rebellion of 1798"—but that it isn't yet grounded in a text, and floats no possible examples, much less generative how-and-why questions. Begin by asking students the most obvious question: what does one do with this? Give them space to consider the range of possibilities. Is there a party line here? Will the professor automatically fail me if I dare to say Irish literature has already escaped? Or is this meant to be a controversial claim that writers are free to confront? Is the prompt simply asking students to demonstrate course knowledge, as might be the case in a take-home exam? Is it possible this wasn't intended as a didactic prompt in the first place? Maybe the instructor was specifying a niche academic debate as the prompt's topic, in which scholars argue about the nature of the Rebellion's literary gravity. But, in this hypothetical, perhaps that's just not clear to the students, who lack the professor's expertise. (In that case, it's a minimalist prompt in disguise, and devising a focused argument in response to your own how/why question would constitute a successful essay.)

The point of facilitating this discussion is for students to learn that the prompt's task is not clear. And so, the most important response to didactic prompts in any course is to ask the professor for clarification. Be sure to address students' likely anxiety about "saying what the professor wants," and channel that energy into seeking a clearer understanding of what task the prompt is asking them to perform.

REFLECTIONS

I run this exercise a few weeks before major essays are due, as soon as I've announced the essay prompts to the students. One aim is to kickstart my students' brainstorming process and show them how they can break their writing process down into manageable pieces. Students who practice crafting their own how-and-why questions often find it liberating to generate questions about the prompt without the pressure of answering them immediately. Similarly, students who hunt for evidence related to a maximalist prompt's how-and-why questions enjoy the process of compiling before they begin analyzing. There can be a tendency for students to pack premature thesis statements into their lists of questions and evidence. You can gently correct for this by suggesting they consider such early-stage theses as hypotheses to be tested as they continue through the writing process.

My main objective with "The How and the Why" is to help students realize that essay prompts invite, and sometimes also model, the type of generative questioning and thinking necessary for strong argumentation. Often, I read student essays that take one of the prompt's speculative claims as their own thesis statement or borrow evidence from the prompt without going back to analyze how and why it functions in the original source. Having students think critically about the structure of prompts helps emphasize their intentional incompleteness as a genre: they *prompt* rather than *perform* argument. Decoding a maximalist prompt together in class will help students understand, when it comes to decoding minimalist prompts on their own, the sort of motive- and analysis-oriented questions they need to be asking. Reacting to the maximalist prompt above, for instance, one of my students remarked, "I've always been interested in how gloomy Stephen is about his past, but I've never considered why or what that symbolizes," before wryly remarking, "I guess that's kind of my job, though." As we moved on to the minimalist prompt, another student observed that, "If it were like the first [maximalist] prompt, it would ask *how* Heaney represents the Troubles." Their small group went on to notice that one of Heaney's poems, "Act of Union," deploys violent birth metaphors and further refined this analytical question to ask, "How and why is giving birth so violent in 'Act of Union'"?

The exercise lends itself to variations, depending on what you wish to emphasize. If your course uses only maximalist prompts, you can end after step two, focusing discussion on how such prompts model, but don't adequately answer, the how-and-why questions that underpin a motivated argument. If your class deals more in the minimalist brand of prompt, you can focus on having students generate their own how-and-why questions. And, if you want the lesson to teach students about how essay prompts vary across courses and disciplines, you can curate a broader array of samples for collective analysis or invite students to bring in examples from other classes they're taking.

Graduate student instructors may find the exercise useful as a kind of reverse outlining process for prompts, especially given that they are liable to inherit prompts they haven't written themselves, some of which may mislead students as to what the task for the essay truly is. For instance, I first developed this exercise as a teaching assistant for a course in which the prompts were all didactic, offering thesis statements followed by an imperative—"discuss"—rather than an invitation to argue how and why that statement holds true. Unpacking these prompts did the work of teaching students to understand that they required more evidence and motivation, but also led them to ask generative how-and-why questions about the essay topics for the first time.

Finally, while I first designed "The How and the Why" as a writing exercise, I also like to point out to my literature students that gathering evidence and inquiring into its function mirrors the process of noticing and interpreting that guides the practice of close reading in literary studies more generally. As one student memorably put it, "You mean, we have to do this all the time?"

Great Expectations

Aditi Sriram

Students try to predict a paper's argument based on its introduction alone.

Writing Focus: *orienting, thesis, structure*
Teacher Preparation: *low*
Student Preparation: *none*
Estimated Time: *40 minutes*
General Disciplines: *humanities, social sciences*

EXERCISE

Prep Work: Select an introduction from a piece of writing that you find particularly effective and photocopy the excerpt as a handout. This may be from a piece of professional academic writing, a magazine essay, a student model paper, or any other piece of argument-driven writing with a strong introduction. On a separate handout, prepare an "X-ray" version of the rest of the piece: in other words, the first and last sentence of each paragraph to show its succession of structural hinge points.

Step One: (10 minutes) Open with a metaphor: a paper's introduction is a handshake offered by the writer to the reader. It should be firm and welcoming, preparing the reader to expect an interesting, important, and well-founded argument to come. In short, it establishes great expectations suitable to the occasion. Now distribute copies of the chosen introduction and have students work in pairs to discuss what expectations it leads them to have about the composition as a whole. What will readers learn from this piece of writing? Why does the author find this topic important, and how will the reader find it relevant? What kind of research has the author done? What structure might the reader anticipate that the rest of the piece will have? Instruct students to identify specific words or phrases in the introduction that support their responses and encourage them to mark up the text.

Step Three: (15 minutes) Reconvene to collect students' responses on the board and facilitate a conversation about their findings. The goal is to arrive at a rough list of elements that belong in a strong introduction (e.g., the introduction of key terms and important figures, the articulation of the main argument, the signaling of its overall direction, etc.) and the relationship of these elements to each other. If you like, you can project a copy of the introduction at the front of the room to annotate as students' share their responses.

Step Four: (5 minutes) Return students to their pairs and distribute the X-ray handout showing the piece's structure. Ask them to trace the progress of the argument and assess how and to what extent they feel it met the expectations set by the introduction.

Step Five: (10 minutes) Reconvene and ask students to point to specific places in the X-ray handout that made them say, "Aha! Just as I expected"—as well as specific moments when their reaction was, "What?! Sure didn't see that coming." (You can also project the X-ray handout if you like.) During the discussion, help students analyze what exactly was present (or missing) from the text that prompted their reactions. Were all the surprises unwelcome? Close by returning to the handshake metaphor. How might they elaborate or nuance that metaphor now that they've seen how the piece of writing intends to deliver on its promise?

REFLECTIONS

The opening of a piece of writing makes all the difference. In fact, writing the preceding sentence has taken me several attempts, as I deliberate how I want to reflect on this exercise. What is the immediate initial impression I want to make on my own reader? Am I trying to signal relevance and urgency, am I asking a question to draw the reader in, am I employing an anecdote to paint a clear visual? The introduction is a chance to earn my reader's interest and trust, and to persuade them to continue reading.

For this exercise, I regularly use a *New Yorker* article titled "How Balkrishna Doshi Bent Le Corbusier's Modernism to the Needs of India" by Samanth Subramanian, though for an example of more conventional academic writing I usually choose a book chapter from a collection or monograph. Almost any introduction will do, though I recommend selecting one that is not too lengthy (no more than a page, two at most) and that students will find interesting or entertaining.

When I project text on a screen at the front of the class, I also invite students to come up to the screen to point to the words and sentences to which they are reacting, while I transcribe their comments live, which are also visible on the screen. When we have finished analyzing an introduction together, words have been circled, sentences have been underlined, and there might be questions in the margins. The students leave class with the momentum and confidence to analyze their *own* draft introductions.

Indeed, you can also expand this exercise by asking students to bring a hard copy of a draft-in-progress to class. After step five, return students to their pairs, have them exchange drafts, and ask them to read just the introduction of their partner's draft. As they read, have them jot down notes in response to questions like these:

- What do you expect this paper to be about, and what specifically in the introduction is generating these expectations?

- How do you anticipate the argument will be structured, and what specifically in the introduction is generating these expectations?
- Overall, what two or three adjectives would you use to sum up this introductory "handshake?" What inspires your confidence and makes you want to keep reading? Where do you get lost or confused or feel skeptical?

Then instruct each student not just to share the "great expectations" prompted by the introduction with their partner, but also to compare how closely those expectations match up with the author's current outline. What might the (likely) mismatches suggest to each writer about how to begin revising their introductions or their structure? Be sure to bring the class back together once more, to invite students to volunteer successful examples from their partner's handshakes, connecting them with the list of strong introductory moves the class generated in step three. You can then finish this version by refining the list in light of students' further discoveries.

In this expanded version of the exercise, students receive peer validation about what makes their paper exciting because of the expectations their readers now have. Students also become aware of how their drafts may be interpreted differently than they intended, as well as the power of an introduction to broach a question, create a framework, and intrigue a reader.

The Scholarship of Strange Sources

Andy Hakim and Emma Ljung

Use strange fiction to teach research strategies as a change of pace from modeling with traditional scholarly sources.

Writing Focus: *motive, sources, evidence, method*
Teacher Preparation: *low*
Student Preparation: *low*
Estimated Time: *50 minutes*
General Disciplines: *humanities, social sciences, sciences*

EXERCISE

Prep Work: Before class, ask students to read two brief fictional portraits of scholarship. These can be complete texts (we are partial to the short stories "Reports of Certain Events in London" by China Miéville and "The Author of the Acacia Seeds" by Ursula K. Le Guin) or excerpts (such as Hermione's use of *Hogwarts: A History* in the *Harry Potter* series, or perhaps certain of the footnoted "historical" sections of Susanna Clarke's *Jonathan Strange & Mr. Norrell*). These works of fiction masquerade as scholarship, offering students surprising and entertaining models of what it means to enter and contribute to scholarly conversations. We typically assign these pieces early in our students' research processes, when they have begun thinking about their research topics in a more focused manner but have not yet written substantial drafts. Don't frame the texts as "strange" or out of the course parameters in any way; their idiosyncrasies and students' unprompted reactions to them are key to this activity.

Step One: (2 minutes) Before turning to the readings, preview the day's class as about the unexpected. Explain that groundbreaking research often happens when scholars go beyond their comfort zones and look at unusual things in strange, new ways. By demystifying that unexpected first encounter, this exercise aims to illuminate how scholars enter and contribute to conversations in their fields. Scholars begin by locating a puzzle or incongruity in the subject matter or existing scholarship and then add to the discussion by the sometimes radically different ways they analyze evidence.

Step Two: (20 minutes) Turn to your first selection. We like to begin with "Reports of Certain Events in London," which presents the attempts of the BWVF, an amateur research society similar to real-world associations that study Jack the Ripper or Henry VIII, to understand the strange, fantastical phenomenon of *viae ferae*, or feral streets. (BWVF likely stands for "British [something]

Viae Ferae," but Miéville never gives the full name of the organization, leaving it to readers' imaginations and adding to the strangeness of our encounter with this source.) Like a work of traditional scholarship, Miéville's story helpfully delineates a primary encounter with a problem in the world, including representation of data in various forms and how writers might enter into conversation with other thinkers in interesting and unexpected ways.

Ask students what problem the BWVF is investigating. The answer is anchored in observed evidence: the streets of London and other major cities across the world are moving!

Divide the class into pairs and ask students to locate evidence of research processes in the story. Questions like these will help them get started:

- How is the BWVF trying to find out why the streets are moving? (Miéville never provides a reason for why the streets move, which highlights that not all research projects lead to tidy solutions.)
- What types of evidence is the BWVF collecting and using?
- What does the presentation of that evidence (as in the table of street appearances) indicate about what the BWVF *does*?
- How is this report engaging in conversations of the sort scholars might enter?

Reconvene and record students' responses on the board. When each group has shared its findings, move on to the next selection.

Step Three: (20 minutes) Repeat step two with the second selection. We like to use "The Author of the Acacia Seeds," in which Le Guin presents three excerpts from a fictional academic journal, *The Journal of Therolinguistics* (or study of animal languages), which can help students see how one enters scholarly conversations by locating research problems and then offering contributions to the ongoing discussion.

Working in pairs again, have students analyze the text by locating evidence of research processes in the story. For Le Guin's story, questions like these might be helpful:

- How do the three excerpts (on ant, penguin, and plant communication) situate themselves in academic conversations?
- How do the authors of the excerpts respond to the work of other thinkers and researchers?

If students struggle, you might ask one to read a passage out loud. (We would suggest reading from the second excerpt, on penguin language, which shows a writer establishing past practice in the discipline, then proposing a way potentially to rethink the field.)

Invite groups to share their discoveries, jotting down their responses on the board. Where appropriate, encourage the students to compare the uses of scholarship in the two texts. (For example, in our pairing, where Miéville's piece offers analysis of primary evidence, Le Guin's story gives us the scholarly conversation in a more fully realized form.)

Step Four: (8 minutes) Encourage students to reflect on their own research processes. In pairs, invite them to describe their research projects to one another, focusing on the discoveries they just made in their analysis of the two "strange" sources. You might prompt students with questions mirroring the main discoveries of the lesson:

- What is your research topic?
- What disciplines are you thinking about engaging? Why do they seem useful for studying this topic, specifically? (In a disciplinarily grounded course, this question isn't necessary.)
- What might scholarly discussions of this subject focus on?
- What are some questions you hope to answer through research?
- What specific types of evidence might help you explore this topic? Why would this form of evidence be useful?

REFLECTIONS

At its core, this activity demonstrates that research writing does not follow one standard formula. Instead, managing the complicated connections between motive, sources, evidence, and method is the key to the quality of the arguments that students put forward. Offering students a radical departure from the ordinary course content, the exercise forces them to focus on the practice of scholarship itself. Strange fictional texts like Miéville's and Le Guin's offer students an effective tabula rasa, liberating them from the course-specific facts and arguments they have begun to internalize as a "scholarly reality." By taking away what they know so they can focus on what they need to do, the lesson helps students develop a deeper understanding of how scholarship functions.

We find that this approach promotes intellectual curiosity as well. Counterintuitively, imaginative works of fiction such as "Reports of Certain Events in London" and "The Author of the Acacia Seeds" help students get excited about their own research projects and begin thinking through how they might complicate and hone their research processes. (For more science-focused classes, you can also offer students "The Case of the Disappearing Teaspoons," a tongue-in-cheek longitudinal cohort study published in December 2005 in the *British Medical Journal.*) Try to pair works that highlight different aspects of the research process. In Miéville's story, the BWVF's attempts to grapple with different forms of evidence challenge students to reconsider the possibilities available for a researcher. In Le Guin's piece, imagining fanciful ways animals communicate, as well as how fictive scholars communicate ideas about these creatures, helps students envision how they might communicate their own ideas on the page. On a biographical level, students find the authors' intellectual range and flexibility an inspiring example of what curiosity can accomplish. Miéville is known for his work in the genre-blurring "New Weird" movement, and science-fiction icon Le Guin refused to pigeonhole herself by working only on a narrow theme or topic. This suggests that one does not have to stick to what one is "good at," but rather that strength in one area can lead to unexpected yet important discoveries in another.

Our students enjoy analyzing these literary portrayals of scholarship. In "Reports of Certain Events in London," for example, they typically notice that the different entries within the text either cite or reference other pieces/fragments of evidence, indicating that the BWVF uses source control, referencing, and note-taking similar to their own practices. They also note the range and variety of evidence collected. Although the society is interested in the streets themselves, its evidence ranges from the physical (pieces of roof tile) to charts (lists of sightings), from eyewitness accounts to newspaper clippings. When students do not make the connection themselves, we suggest that investigating one topic through multiple forms of evidence may enrich their own inquiries.

In "The Author of the Acacia Seeds," students quickly see how the extracts, although fictional and strange, mimic scholarly practices they have seen in nonfiction scholarly writing. For example, in the first extract, they notice that "Dr. Rosbone" advocates for the reconsideration of the scholarly community's approach to understanding ant communication via the sequential arrangement of acacia seeds, a bold scholarly move that both questions the established consensus and revisits important core evidence in a new way. For our students, this is quite easy to understand as a motivating move, but we invite them to discuss the other sections of the story as well. Sometimes, for instance, they note that Anna Serebryakova attempts to interpret penguin language via dance in the second extract, which indicates that bringing a new disciplinary perspective can lead to a fresh understanding of particular evidence in unexpected ways.

Why use fictional works to teach scholarly evidence and motive? Because fiction softens scholarly authority in positive ways and encourages students to define themselves more actively as young scholars. Since the story content is clearly fictional, it resets their assumptions about scholar/student hierarchies and implicit appeals to authority. ("Freud/Marx/Gibbon has already talked about this so there is nothing I could possibly add.") The sheer strangeness of the subject matter can build scholarly confidence in students, as they see how the conventions of academic work can be applied to seemingly absurd subjects in convincing, evidence-based ways. Consequently, students have nothing to lose in their discussion of the material yet begin to see how they might engage in a scholarly practice. As a result of this fun excursion into the unexpected, students come to see scholarship as something attainable not just for their professors, but also for themselves.

Thesis Improv

Benjamin Widiss

Demystify and streamline the process of thesis creation and encourage substantial rethinking.

Writing Focus: *thesis, structure, key terms*
Teacher Preparation: *low*
Student Preparation: *none*
Estimated Time: *35 minutes*
General Disciplines: *humanities, social sciences*

EXERCISE

Prep Work: None. Ideally, the exercise should be introduced shortly after an essay has been assigned but well before its due date. In class, it should follow an extended discussion of any source material that might ground an essay for your course.

Step One: (5 minutes) Ask the students to take a moment to reflect on the ideas they've arrived at as a group in the last few minutes of your discussion. Then ask them to compose a possible thesis *jointly*—through the contribution of one word by each student, moving around the room and circling back for multiple passes as necessary. Make clear that the resulting sentence will be no more than an ungainly starting point, that nothing rests on the particular formulations they arrive at on the fly—except for the magical transformation of nothing into something. Don't allow more than a couple seconds of hemming and hawing, and don't allow people to pass; the whole point is to get words out even when doing so might feel awkward or premature. If nothing else, the momentum of grammar alone can carry the process forward, providing ample material for emendation thereafter. Write their composition on the board as they go. Here's the result from my last outing: "Grief is prominent in both poems showing the different losses experienced by various mothers in moments of grief."

Step Two: (20 minutes) Ask the students to take a couple minutes mulling over the statement they've created, and encourage them to think back to earlier points in the discussion that might be germane to the statement but not adequately reflected in it. Then invite editorial revisions of all kinds—not just to say what's already on the board better, but also to say something that more fully engages the preceding conversation or the original material under debate. Since it's often in measuring the shortcomings of our drafts that we finally grasp what we are trying to say, these steps in sharpening the thesis often double as or open into continuations of the preceding conversation. Encourage the students to pursue precision, nuance, and responsibility to the complexity of their discussion. But have them think about style and panache, too: how can a thesis statement getting weighed down by particulars or prudence achieve verve and quotability, even memorability?

Be sure to keep an original version of the thesis on hand. Then create a space to record their alterations on the board as they propose them, so that the most up-to-date version of the statement is always there in full in front of them. Alternatively, one can permit multiple formulations to branch off, at least to consider competing options. Doing so helps students to see the implications of more or less subtle differences of opinion or articulation, and sometimes helps pave the way toward a more finely calibrated endpoint.

Step Three: (10 minutes) Whether or not everyone is entirely satisfied, be sure to leave time to facilitate a discussion about how the claim on the board has developed and what has made it stronger. Many particulars of that improvement will already be clear to everyone in the room; this conversation offers the opportunity to help students translate those specifics into a broader conceptual understanding of the nature and process of revision—an understanding that they can subsequently bring to bear on their individual writing projects. Very possibly, you will have charted a path from description to argument, from loose generalization to increasingly precise vocabulary, and from simple parallels or divergences to more exacting logics. The opening formulation I've quoted above, for example, evolved into: "Although both poems depict grieving mothers, the way that we experience closure as readers shifts our interpretation of blame for the children's deaths from a social context to a more abstract approach to trauma." Still a work in progress, but much progressed! I don't allow students to use our collectively produced thesis as the basis for individual papers, but you might on the other hand permit them to adopt that claim as a starting point—with the clearly enunciated expectation that a faithful and rigorous engagement with the evidence will lead them to more nuanced, specific arguments of their own.

Step Four: (homework and next class, optional) Alternatively, you might actively call on the class to illustrate those myriad paths forward by means of the production of several hypothetical papers. Set up pairs or teams to chart out component parts of an essay following from the final collective version of the thesis, making use of the conversation that preceded it and relevant source material. You might ask them to create traditional outlines for these imagined essays, or you might offer other structuring devices. For instance, you could decree that the essay will be grounded in four quotations from a primary text you've been discussing and two from secondary sources you've read together, and have each pair or group come to class with their selections and a justification for the order in which they'd propose to make use of them. Or ask them to propose three key terms for the essay and write a paragraph explaining their relationship, considering also how these words overlap with or depart from the language of the draft thesis. Or have them come prepared to explain how they might introduce and manage three possible complications or apparent exceptions to the thesis. Or mix and match. There is an endless series of options—the point is to get students to use the next steps in the essay-writing process to refine the thesis they started with.

Begin the next class session by talking through the strengths and weaknesses of how each imagined essay follows through on the promises of the original joint thesis, how each manages the evidence and interpretation from the class discussion, and what further suggestions each implicitly (or explicitly) makes for further alterations to the thesis.

REFLECTIONS

I've suggested that this exercise takes about half an hour. In truth, the first time I undertook it, we flew through in no more than ten or fifteen minutes—precisely because we didn't have enough time left for the longer version of the exercise I had planned. My original intention was that students would compose possible theses in pairs or small groups. They would have worked in a more leisurely give-and-take fashion, fine-tuning as they went. Then we would have put three or four theses on the board simultaneously and talked about their comparative strengths. I've timed things correctly to use this small-group approach on other occasions, and it works well too. The full-class improv alternative, however, engenders a strong sense of universal buy-in; everyone has a hand in the creation of the thesis, and everyone can contribute to improving significantly on its original haphazard form.

At the outset, of course, this approach also engenders a strong sense of universal incredulity. No one believes that a good thesis will emerge from the opening collaborative compositional gambit, and I have sometimes had to prod my students to play the game. The one-word-per-speaker method comes from an improvisational-comedy routine that I saw in college, where it indeed did not seem intended to be taken very "seriously." I think that's where its utility enters for this exercise though; paper-writing can be so terribly serious, and therefore stultifying, for many students. Not only can this weightiness produce risk-averse writing strategies (and risk-averse theses!), but it can also make the writing extraordinarily slow and painstaking for fear of wrong steps. Generating a claim headlong and pell-mell gives students an experiential sense of possibility: one can dare to commit an opening set of words to the page hastily, and it's okay for them to be imprecise, repetitive, even uninspired—because then, they can actually be revised quite quickly. I make a point of highlighting at the end of class the fact that we've moved from a freewheeling and multifaceted discussion, usually dotted with incompatible claims, to a significantly more pointed and actionable working thesis in the space of half an hour or so.

I encourage students to experiment with giving themselves tight time limits for the same agenda at home, or indeed to interrupt what they would otherwise take to be antecedent stages of brainstorming or mapping their thoughts to formulate theses that they explicitly understand in advance to be provisional or partial. For example, I often ask students in the earliest stages of composing a long essay to choose three passages from the primary text(s) they'll be using, to annotate them as heavily as possible, and to create a temporary thesis statement based on that work. This temporary articulation sometimes becomes a steady guide for all the work that follows, but it's equally useful (and perhaps more exciting) if it turns out to be an early conception that a student ends up writing against or otherwise outflanking.

With luck, the experience of successfully and efficiently moving from a sloppy start to a clear expression of even a provisional thesis gives students the incentive and the wherewithal to undertake similarly ambitious revisions of the rest of their writing. (I was recently delighted to receive an email from a former student working on her medical school application essay two years after graduation, quoting back to me my statement—made more than once, it appeared—that "revision is where the magic happens.") It would be easy to apply this exercise to topic sentences, or other important moments of transition or summation. I suspect that any practice with translating somewhat inchoate thinking into functional, sharable language pays dividends in classroom discussions down the line, too, helping spur students to exchange ideas more comfortably and productively even when their thoughts don't yet feel fully baked.

DRAFTING

It's easy to feel paralyzed by perfectionism or the myriad routine questions that every writer faces: "How should I organize my ideas?" "What do I do with all these sources?" "Will this point make any sense to my readers?" "Does it make any sense to *me*?" One of a teacher's most important jobs is to encourage students to view with celebration rather than shame the deeply imperfect results of any initial, sustained writing effort: what Anne Lamott calls the "Shitty First Draft." The apparent emergence of something from nothing marks a key transition in the process. It's not really from nothing, of course. Only through all the work leading up to a draft—work that should *also* be understood as writing—does the iceberg just start to shimmer into view above the water, far from complete but also an incredible accomplishment. To get there, students must tame the somewhat disorderly thought-work of the early stages of a writing project as they piece together their argument on the page, develop their analysis, experiment with structure, and integrate source material as they go. "Drafting" is an ill-defined hinge between "Starting" and "Revising"; at no point do writers fully abandon the open-ended thinking work of a project's genesis, and words committed to the page are immediately subject to revision. Even so, a welcome sense of grounding comes with that first draft, a feeling, perhaps, that the hard part is over. That intuition is only partly true—radical revision awaits!—but let's not spoil the victory of drafting. This section focuses on how to reach that victory, featuring exercises in which students learn how to define key terms, stage a scholarly conversation, analyze evidence, decode graphs, and other strategies for interpreting texts and engaging with sources.

INTERPRETING TEXTS

Teaching Textual Irreverence

Marion Wrenn

Use choreographed writing to help students crack a source's meaning and engage another writer's ideas to motivate their own inquiry.

Writing Focus: *analysis, evidence*
Teacher Preparation: *low*
Student Preparation: *medium*
Estimated Time: *50 minutes*
General Disciplines: *humanities, social sciences*

EXERCISE

Prep Work: Choose a professionally written text—either something the whole class has read together or something they have selected and read on their own. Ideally the text should be complex and should reward rereading. (I have used everything from Theodor Adorno and Max Horkheimer's "The Culture Industry: Enlightenment as Mass Deception" to excerpts from Matthew Goulish's *39 Microlectures: In Proximity of Performance*.) Before class, students will need to have carefully read and annotated the source they want to use for the exercise. Ask students to identify a key, paragraph-length passage in the source. I ask my students to find moments that haunt or delight: "This could be a piece of the text you don't understand but feel is critical, a passage that gets you riled up, an image that stays with you long after you finish reading. Pick a paragraph-sized moment." Prepare the seven-point handout below and make the necessary number of copies to bring to class.

Step One: (5 minutes) Give students time to reread their notes and the passage itself. Ideally, they will have marked it up—identifying key terms, noting style and craft, and thinking about why they identified this passage. Is it important to the text's ideas? Does it charm the reader? Or baffle the mind? (The good news is that answering yes to any of these questions will do just fine.)

Step Two: (45 minutes) Ask students to pull out a notebook and open it to a blank page. Then distribute the handout for them to complete. Tell students they should anticipate five to seven minutes for each of its seven instructions.

As students complete the workshop, periodically circulate around the room to answer questions or give anyone who might be stuck a little boost. Alternatively, instead of providing a handout, you can simply read the prompts aloud, moving step by step and timing each new prompt. Either way, your students should come away from this work with a sizeable and complex paragraph (or two!). You might ask them to repeat this choreographed close reading again at home using another part of the essay.

REFLECTIONS

I'll confess that when I ask students to summarize sources, I'm afraid I'll wind up with a stack of obedient paragraphs that get stuck on theme or plot rather than explore claim, argument, or idea. These looming, potentially lifeless paragraphs are full of declarative sentences like: "This essay is about X" (where X is always only a single word) or "I agree with the author." Overgeneralizations are safe and they create a sense of authority for the student writer. But it is sentences like these that stand in for a more nuanced representation of the source material and keep students from finding an analytical edge. It took me a while to realize it was my job to help students learn to do something different.

This workshop stages an embodied experience of close reading in order for students to decipher the textual complexity of a single source and then do something with those findings. That "something" can be anything from coming up with a good analytical question to arriving at a deeper understanding of a primary source's ideas to taking a stance on those ideas after carefully rendering and representing them. (Look at the fourth prompt and you'll see that you can tailor the bracketed part of the sentence to serve the work you want your students to do for the particular writing assignment in your class).

I've found this workshop works really well in the rough-draft phase of the writing process, especially for analytical essays drawing upon complex source material. When I tried it recently, a first-year student writing an essay about a Woody Allen film was able to draw upon and resee what Adorno and Horkheimer meant by their claim that "the culture industry cheats the consumer of what it perpetually promises." She had come to class with a draft in which she'd attempted to integrate "The Culture Industry" in the service of her analysis of the film. By looking back at the passages she'd tried to draw from, and (re)writing her reading of them in class, she went home with targeted work to do based on what she'd discovered. She had a practical starting place to rework her source integration, and the insights that emerged helped her develop and refine her thesis.

The results were impressive: the student used the authors' claims to critique and refine an underlying idea about the social construction of taste that she found lurking in Allen's *Midnight in Paris*. By dwelling on the complexities of one text she was inspired to reassess another. She was also, crucially, able to name this work in the cover letter she wrote for her final essay. She noted that this in-class writing helped her figure out an analytical question that ultimately led to a thesis, signaling that she could now see—and perform—the relationship between careful source use and her own ability to make powerful, insightful claims.

Ultimately, the workshop—which I originally developed with my colleague Christopher Stahl—can be adjusted to suit your students' needs. I have used it early in the drafting process, as an idea-generating tool. I have also used it slightly later, for a second-draft workshop, to highlight that good source use demands careful thinking and a robust expression of that thought process. Even late in the drafting process it can be helpful for students to check to see if they have gotten the most out of their sources. It is also worth noting that the series of prompts in the handout acts like an accordion: it can take forty minutes, or it can be stretched across multiple classes, repeated, and varied as needed. (It also serves a culturally diverse, multilingual student body surprisingly well, as I have discovered at my current institution.)

Gerald Graff and Cathy Birkenstein's *They Say/I Say: The Moves that Matter in Academic Writing*—as well as "A Writing Lexicon"—serve as the pedagogical and conceptual background for this assignment. What your students will begin to notice is that they can establish their credibility as thinkers and writers by performing engaged, sustained attention to the text at hand *on the page*. The prompts set them up to write for an imagined reader who can follow the steps of their observations and reflections, the flow of insights based on the close reading of text(s).

But more importantly, this assignment sparks and activates students' analytical minds by asking them to slow down and pay attention to a small piece of potential evidence. Doing so—slowing down—creates the illusion of infinite time. If your students are feeling pressed with deadlines or stressed by exams or overwhelmed by the range of sources they have gathered for their research papers, they might not know where to start, so they are apt to skim the surface rather than risk drowning in material. The in-class exercise creates space and time for them to mull, dwell, dive in, and deal directly with source material—to see what the source says before they say something about it.

HANDOUT

1. *Introduce* and *restate* the passage in your own words, in four or five sentences. Do not try to interpret the passage at this point. Your goal is simply to make the author's words into your own. As you do this, ask yourself: What are the paragraph's important ideas and key concepts? What is the author saying in this paragraph? What key terms would readers need to chew on so that they might better understand the passage?
2. Restate your four or five sentences in one sentence that begins with "In other words . . ."; your goal here is to pay closer attention to the important parts of the author's text. This sentence should both *compress* and logically *emerge* from your initial paraphrase.
3. Challenge yourself to press your restatement further. Begin your next sentence with "Not only that, but . . ."; as above, this sentence should logically emerge from what has come before.
4. Begin your next sentence with "This leads me to consider that, for [this author's ideas, or in this essay . . .]." Again, the sentence will logically emerge from what has come before it and deepen your initial understanding of the author's idea.
5. Push yourself further. Add a sentence that starts with "However . . ." and see if you can locate a contradiction or complication within the selected text.
6. "Perhaps . . .": Now would be a great time to riff on a tentative claim. Articulate an insight based on the contradiction you just noted. Don't try to fix, resolve, or shut down this puzzle. Aim to open it up, articulate what makes it worth thinking about, and reflect on the stakes of your inquiry.
7. Finally, strive to clarify the sense you've made. Start the final sentence with "What I'm really trying to say is . . ." and see how you might compress or restate what you are coming to understand.

Put On Some Clothes!

Megan Brankley Abbas

Introduce the interpretive mode of argumentation by contrasting it with the debate mode for engaging with texts.

Writing Focus: *analysis, method, evidence*
Teacher Preparation: *low*
Student Preparation: *none*
Estimated Time: *60 minutes*
General Disciplines: *humanities, social sciences*

EXERCISE

Prep Work: Locate a short text or excerpt that is ripe for interpretive analysis. The text should invite students not only to argue for or against its claims but to move toward interpreting why and how the text functions as it does. Many different texts will work well for this exercise; I use a selection from the Indian nationalist manifesto *Hind Swaraj* in which Gandhi denounces railroads on the basis that they spread famine and disease and because "good travels at a snail's pace" whereas "evil has wings."

Step One: (10 minutes) Divide students into small groups. Ask them to read the text individually, making sure to take notes about the main argument(s) and their initial reactions. Next, invite them to share their reactions within their group. After a few minutes of unstructured discussion, pose a more specific question to the class as a whole: how would you argue *with* the author of the text?

Step Two: (10 minutes) Draw a version of Table 3 on the board. Direct students to the first empty space in the "arguing with" column and ask them to share their ideas for how to argue *with* the author of the text. Record their suggestions in the appropriate box on the chart while leading a short discussion about the merits of their ideas. (The purpose of the remaining boxes will become clear in the next steps, and an example of a filled-in chart appears in Reflections.)

Step Three: (10 minutes) Now direct students to the next empty space in the "arguing with" column and introduce a silly but accessible everyday life example: a roommate who likes to sleep in the nude. An argument *with* such a roommate would usually entail trying to persuade them to wear some clothes. What are some of the strategies students might use to convince this imagined roommate to alter their sleeping habits? Solicit some potential arguments from

Table 3 ("Put On Some Clothes!")

	Arguing with	Arguing about
In the text		
Roommate example		
General principles		

your students and write them in the appropriate box on the chart. Encourage students to consider a variety of strategies, including arguments about social norms, the impact that the nude roommate's behavior might have on others, and any inconsistencies/hypocrisies in the roommate's possible defenses. If students do not arrive at this diversity of responses on their own, feel free to suggest some examples of your own.

Next, turn to the last empty space in the "arguing with" column and ask your students to propose some general principles for this mode of critical engagement. How does an "argument *with*" a text or person work in the abstract? Record their suggestions in the appropriate box on the chart. Since your students have already used this form of argumentation for the original text and the nude roommate, examples should readily come to mind (e.g., persuade the author/individual to change his/her mind, provide counterexamples, identify inconsistencies or hypocrisies in the argument, and so on). If students find this abstracting work difficult, walk them through one example and then ask them to brainstorm another suggestion individually or with a partner.

Step Four: (10 minutes) After acknowledging your students' existing talents for arguing *with* an author, explain that academics practice a second mode of argumentation that we will refer to as "arguing *about*" a text. Direct their attention to the second column and pose this question: what might an argument *about* the nude roommate's behavior look like? Ask students to imagine chatting about the situation with a parent or a friend from home. What would they discuss? Gather a range of responses and enter them in the appropriate box on the chart. Encourage students to address the roommate's possible motives, background, personality, and worldview, as well as how the roommate's behaviors may impact or be interpreted by others. Write these answers in the "arguing about" / "roommate example" box on the chart.

Next, ask students to abstract these specific examples into general principles for "arguing about" a text. If students seem stuck, provide a model to jump-start the conversation. For example, you could ask them how they would translate a bullet point like "why does my roommate prefer to sleep in the nude?" into the more general principle of investigating motives. Walk through the "roommate example" responses one-by-one until you have identified several principles to enter into the "arguing about" / "in the abstract" box on the chart.

Step Five: (20 minutes) Now ask students to return to their groups and devote five or ten minutes to brainstorming ways of "arguing *about*" the original text. After the groups have had a chance to discuss, reconvene the class and ask for initial ideas for filling in that final space in the chart. If students have promising angles for interpretive analysis, then simply summarize their ideas on the chart. If the responses seem a bit lackluster, push them to deepen their analysis with some prodding questions. For example, when I teach Gandhi's *Hind Swaraj*, I ask them to think about Gandhi's motives for using such a simple argument about good traveling slowly. I remind students that Gandhi was a British-educated lawyer, so he clearly possessed the ability to construct a more nuanced and evidence-based argument. Why might he have chosen not to do so in this moment?

Make sure to gather at least three promising angles for analysis on the board. This diversity will highlight for students the range of possible interpretive arguments for any single text and therefore encourage them to deepen their own engagement with complicated historical and/or religious texts in the future.

REFLECTIONS

I developed this exercise after hitting a wall with the quality of interpretive arguments in my writing courses. In essay after essay on *Hind Swaraj*, students advanced arguments such as "Gandhi was wrong about the evils of railroads" or "Gandhi was a hypocrite because he denounced railroads as evil but then often rode on them." I admit that there was nothing inherently wrong with these arguments, and students were able to muster evidence from the text or outside sources to support their claims. However, I was troubled by the serious disconnect between my students' arguments and those that historians, anthropologists, and scholars of religion usually make about texts. Many scholars in the humanities do not directly challenge the claims of their primary sources but rather seek to interpret the motives, assumptions, worldviews, and unintended consequences that undergird such texts. In other words, we generally "argue *about*" primary sources and "argue *with*" scholarly secondary sources. I wanted to introduce students to the logic of these disciplinary methodologies so that they could appreciate the difference between interpretive and debate-mode arguments. This distinction was initially a tough sell. Many students resisted the notion that interpretive analysis even counted as a form of argumentation; they believed that the only way to make an argument was to defend a text as right or to attack it as wrong. This view was inhibiting their ability not only to develop interpretive arguments but also to recognize this mode of argumentation when they read academic books and articles in history, religion, and other related fields.

This exercise aims to make the implicit rules of interpretive analysis and argumentation explicit for college students who are new to humanities and social science disciplines like history, religion, and anthropology that rely on these rules. It uses two examples to illustrate the practice of interpretive analysis: the

Table 4 ("Put On Some Clothes!")

	Arguing with	Arguing about
In the text (excerpt from Gandhi's *Hind Swaraj*)	Speed can be a good thing—it makes chores more efficient so we have time for what matters. Some good things do travel quickly, like ambulances and firetrucks! Why did Gandhi use trains himself if they were evil?	Gandhi is using this simplified example to communicate a larger point to the masses. Gandhi is challenging whether efficiency is a virtue because he wants us to live simple, reflective, community-oriented lives. Gandhi wants to challenge fundamental modern values but needs to use some modern means to do so. Is this a logical or self-defeating move?
Roommate example	Put on some clothes! Everyone else wears clothes. Sleeping in the nude makes me uncomfortable and is thus unfair to me and my guests. Wait, if you say you're too hot, why don't you just take off one of your many blankets?	Do you think they're just hot? Or are they doing this to annoy me? Maybe they come from a family or culture where this is normal? Are they a philosophical nudist? Am I over-reacting? How would other college students respond to this habit? They don't like it when I take off my clothes. Why are they such a hypocrite?
General principles	Persuade the author to change their mind/behavior. Provide counterexamples. Point out the (unintended) consequences the argument/behavior might have on others. Identify inconsistencies and/or hypocrisies in their argument.	What might the author's motives/intentions be? What might this tell us about the author's background, culture, and/or worldview? How might others respond to this? Would that be a fair response? What might those inconsistencies reveal about the author and context?

accessible real-life case of the naked roommate and a short text. The roommate example enables students to recognize that they already practice interpretive analytical skills in their everyday lives, which makes this seem less like a foreign or arcane mode of argumentation. The textual example, in turn, demonstrates how they can translate those existing interpretive skills into a new academic register.

When I recently used the exercise with my students, this is how they filled in the chart (see Table 4). Ideally, this exercise helps demystify for students why certain academics write the way that we do. I try to underscore two points in particular. First is the all-important issue of audience. Historians and scholars of religion often analyze texts that, because they were written in different time periods and/or in different cultural contexts, present claims that fall outside the scope of contemporary academic argumentation. For example, most of us are so dependent on technology in our daily lives that we are not likely to agree with Gandhi's denunciation of the railroad. Consequently, an essay that argues that Gandhi is wrong about the evils of train travel is preaching to the choir. I encourage students to reflect on who their audience is and what types of assumptions they may have so that they can construct arguments that are more compelling to their potential readers. Second, interpretive arguments can raise the stakes of an essay's analysis because, rather than focusing on the strengths and weaknesses of only one text, they often point toward larger and more complicated questions. I highlight how students might raise their essays' stakes with the example of Gandhi's supposed hypocrisy regarding railways. While it would not be wrong to argue that Gandhi's willingness to travel by train was rather inconsistent with his denunciation of trains as evil, such an argument focuses on Gandhi and Gandhi alone. I suggest that students consider *why* Gandhi might have been inconsistent on this matter. Was he trying to use the system to dismantle the system? Is that a clever or a problematic strategy? Most students will quickly see the higher stakes behind this latter mode of analysis.

While I designed this exercise as an introduction to interpretive argumentation, it can also serve as a timely intervention in the middle of the essay writing process. The abridged, twenty-minute version consists primarily of steps three and four. Afterward, I encourage students to reassess their working drafts. Which sections of their essays fall into the "arguing with" rather than the "arguing about" mode? How could they revise an "arguing with" claim into an interpretive argument? Posing these questions enables students to translate their new methodological and analytical skills directly into their own writing.

Cloudy Key Terms

Leah Klement

Crowdsource your course's key terms to reveal their potential for ambiguity and to practice defining them explicitly.

Writing Focus: *key terms, analysis, orienting*
Teacher Preparation: *medium*
Student Preparation: *low*
Estimated Time: *80 minutes*
General Discipline: *humanities*

EXERCISE

Prep Work: Students bring drafts in progress about a primary source. The ideal primary source dwells on but does not settle big ideas or concepts that can be captured by key terms. Fiction will often provide the most fertile ground. Bring a stack of blank Post-it Notes and choose a few key terms you'd like your students to think more deeply about, ideally those with potential as strong analytical tools but that were undefined or under-defined by students. In my course on apocalyptic fictions, for example, students wrote on the 1999 film *The Matrix*, so we focused on the key terms "identity," "humanity," "justice," and "reality."

Also find and bring copies of at least one excerpt of academic writing that shows key terms in action. It is helpful if the excerpt has clear relevance to the primary source in question. (This allows the exercise to remain focused on developing clarity in key terms, and not on the potentially thorny question of establishing a secondary source's relevance to the primary source.) For my course on *The Matrix*, we used an excerpt from the prologue and first chapter of N. Katherine Hayles's book *How We Became Posthuman*. The connections between this piece and *The Matrix* are clear: both address the shifting lines of the "human" in science fiction, and the way technology mirrors and extends our selves. The excerpt from *How We Became Posthuman* also illustrates multiple strategies for developing clear key terms from both primary and secondary sources, which makes it a useful model for this exercise.

Step One: (5 minutes) Write the key terms you've selected for the day's lesson on the board, spaced away from one another—students will be pasting Post-it Notes around them in step two. Ask students to spend no more than sixty seconds brainstorming the everyday meaning that comes most readily to mind for each key term. In other words, how do they think they would have defined the terms *before* they encountered the primary source? Or, how do they imagine someone they meet at random on the street might define them? Invite students to share a few definitions for each term before moving on. The point is for them to observe the plurality and imprecision (cloudiness!) of the competing definitions. Once that is visible, move quickly to the next step.

Step Two: (10 minutes) Distribute the Post-it Notes (one per term for each student) and draw a cloud surrounding each word on the board for students to stick the notes in. Ask them to write down a new definition that captures a meaning of the term *in the context of the primary source*. The Post-it Note is a useful constraint on the length of their response; their definition must fit on a single Post-it. If they're stumped, encourage them to think of a specific scene or moment from the source that illuminates something about the key term—even if it seems in conflict with another scene or moment. (Spoiler alert! This is, in fact, the takeaway of the step.) When students look like they are finishing up, ask them to go to the board and post their definitions around the key terms inside the cloud shape.

Step Three: (20 minutes) Recruit a few volunteers to lead the class through the definitions. There will inevitably be a wide divergence in the way that students have defined the terms, and you'll want to point out the trends and contradictions, drawing out similar definitions but also emphasizing the differences. In this round, it's likely that the definitions have become more precise and perhaps also even more contested. The work of the primary source is to stage different perspectives: the force of the plot, characters, world building, and so on makes the shape and stakes of different abstract concepts be felt in immediate, urgent, intuitive ways.

Step Four: (25 minutes) Having looked at a wholly open version of defining key terms and a version that is anchored in the world of a primary source, turn next to the function of key terms in scholarly writing. Begin by explaining that key terms should be clearly and explicitly defined to fully realize their power as analytic tools and signposts within an argument. You might also note that clarity is not the only requirement for effective key terms in scholarly writing; academic writers are usually expected to engage with prior voices on the topic to establish their credibility. Now distribute your excerpt and write the key term you want your students to consider on the board. It is helpful, though not essential, to choose a key term that overlaps with a term from your primary source, especially if you anticipate students using the excerpt as a potential analytical tool in their own essays. (In the excerpt from *How We Became Posthuman*, we discuss the main key term "posthuman," which offers a powerful way for students to add depth and nuance to their analyses of competing conceptions of "the human" in *The Matrix*.) Using the excerpt as context, ask them to compose their best, most succinct definition of that key term on the Post-it Note *as it is defined in the secondary source*.

Ask for a first volunteer to come up, stick their Post-it to the board and read their definition aloud. Then ask for a second volunteer who has a substantially *different* definition to do the same, placing their Post-it at some distance from the first. Continue to call up volunteers so long as there remain serious differences in definition. Once those major differences are exhausted, ask the remaining students to come up to the board and place their definitions where they seem to fit best in relation to the existing points already established.

Lead a short discussion about what this "heat map" reveals about the key term. Unlike with your primary source, the point of this step is to converge on the excerpt's definition of your chosen term. Depending on how succinctly and effectively your excerpt accomplishes this definition, the length of this step can vary, especially if the students disagree or are unsatisfied with the answers on the board and want to revise the key term definition. Encourage them to do so.

Step Five: (20 minutes) Have students turn to their drafts and identify two or three key terms that drive their own argument (circling them on paper or highlighting them digitally). Ask them to exchange drafts with a partner and have the partner attempt to define the key terms on Post-its, using only the essay as context. When finished, have them talk through both sets of definitions to test for the match between the writer's intentions and the reader's reception. Where there isn't a strong match, invite partners first to discuss where and how in the draft the reader came to their (unintended) understanding, and second to develop a plan to revise the introduction of the key term to better facilitate its intended meaning.

REFLECTIONS

Student writers are often excited to tackle big ideas in their papers, but they also frequently assume that readers will readily understand what they mean in invoking certain terms, or they do not yet envision an audience at all. This exercise illustrates vividly both how key terms function differently in different contexts and why clear definitions are necessary in our own argument-driven writing. It does this first by walking students through three contexts in which key terms will function differently: out in the everyday world, in a primary source where meaning is intentionally contested or ambiguous, and in scholarship where a precise, transparent meaning is vital for clarity and analytic power. It gets them talking in a fun, lively, and often profound way about big ideas, first drawing on their own experiences and personal definitions of key terms, before delving into the primary and scholarly sources.

In my class, it doesn't take long for the early steps to turn into a useful anarchy. The terms we discuss from *The Matrix* are fundamental to the course topic and its home discipline, as well as to our understanding of the human experience more broadly. We've already been discussing them together for weeks—and yet, isn't it hilarious that we still can't agree on a definition? In fact, much academic endeavor comes from interrogating, redefining, and justifying a particular definition of these key terms. It matters that "justice" means *this* and not *that*. The kind of diversity of thought that students see represented on the board is what drives scholarship forward. Some of my students have defined "justice" in religious terms; others in moral or punitive ones. Some have understood it as equal treatment, some as proportionate treatment, and some as fundamentally related to retribution. Student definitions of "reality" are frequently antithetical: some see it as a construction of the mind, while others define it as everything that exists outside the mind. The range of definitions is always surprising and often funny, and my students usually laugh at contradictory or particularly bold definitions.

At the same time, this exercise opens up a can of worms: if every reader brings a different definition of key terms to the table, are writers doomed to be constantly misunderstood? I find it useful to point out to students that this is where the differences in function matter. *The Matrix* intentionally, explicitly *unsettles* our definition of "reality," but that is one of its goals as a work of fiction. Scholarship uses key terms differently; it *settles* meaning for its own local purposes. Sometimes that purpose is to leverage a settled meaning, stated up front, in order to advance analysis. Sometimes the central argument hinges on contesting another scholar's definition of the key term ("No, 'justice' means *this*, and here's why"). Sometimes a scholar might even stage the complexity of the key term by allowing its nuances to unfold throughout the argument. Beginning with a provisional definition of a key term, the scholar might examine evidence to show that the key term should be understood differently, revising the term iteratively before landing on a final definition. However, whatever the exact role a given key term plays, using it effectively requires precision and transparency.

Students often ask why they cannot simply define a key term based on their own personal beliefs. I remind them that as analytical writers they have a responsibility to their audience. To be persuasive to readers, the choice of key terms, and how to define them, must be appropriate and well-supported by evidence in the context of an essay's sources. In an analytical essay on reality in *The Matrix*, an argument that defines "reality" without reference to the film itself would render the essay's primary source material irrelevant. After completing this exercise, however, students should be able to better visualize an interested but skeptical audience as they write. The first step in defining key terms persuasively might therefore be to consider: what evidence would they present in order to convince a reader that they should define a key term in a certain way? Showing readers that their use of key terms is appropriate and well-supported by their sources is a strong first step toward a convincing thesis.

As I discovered in the excerpt my class read from the prologue and first chapter of Hayles's *How We Became Posthuman*, students were quick to recognize a helpful, clearly signposted and numbered list that transparently lays out several defining aspects of the posthuman view, and also quick to register remarks written in the first person ("I think he is wrong about . . . but right about . . ."). Yet they were more hesitant to chime in at those points when Hayles more obliquely paraphrases or engages the voices of other scholars. In our "heat map," it was common for students, at first, to identify opposing viewpoints as those of the author. However, through discussion and rereading, students can and do begin to recognize the more subtle signposting that signals a shift in voice ("We can recall . . ."; "It is important to recognize . . ."; "One could argue . . ."; "The posthuman deconstructs . . ."), thus gaining experience with the kind of careful reading that will allow them to engage accurately with other scholarly arguments in their own writing. The heat map in general can be revealing. Usually, the "hot" answers (those with the most sticky notes surrounding them on the board) are the most correct definitions, or close to it, but students occasionally realize they're not satisfied with their answers. And sometimes students will converge on a not-so-accurate definition, which is also useful (even if it prolongs the process) since it often highlights a common misunderstanding of the source and offers an opportunity to return to the text together to read more carefully.

The subject matter and terminology of Hayles's work was unfamiliar enough that we all had to stick close to the text, even as students' imaginations took over to debate the broader implications of the argument ("Does this mean my cell phone is actually a part of my posthuman body? Does that make me a cyborg?!"), and so we got to observe in detail the emergence of her key terms from primary and secondary sources, and how she carefully positions herself at each juncture. The payoff for all of this hard work emerged as students came to realize how Hayles's argument is encapsulated in the moves she makes with her central key term. If they can understand and unpack the complex layers of her definition of "posthuman," they've already grasped the overall argument.

The purpose of "Cloudy Key Terms" is to provide a strong illustration of the centrality of key terms in argument-driven, scholarly writing and set students up to engage in some ambitious refining of key terms in their academic work. Academic writing involves a landscape of other secondary sources that inform and shape our arguments; in this chorus of voices, clarity and consistency in one's own position becomes even more critical. As scholarly writers, it's important to hold our key terms constant, and to transparently reveal to our readers what we mean when we use them.

Picturing Analysis

Sarah Case

Help students visualize analysis—and ultimately argument—by way of taking photographs.

Writing Focus: *evidence, analysis*
Teacher Preparation: *medium*
Student Preparation: *medium*
Estimated Time: *50 minutes*
General Disciplines: *humanities, social sciences, sciences*

EXERCISE

Prep Work: For homework before class, ask students to visit and take a picture of their object of study. For example, in my course on urban green spaces, I have students pick a site on or near our college's campus, but in other classes students might photograph a thematically relevant object. Their task is to identify what they find most striking or problematic about the site or object of study, and to compose their photograph in a way that makes the striking or problematic element obvious for the audience. Reassure them that you're not expecting professional-quality photos—just thoughtful, interesting compositions.

Depending on the topic of your course, you might have all students photograph the same site or object of study, or you might have them pick their own. Have students submit their photos before class so you can pick two examples for steps one and two below. The opening of the exercise works best if you select two photos that depict the same subject—or same kind of subject—in notably different ways.

You'll also need a short excerpt of analytical writing about a non-textual piece of evidence to use as a model. It should be on a related but ideally slightly different topic to avoid direct overlap with the writing you'll be asking students to produce at the end of the exercise. In my course, I pick a recent op-ed about access to public or national parks that engages specific evidence from the park throughout, though brief excerpts of scholarly visual analysis also work well.

Step One: (10 minutes) Noticing details and finding tensions is the objective of steps one and two. Start by showing one of the photos you selected in advance and ask students to spend a few minutes "annotating" the details they notice in the photo as they would annotate a text. In my course on urban green spaces, I encourage students to notice details like the presence or absence of people, accessibility of the site, options for seating, types of plants and greenery, scale and architectural style of any buildings, appearance of public art, and transit features like walkways, bike paths, and roads. Have students share their annotations in pairs.

Next, help them move from description to analysis by asking, "What is interesting or problematic or puzzling about the details you noticed in your annotations?" Have them discuss in pairs before gathering answers as a class. Ensure that students are taking the leap from description to analysis by helping them identify points of tension rather than merely saying what the photo depicts. This is probably the hardest part, so seed the conversation with questions. If someone notices that a space doesn't have many people and seems deserted, I might ask a variety of both specific and broad questions: How big is the space? What's in it—seating? pathways? trees? plants? What's surrounding it? In what ways has the natural landscape been altered, and how can we tell? In what ways does the space seem welcoming? In what ways unwelcoming? Why might we value—or want to change—a space like this? These questions are meant to help students develop their analysis of a specific piece of evidence (the photo of the campus space) while also thinking about the larger stakes of the discussion. In a class about public monuments, for instance, you might ask about how the monument memorializes its subject and how it functions as part of its surroundings.

Step Two: (10 Minutes) Continuing the class discussion, invite students to examine the second photo you selected in advance, asking how this one leads them to notice different details. It's usually at this point that students really start to see how much composing their photos matters, how photographs take complex subjects like physical spaces and turn them into a variety of fixed perspectives. Depending on logistics, you might even want to visit the site being depicted to have this conversation.

Step Three: (10 minutes) Now that they've had some practice with the samples you've curated, ask students to take out their own photos and spend a few minutes annotating the details. Then have students pose two or three analytical questions out of what they've noticed. In my class, for example, a photograph of an empty lawn elicited questions like: Why no benches or picnic tables? How does the layout of a space impact people's use of it? What makes green spaces seem inviting or uninviting? Once they've done this individual work, have students share their analytical questions with a partner, seeing if their partner notices anything different or has other questions.

Step Four: (20 minutes) With evidence and analytical questions in hand, students are almost ready to draft a paragraph of analysis. Begin by distributing the analytical writing sample you picked and have a student read it aloud. Ask students what they notice. How is the author using evidence? Since the writer can't quote, what are they doing? How finely grained is the description? The model excerpt should help students see that, when they're writing about their own sites, they need to do the work of translating what they see for their readers, being as specific as possible by describing details and then giving a sense of why they matter. This is where you can emphasize that the photos are a useful tool to help notice details, but ultimately the goal is to be able to communicate these details through words.

Once students have discussed the example, it's time to try it for themselves. In the time remaining, invite students to pick one of their analytical questions generated in step three and start answering the question using evidence from their photo. Doing so is a first step toward the kind of analysis that serves as a building block for a larger argument.

REFLECTIONS

"Picturing Analysis" helps students gather evidence and develop ideas, setting the table for analytic thinking and writing. I use this exercise on the second day of my first-year writing course and build on it by integrating other photography assignments as the semester continues. Having students take their own photos can be especially rewarding because it is a familiar and creative practice that encourages them to notice nitty-gritty details that they can then use as evidence in their essays. Keep in mind that this exercise is not primarily about teaching students how to close read photographs. Rather, the photos provide an opportunity for students to think about their sites or objects of study and find points of analytical texture.

While students have likely taken thousands of photos, this may be the first time they've been asked to do so for a course. When students don't have a text to quote from, conceptualizing what constitutes evidence can be a big jump. You may want to offer a brief introduction to the kinds of choices they'll need to consider in composing their photos, like scale (a wide shot versus a close-up) or framing (symmetrical or asymmetrical). I illustrate a few photographic techniques in the previous class by showing some examples of photos I've taken myself on campus. Using the example of a busy lawn, I juxtapose a blurry, zoomed out shot with one that focuses on an individual element, like a group sitting on the grass. Students quickly see that effective photos emphasize something specific, while less effective photos don't orient their viewers to what they should focus on. The goal of these examples is to help students understand that taking a photo is an act of interpretation; the way they compose their photos will shape what their viewers notice and pay attention to.

The move from general description to analytical question in this drafting exercise is particularly productive, and critical. The best examples of photos my students have taken capture something vivid and specific, such as footprints left in the dirt on a running path along a river. Framing this photo helped a student gather evidence for a larger argument about the importance of exercise in nature for student health. Another student photographed a quad from inside a nearby building to capture the scale of the space, which helped him come to the argument that the campus could seem intimidating and hard to live in comfortably. The visual pop of color provided by red chairs in an outdoor seating area helped still another student notice the importance of outdoor gathering spaces on campus. The best photographs complement and build upon what students notice when they spend time in their spaces.

Encourage your students to take more than one photo of the same site to help them uncover a possible counterargument or alternative interpretation—an especially effective technique for complicating their claims. One of my students, for example, was making an argument about the lack of green space in the university's urban setting. Taking a photo of a plaza by zooming in on the few trees present seemed to suggest nature in the city, but her other evidence, a photo that took a wider view of the same plaza, suggested that the close-up image was misleading. The contrast helped her develop a compelling argument about experiencing nature in a fuller and more multisensory way by thinking about what neither photo ultimately captured—the noise and smells of traffic and air pollution. Having your students return to photograph their sites again after they've developed a tentative argument can be a productive follow up assignment.

In their course reflections, my students have pointed to the value of writing about non-textual sources, types of evidence that get away from "quotation overload," as one student called it. Another student pointed out that taking photos helped her think about the viewer of the photo as a proxy for the reader of her essay. As she was writing about her campus site, she was able to think about how a reader would understand her sentences just as a viewer might understand her photo. Practicing analysis with non-textual sources ultimately translates productively when students shift their attention back to analyzing texts. The act of taking the photo becomes a useful metaphor for capturing the interesting questions or tensions at stake in any object of interest.

Making Analytical Connections

Anne Freeland

Put course texts into conversation with each other with a comparative analysis exercise that can serve as a springboard for formal writing.

Writing Focus: *analysis, sources, key terms*
Teacher Preparation: *medium*
Student Preparation: *none*
Estimated Time: *45 minutes*
General Disciplines: *humanities, social sciences*

EXERCISE

Prep Work: Select passages of between two hundred and five hundred words from course texts that allow for several different pairing possibilities—that is, students should be able to draw meaningful connections between them that could be elaborated in substantial paragraphs, and they should have some freedom in deciding how to do this. Depending on your class size, you'll likely need between four and eight excerpts. I typically use a group of primary sources, but the exercise is also valuable for scholarly and theoretical sources. Humanities and social sciences texts orbiting around a common theme are especially effective. You can mix genres or keep them consistent, depending on the type of analysis you're asking students to do. It's helpful to include some passages that you have read closely as a class in a previous session.

Print one passage per sheet, and enough copies to give each student one passage. For example, for a class of twenty, you could have five passages and print four copies of each. Prepare one or two more handouts: 1) a set of questions to guide students in discussing the passages before pairing them (optional); and 2) a "Passage Analysis Chart." See samples of both below.

Step One: (5 minutes) Distribute one passage to each student and make sure each passage has at least two readers in the class. Give students a few minutes to read and mark up their passages. Offer active reading strategies as needed. For example, invite them to circle key terms, underline a sentence or two that they would quote in responding to the passage, and jot down a few words in the margin explaining the significance of the parts they underlined.

Step Two: (5 minutes) Have students turn to a partner with the same passage. Give them a few minutes to discuss.

Step Three: (20 minutes) Hand out the "Passage Analysis Chart." There are two ways to proceed here.

Option A: Have students work in pairs or small groups where only two passages are in play.
Option B: Allow students to form their own groups in which three passages are in play.

Allowing students to circulate and form their own groups (option B) works well when students have a good grasp of the themes of the course and have practiced analyzing them through close readings of primary texts, and when there is an established sense of classroom community and a habit of self-directed groupwork. Many of the key terms and concepts that helped my students to form groups were familiar from prior class discussions. If that is not the case, and students are new to the texts, step in and form the groups yourself.

Once pairs or groups have been formed, have students work with the chart to analyze the relationship between the texts.

Step Four: (15 minutes) Reconvene the class and facilitate a discussion among the groups, using the board to track common threads and differences across texts. The goal is both to build a deeper, more nuanced understanding of the relationship between a given pair of texts *and* to give students a broader grasp of the complex network of multiple sources in conversation with each other. Students' completed charts, together with the diagrams you sketch on the board, could serve as navigational tools as they work to develop their own arguments amid a complex web of sources. Or students might want to start afresh with new sources, but armed with a procedure for developing a thesis from close readings of the texts that most interest them.

REFLECTIONS

I've used this exercise in a course on the intellectual history of Latin America, toward the end of the semester, in preparation for an essay exam that would require students to draw on multiple texts. I made an initial selection of passages that I had already highlighted in my notes as particularly rich (we had discussed most of them in class, but some we hadn't gotten to), and then cut the ones that seemed to offer fewer avenues for comparative analysis within the set. My final list included Christopher Columbus, Hernán Cortés, Alexander von Humboldt, Domingo Faustino Sarmiento, Andrés Bello, José Martí, and Octavio Paz. I've done a similar passage-pairing exercise (without the element of choice) in a social theory course on Marx, Durkheim, Weber, and Freud. The exercise would work for any course that focuses on a corpus of primary texts that participate in common discourses, including political theory, philosophy, or literature.

The exercise gets students thinking about how texts speak to one another, either at close range or across time and even across genre. A few of the passages I chose cite or allude to others, and students identified this kind of intertextuality—recognizing, for example, that when Martí writes that "the struggle is not between civilization and barbarity, but between false erudition and Nature," he is responding to Sarmiento, who describes "an awesome struggle in America" "between European civilization and indigenous barbarism." Key terms help to establish these kinds of connections, even when they don't allude to a particular author. From there, students began to question how much Martí's "natural man" in fact differs from Sarmiento's barbarian, since, while Martí's thesis is that the form of government in the Americas must conform to its "native elements" and not be imported from Europe, he stops short of attributing to them the capacity to govern themselves ("The uncultured masses are lazy and timid in the realm of intelligence, and they want to be governed well"). Students start with surface differences or similarities but then, sometimes with a little prodding, go deeper into the complexities of these relations.

Students have to pay attention to different elements of a text—its purpose, its position within a larger discourse, its explicit claims, and the connotations embedded in its language—to identify similarities in some aspects and differences in others. One group tracked Orientalist tropes from Humboldt ("In Mexico, as in Hindostan, it was not allowable in the faithful to change the figure of their idols in the smallest degree") to Paz ("The impression we create is much like that created by Orientals. They too . . . are hermetic and indecipherable"), noting the important differences in genre and style, which led to a discussion about how claims can be embedded in methodological or aesthetic choices. This exercise helps students read for tensions within a text but also across texts, to get to underlying assumptions or unstated implications.

In their small groups and in the whole-class discussion, students move from the particular to the general, linking their observations back to the big questions that have guided the course. The exercise walks students through a sample-sized version of an inductive process of generating an essay question, hypothesis, or thesis based on close readings of multiple sources, serving as a model or springboard for future writing tasks.

HANDOUTS

Discussion Questions

Use the following questions to guide your discussion, focusing on the ones you find most relevant. You will not have time to answer them all!

- Who is the intended audience?
- What purpose does the text serve?
- What is the author's thesis?
- What evidence does the author use to support the thesis (if any)?
- How would you describe the style and tone of the passage?
- Which metaphors or other figures of speech stand out for you?
- What assumptions does the author make?
- Create a list of any internal contradictions you identify in the passage.
- What do you find most significant, interesting, or surprising?
- What questions do you have?
- What are some of the key terms or concepts at work?

Passage Analysis Chart

Authors of passages compared:		
What common thread connects the passages? It can be a term, concept, metaphor, theme, or some other element.	**Common element:**	**Textual evidence:**
How does the common element differ from one text to another?	**Difference:**	**Textual evidence:**
Why are these similarities and differences interesting or significant? What follow-up questions does your analysis raise for you or prompt you to explore next?	**Analysis:**	

The Principle of Charity

Fannie Bialek

Apply the principle of charity to interpret and refine complex arguments.

Writing Focus: *analysis, motive, ethos, orienting*
Teacher Preparation: *low*
Student Preparation: *medium*
Estimated Time: *50 minutes*
General Disciplines: *humanities, social sciences, sciences*

EXERCISE

Prep Work: Assign a complex philosophical or theoretical text to read as homework, and bring copies of a short, analytically meaty excerpt. I've used Hobbes on the equality of vulnerability in the state of nature, Sylvia Federici's descriptions of marriage in *Wages Against Housework*, and Descartes's "Second Meditation," but the possibilities here are endless. When choosing a sample text, look for an unexpected move in the train of argument, especially if at first it *seems* like a tangent or digression. You want both the thesis of the broader text *and* the analysis in the excerpt to be open to multiple plausible interpretations, and for those interpretations to depend on one another.

Step One: (15 minutes) Put your students in small groups and have them read the excerpted passage carefully. Ask them to choose one thing about it that they find strange, interesting, or confusing, especially in light of their understanding of the argument as a whole. Then have them try to answer the (deceptively simple) question: Why did the author do that?

While I don't say this up front, the question is unanswerable. Give groups time to develop competing explanations for why this strange author did this strange thing, and then reconvene. Try to elicit the disputes that emerged within the groups—they shouldn't be able to arrive at a consensus (and if they do, they won't be able to defend it). I want my students to discover that the question is a dead end: we can't read the author's mind, only the text at hand.

Step Two: (15 minutes) We simply can't resolve the question when it's framed in terms of authorial intention, which suggests a subtle but important reframing: Why *would* the author do that? In other words, by what interpretation does the text's apparently strange move make sense? Use this reframing to introduce philosophy's *principle of charity*: choosing to interpret both the argument and the excerpt in such a way that the confusing move becomes as coherent as possible. Applying the principle involves asking questions like: How can I understand the text so that this move is reasonable, right, or good? What *could* the author mean by this confusing or seemingly misused word, for example, or this strange line of reasoning? Given the possible meanings, which *would* the author use if he or she were trying to make the most reasonable and compelling argument? The charitable approach often unlocks meaning that is inaccessible when we lead with our critical, rather than generous, faculties, actively looking for internal contradictions, lapses in logic, or other moments of confusion.

Send students back to their groups to discuss possible answers to the revised version of the question: Why *would* the author do that?

Reconvene and discuss what students found. How well can the principle of charity produce clarity or coherence for both the larger argument and the particular move in the excerpt? Did they uncover a more plausible interpretation of the text? Or did they find multiple charitable interpretations, and if so, what should they do with them? Do they feel they had to stretch the principle beyond its breaking point to rescue the text?

Step Three: (20 minutes) In the same small groups, ask students to identify another moment in the text that makes them wonder, "Why *would* the author do that?" and practice applying the principle of charity there. Ask them to be ready to share three things from their discussion: First, what is the difficulty they've located in the text? Second, why might asking about that difficulty be important? Third, what insight does the principle of charity offer into how you might interpret the difficulty you identified?

Reconvene briefly to workshop one or two student examples, reinforcing the steps they've just practiced as useful for the task of finding motive in a text and as a first step in textual analysis.

Before wrapping up, note the important limits to the principle of charity. It's a valuable interpretive tool, but it neither gives us access to the author's original intended meaning, which can't be known, nor means we should indefinitely suspend our critical mode of interpreting texts. Its value lies in allowing us to read for meaning and reconstruct arguments in their strongest form. When applied to our own writing, it can help us develop stronger, clearer arguments as well. But while it is something we should always use in our reading of others' work, it is not a principle we as writers can invoke to demand that our readers make up for our mistakes and moments of opacity: we must revise with the reader in mind, without relying on their charity.

REFLECTIONS

This exercise sprang from teaching the principle of charity as a philosophical idea and discovering thereafter that every conversation about writing improved dramatically. Misunderstandings of texts could be approached by asking students to interpret the text more charitably, leading them to discover their misreading. Overstated thesis statements could be redeveloped to argue first what the author *might* mean, instead of asserting only what they got wrong. Students see how the charitable interpretation refines rather than dilutes their arguments—and makes their arguments more convincing because they've given the author a full and generous hearing. Through the principle of charity, my students understand themselves as engaged in a different task when working with a text or argument: trying to make it make sense instead of trying to show all the ways it doesn't. It shifts them away from a tendency to lead with criticism, thinking that's the best way to make a hard-hitting argument, when what they actually accomplish is the dubious distinction of taking down a strawman.

Teaching charitable interpretation often reorients the way students engage with texts and develop arguments. In a mode akin to Peter Elbow's "believing game," they learn that they need to understand those claims as deeply and charitably as possible, giving the argument even more credit, perhaps, than it is due (charity as opposed to justice) before they can mount a convincing response. By reconstructing their arguments through charitable interpretation, students find themselves doing some of the author's work, and maybe doing it even better than the author did it themselves. They feel like part of the project, and thus empowered. A student once compared this to performing classic chemistry experiments in his lab courses: he may not have come up with the idea, but by doing it, and doing it sometimes more precisely than it was originally done, he saw that he was capable of doing things in the lab that lead to real scientific understanding.

Students also learn that many of the most convincing arguments take a charitable form: "*Even* if the author were saying X (which he or she barely manages to say), the author *still* can't resolve the problem I'm pointing out . . ." (e.g., "*Even* if we do these gymnastics to make this part of the argument square with this other part, we *still* can't make sense of the connection . . ."; "*Even* if we were to fill in this evidence here and this definition here, the author *still* can't justify that claim . . ."; and so on). These are powerful sentences. They offer convincing evidence for the criticism being made, and they make the reader trust that the critic has tried to give the author's argument a good hearing—not just a fair one, even, but a charitable one—and thus is likely trustworthy in his or her representation of the text.

I find the exercise works best when we discuss a text that students are spending substantial time on in the course, so that they have a good sense of its overall argument and aims. One of the most productive sources for this exercise in my courses has been Descartes's *Meditations*, particularly the paragraph about melting wax from his "Second Meditation." Students find much of the text strange, interesting, and confusing, but also can follow the argument quite well. They have a lot of "why does he do that?" questions, which can be productively reframed as "why *would* he do that?" questions. The text's first-person voice invites readers to identify with the thinker through his meditation, easing students' way into the role of charitable interpreters. The exercise also facilitates teaching secondary sources, where students often struggle to engage an argument critically without walloping it with critiques, leading them to overstate their distance from existing scholarship or their contribution to the conversation.

While this exercise emerges from teaching philosophy, it can transfer to any course with texts making arguments. Why, for example, would Gayatri Spivak choose the word "subaltern" among other terms for colonial subjects, in her famous essay "Can the Subaltern Speak?" and why would J. M. Coetzee choose to make the argument of *The Lives of Animals* in the voice of the fictional Elizabeth Costello, instead of his own? You can also go beyond argument-based works to include fiction, poetry, drama, and even film or television (e.g., the last episode of *Game of Thrones*), as well as visual representations of data in the social and natural sciences. Though the sense-making standard may need to be redefined in different fields and with different kinds of texts, that redefinition itself makes for a productive preliminary discussion.

In my introductory courses, I have students write multiple short papers developing charitable interpretations of a text before they develop a longer argument-driven paper in response to an original question. Charitable interpretation allows them to develop genuinely motivating questions about the interpretation of a text through a process of reading and interrogating, instead of waiting, as one of my students once put it, "for whatever divine inspiration gives other people their good questions."

ENGAGING WITH SOURCES

What Makes ToCs Tick?

Trust Your Gut (But Not Too Much)

Epistolary Experiments

Click to Reply

Don't Forget Your Backpack

Synthesizing Science

Puzzling Out Structure with a Jigsaw

The Data Never Speaks for Itself

From Graphs to Questions

What Makes ToCs Tick?

Dael A. Norwood

Teach students to assess scholarly sources using Tables of Contents (ToCs) and to expedite their research by mapping the scholarly landscape.

Writing Focus: *structure, conventions*
Teacher Preparation: *medium*
Student Preparation: *medium*
Estimated Time: *55 minutes*
General Disciplines: *humanities, social sciences*

EXERCISE

Prep Work: Gather examples of ToCs from three different scholarly works on one subject and prepare photocopy packets that include the title page, copyright page, and ToC for each work. Make sure your examples represent different genres of scholarly work and exhibit different organizational and methodological approaches to the topic. (A textbook, an edited essay collection, and a monograph work well as a trio—it's what I usually use—but conference proceedings, journal issues, primary source readers, dissertations, and so on, would all serve just as well.) Avoid works already read in class, as the purpose of this lesson is to learn how to make smart, rapid assessments. You will also need to prepare a slide or handout of the demonstration chart used in step two, plus blank copies of the chart for each student to use in step three.

For homework, ask each student to borrow a book from the library and find a review of it in a scholarly journal. Setting a focused theme for their research will allow you to model the work of making connections between different pieces of scholarship during step three. While the exercise focuses on the book, the review provides a means of getting purchase on an unfamiliar work before discussing it in class, and also offers students additional practice using research tools. Have them bring both the book and the review to class.

Step One: (10 minutes) Open with a brief discussion about the purpose of ToCs. What are they, and who writes them? What purpose do they serve? What conventions are there for ToCs? What can readers learn from them?

If you have time, you can also have a similar discussion about other parts of a book's front matter (e.g., title page, copyright page, acknowledgements), all of which shed light on scholarly texts as purposeful creations designed and produced in conversation with genre structures, scholarly networks, reader audiences, and (often) markets.

Table 5 ("What Makes ToCs Tick?")

Source (format):	Who produced it?	What's the scope?	How is it organized?	Who is the intended audience?
[Source type 1]				
[Source type 2]				
[Source type 3]				

Step Two: (15 minutes) Distribute the photocopied packets to students and put a version of the chart in Table 5 on the board or screen, filling in the column and row headers but leaving the rest of the boxes blank. (On your chart, instead of "source type 1," etc., you'll write "textbook," or "monograph," or whatever descriptors are appropriate for your examples. Alternatively, you can fill in the four column headers but leave the row headers blank, so that students can be invited to guess each "source type" simply by skimming the three ToCs in the handout.)

Now invite the students to help you fill in the chart, guiding them through the process of categorizing scholarly works and identifying genre. Most importantly, focus on why this is worth doing: knowing what kind of scholarly book you're dealing with helps frame a text's purpose, gives you details about its intended audience, and sets expectations for the kinds of arguments—and level of detail—you can expect.

Ultimately, by helping one quickly evaluate what a book does, and what specific components of the work are relevant, a competent scan of a ToC enables a researcher to make quick decisions about the utility of a given work. While using ToCs in this way may seem like judging a book by its cover, it's actually an important disciplinary practice that distinguishes expert readers from novices.

Step Three: (15 minutes) Ask students to spend five minutes assessing the books *they* brought, using the ToC and book review to answer the chart questions for their own books. Then gather them into pairs or small groups to discuss their findings and invite them to propose ways that their books could be put into conversation. For example, a monograph on the history of the national bank and one on tariff policies could be put into conversation because they investigate different aspects of economic history—and perhaps share methods, or sources. Or, for example, a textbook on early US history might contextualize a monograph about nineteenth-century Christian revivals.

The task of putting different books into conversation is a difficult one for beginners—especially when they haven't yet read the works in question! But this is precisely the challenge that wise engagement with ToCs is designed to help facilitate. Remind students that there are lots of different ways books might connect—on topic, theme, geography, chronology, methodology, sources, and so on—and to think broadly about potential links.

Step Four: (15 minutes) Reconvene the class and ask each group to report on their findings and explain their conclusions. How did they classify their books, and what characteristics led to that classification? What connections did they propose between their books? If a student has brought an example of a scholarly genre that wasn't in your photocopy packet, add the new genre to the chart from step two. Don't be shy about helping students draw links between the works under discussion. As a specialist, you will see many more connections between works than students will, and of many more types—make these visible.

End the discussion by turning the students' attention back to imagining their own work as a scholarly genre: where and how might the research papers they write for this class appear in a scholarly book? (A chapter in an edited collection? Part of a monograph? An article?) Use this to underscore how the scope of a scholarly work helps define its argument—and emphasize that these are visible on the ToC.

REFLECTIONS

Students often imagine ToCs to either be unauthored (simply the "obvious" arrangement, rather than the result of conscious thought) or the author's idiosyncratic creation, divorced from any consideration of audience or genre. Debunking these assumptions frees students to use ToCs more effectively in their own work, helping them to distinguish between types of scholarly sources, and to quickly zero in on what might be useful for *their* research.

If you know that a book is a monograph, for example, you can be fairly sure it's intended to communicate new knowledge, aimed primarily at an audience of other scholars, and will make targeted arguments about a specific subject. It will be useful if you're looking for theories, data, or an interlocutor to engage on a subject; it can be a critical resource as you're coming to grips with a subject and writing a paper. A textbook, by contrast, synthesizes existing scholarship on a broad range of topics for an audience of nonexperts. It is better for context, or as evidence of the prevailing or consensus view among scholars, and can be useful for the very beginning of research, as orientation—but less so in making an original argument.

When I prepare the photocopy packet for my class on early US history, I include a survey textbook (Eric Foner's *Give Me Liberty!: An American History*, vol. 1), an edited collection of scholarly essays (Andrew Shankman's *The World of the Revolutionary American Republic: Land, Labor, and the Conflict for a Continent*), and a monograph (Emily L. Conroy-Krutz's *Christian Imperialism: Converting the World in the Early American Republic*). Foner's widely used textbook is a classic example of the genre: written by one author and produced by a commercial press, it has a broad scope and aims to organize an accessible, comprehensive synthesis of scholarship into a coherent narrative. The ToC reflects these goals: each chapter covers many topics and places within a period of US history, advancing in chronological sequence. Shankman's collection of essays has one editor but many authors; though produced by a scholarly publisher, it was not published by a university press. The ToC catalogs the varied, specialized approaches professional researchers take to the topic of "early America." Instead of providing a smooth, comprehensive narrative or a single, focused argument, it illustrates the spirited conversation in the field. Conroy-Krutz's monograph is a scholarly study of one subject, by one author, published by a university press. The ToC demonstrates how a scholar can examine a single topic in-depth, using an organizational structure that breaks down the broader topic into more limited case studies, rather than one chronological narrative.

When I've run this exercise, students have been quick to see differences between the books, but (usually) find matching the differences they observe to the genres on the chart difficult. They see very readily that monographs are more focused than textbooks—and that textbooks are often "wordier" in their section titles—but they don't always know how those observations connect to differences in production or audience. When one of my students noted of an edited volume ToC that "it seems to be written by a whole school of people," I used that as an opportunity to talk about how edited volumes are typically produced (i.e., originating at conferences or themed panels), which then helped me explain why an edited volume might be on a "theme" or, indeed, an expression of a "school of thought" in a different way than a textbook or a monograph. My students have been particularly pleased in completing this exercise to learn some of the smaller tricks in quickly assessing a book (namely, knowing that the subtitle of a book is almost always more descriptively useful than the portion before the colon break; or how chapter breakdowns differ, visibly, between textbooks and monographs). Table 6 is an example of a filled-in chart from one of my class sessions.

I always require students to bring a physical book to class because they come away with a greater familiarity with the library catalog and databases. Besides, going to the library is fun! It's also a low-stakes way to push students out of their comfort zone (and into the stacks). My students have described the visit to the library as a "treasure hunt" and many characterize it as a "real college experience."

The exercise usually works best before students begin significant research on their own or as they are working through the scholarly literature on a topic. But it could also be used between the draft and final revision stage to help them consider the hard choices they must make about the organization of their own work. If students are just beginning their research, they could follow the exercise by locating four potential sources and then deciding on which two of the four to keep based on their assessment of the ToCs. If the class is on a well-defined theme, you can have students create a lightly annotated shared bibliography out of the books they brought to class, possibly using Google Docs or other collaborative word-processing tools. (On developing annotated biblio-

Table 6 ("What Makes ToCs Tick?")

Source (format):	Who produced it?	What's the scope?	How is it organized?	Who is the intended audience?
Textbook Foner's *Give Me Liberty!*	One author; published by a commercial press	Broad: covers a long chronology, large geographic area, and multiple themes	Each chapter covers many topics and places within a period of U.S. history, advancing in chronological sequence. No footnotes, but a list of suggested readings for each chapter at the end of the volume.	Students
Essay collection Shankman's *The World of the Revolutionary American Republic*	One editor, but many authors; a scholarly publisher, but not a university press	Medium: the volume as a whole is focused thematically, but the essays range widely in geographical and chronological scope.	Each chapter is its own self contained argument, focused on a geographic, thematic, or chronological topic. Endnotes are included with each chapter.	Other scholars; some students
Monograph Conroy-Krutz's *Christian Imperialism*	One author; published by a university press	Small: an in-depth study of one subject; each chapter contributes to one larger argument	A series of limited case studies rather than one chronological narrative. Endnotes but no bibliography.	Other scholars; students; some nonspecialist readers

graphies, see "Trust Your Gut [But Not Too Much].") If students are closer to the end of a research project, ask them to produce a ToC for their own draft and explain its logic.

On one occasion, a student brought in a book foundational to the field. It provided a great opportunity to discuss the ways in which a book could be influential, not only through the ideas it communicated, but also through its social context. In this case, not only had the author provided a foundational interpretation that many other works had used as a springboard, they had also mentored many graduate students and thanked them in the acknowledgements—some of whom were authors of other students' show-and-tell books. Seeing that books are social as well as intellectual texts can be a revelation—and help students see *their* research project as participating in the world of scholarship (which of course, it does!).

Trust Your Gut (But Not Too Much)

Nimisha Barton

Help students see how personal intuition can jumpstart scholarly critique.

Writing Focus: *analysis, sources*
Teacher Preparation: *medium*
Student Preparation: *low*
Estimated Time: *50 minutes*
General Disciplines: *humanities, social sciences, sciences*

EXERCISE

Prep Work: Prepare two handouts: 1) "Sample Entries for an Annotated Bibliography," featuring three entries of varying quality; and 2) the "Drawing on Your Intuition" worksheet. (Samples of each are provided below, along with suggestions for crafting your own.) Ask students to bring a copy of a secondary source they have read to class, ideally one they plan to use for a research project.

Step One: (5 minutes) Because students may struggle to keep track of multiple secondary sources when first undertaking a long research project, begin by asking about their progress managing their sources. What challenges have they encountered so far? Assure students that all academic writers experience difficulties when trying to keep track of numerous sources while a) remaining attentive to each author's thesis, sources, and methods, and b) trying to foresee how the sources will eventually fit into a broader scholarly conversation.

Be sure also to ask what role, if any, they think their personal reactions should play in evaluating their sources or building their own arguments. Even if they're not sure how to answer this question, introducing the idea will help prepare them for the turn to intuition later in the exercise.

Step Two: (20 minutes) To demonstrate the utility of annotated bibliographies, distribute the first handout, which provides three sample entries ranging in quality from "not so useful" to "very useful." Ask students to spend about five minutes reading through, marking up, and comparing the three entries to one another. Then divide the class into small groups and invite them to spend another five minutes or so discussing their responses. What makes some entries more useful than others, and why? What questions do the more useful entries answer, and how? Which entries will be helpful in the weeks and months after you've read them, and why? Reconvene the full class to share reflections and develop a list on the board of the most important attributes of useful annotated bibliography entries. While the specifics of each discussion will vary, the essential components typically include: 1) a summary version of the author's thesis, 2) a *with*-the-grain analysis of the argument, 3) an *against*-the-grain analysis, and 4) a short reflection about how the source fits into one's own research project. Note that only the third entry in the sample annotated bibliography handout meets these criteria.

At a basic level, for students undertaking a long research project for the first time, annotated bibliographies hedge against forgetting about sources read weeks, perhaps months, earlier. As students will see in the next step, annotated bibliographies can also be a place for them to draw on their initial intuitions about their sources, even if they aren't already experts in the topics they are researching.

Step Three: (10 minutes) Now distribute a sample completed version of the "Drawing on Your Intuition" worksheet based on the "very useful" entry from the sample annotated bibliography handout. As you review the sample worksheet, you may want to suggest the following process for students when they proceed to complete worksheets for their own sources:

- In part 1 ("Paraphrase the Thesis"), locate the author's thesis and restate it in your own words.
- In part 2 ("Record Your Intuitions "), sort your initial responses to a text into two general categories: what you "agree with" and what you are "skeptical of." These initial responses may concern any aspect of the source text, including the author's motive, thesis, source use, analysis, etc.
- In part 3 ("Bring Critical Scrutiny . . ."), be cautious about the leap from intuitive agreement to with-the-grain (WTG) analysis. What we initially agree with might not turn out to be the fullest and fairest interpretation of an author's argument, or we might agree with an author's conclusions for our own, very different reasons. Attentiveness to *why* we agree or disagree is often more important than the mere fact of (dis)agreement.

  Use the against-the-grain (ATG) box to highlight exactly what you find strange, surprising, puzzling, and/or problematic about a text. For instance, do your skeptical intuitive responses point toward assumptions, contradictions, or oversights in the text? Do they reveal something about the author's choice of evidence, analysis, or methodology?
- In part 4 ("Combine Your WTG and ATG Analyses . . ."), the WTG and ATG analyses, when combined, should look fairly similar to the "very useful" annotated bibliography entry.
- In part 5 ("Build Out Scholarly Connections"), you have an opportunity to establish links among individual annotated bibliography entries. (The worksheet sample below includes two rows for making connections, but you can include more or fewer depending on the makeup of your sample annotated bibliography.)

Step Four: (10 minutes) After you have shared the sample, ask students to fill out their own "Drawing on Your Intuition" worksheet, using the secondary source they have brought to class. This will give them the opportunity to try translating their own intuitions into specific with-the-grain and against-the-grain analyses. (Students who don't have time to complete their worksheets in class can finish them for homework.)

Step Five: (5 minutes) Invite students to reflect briefly on the exercise. This might be a good opportunity to facilitate a discussion about how far personal intuitions can pave the way for scholarly critique, and especially how much of one's initial intuition winds up in the final scholarly product, with a reminder that annotated bibliographies are a good place to "store" personal observations that may not make it into the final research paper.

REFLECTIONS

I first implemented a version of this exercise to provide relief to students drowning in a sea of secondary sources. Rather than constituting unnecessary busywork, I wanted to demonstrate that annotated bibliographies were a useful organizational tool during the research stage that students could return to later in the writing process to refine motive and thesis. During class discussion, however, many opened up about their difficulties finding a way into a scholarly conversation. Their concerns were only partially about the stresses of information management. Rather, they had to do with students' unfamiliarity and even discomfort with the practice of scholarly critique as opposed to "mere" summary. Moreover, as novices to a subject, field, or discipline, college students understandably find it more difficult to spot gaps, oversights, or assumptions in a text than experts who have read in their field for years.

These feelings are frequently amplified among students from first-generation, low-income, and/or minority backgrounds, some of whom, as research shows, may hold deeply ingrained beliefs about deference to authority. In other words, learned obedience toward authority figures, including established authors and well-known scholars, hampers students' critical engagement with texts. In my classrooms, I have seen clearly how this discomfort can compromise students' ability to engage in academic spaces more generally. This exercise not only gives students "permission" to critique scholars in their field; it also provides them with an opportunity to discuss the tension they may encounter between an engrained, deferential attitude toward authority figures and the norms of active engagement expected of them in a college environment (e.g., participation in seminars, office hours, and so on).

Annotated bibliographies can be challenging to prepare, particularly for novice academic writers. Remind students that developing the skills that aid us in scholarly critique takes time, and that in the early stages of a research project there is value in working outward from intuitions as long as we subject those intuitions to careful scrutiny.

I have found that steps one and three especially offer in-class opportunities for instructors to share their own past challenges as novice writers. These steps also provide instructors with the occasion to reframe students' writing-related anxieties in terms of a growth mindset. For example, in my classroom, many of my students were surprised to learn that their intuition could serve as a valuable—and valid—"tool" to jumpstart the research and writing process. For students from historically marginalized backgrounds especially, the idea that they bring their own wisdom to the classroom can come as a relief and, more importantly, a reminder that they already have what it takes to succeed in college.

If you prefer to create a sample annotated bibliography handout in keeping with your own course themes, I recommend that the "very useful" annotated bibliography entry consist of a strong summary, analysis, and reflection; that the "not so useful" entry include shoddy versions of each, or perhaps lack one or more components; and that the "sort of useful" entry fall somewhere in between. (If you have less time available for this exercise, you can also include just one annotated bibliography entry on the handout—specifically, the "very useful" one.) When using the "Drawing on Your Intuition" worksheet in class, consider providing each student with a few copies of the handout so that they can complete one for each secondary source they read.

This exercise works well with several others in this volume. You might consider using it after students have learned how to choose and assess secondary sources, a task addressed in "What Makes ToCs Tick?" The exercise also evokes themes found in "Mapping Personal and Scholarly Motive." Both render visible students' personal intuitions while creating space to consider how and why scholars translate the personal to a broader academic audience. Rather than begin from the premise that students are empty vessels in need of total assimilation to the norms of higher education, these exercises communicate that students' experiences bring value to the larger scholarly community. As such, the exercises can benefit all college students, particularly those from nontraditional backgrounds as they learn to develop a critical scholarly voice and to see themselves as part of an inclusive academic community.

HANDOUTS

Sample Entries for an Annotated Bibliography

Desan, Suzanne. *The Family on Trial in Revolutionary France*. Berkeley, CA: University of California Press, 2004.

> This book examines the French Revolution (1789–1815) as an extended family melodrama. Each chapter looks at a discrete episode of the revolution through the prism of "family drama."
>
> Chapter 2 was not very interesting, but I thought chapters 4 and 5 were well-written.

Cage, Claire. "'Celibacy Is a Social Crime': The Politics of Clerical Marriage, 1794–1799." *French Historical Studies* 36, no. 4 (2013): 601–28.

> Cage argues that during the Terror phase of the French Revolution (1794–1799), "The campaign against clerical celibacy sought not only to incorporate priests into the nation through marriage but also to transform priests, whose celibacy they viewed as a flagrant violation of the laws of nature, into ideal [fathers] and paragons of public and private virtue" (604). But the article concerns itself with a very short period of time, which could be problematic . . .
>
> This article could be useful in a research paper about France.

Tuttle, Leslie. *Conceiving the Old Regime: Pronatalism and the Politics of Reproduction in Early Modern France*. New York: Oxford University Press, 2010.

> Tuttle studies emerging pronatalist (or pro-birth) thought in seventeenth-century France. She argues that marriage and the family became salient social and political categories to rulers and administrators much longer ago than we previously thought. Starting with Louis XIV's 1666 Marriage Edict, the French monarchy began to engage in population experiments which incentivized marriage and heterosexuality as the basis for a stable, reproductive order. For example, the king offered tax breaks to fathers of twelve or more children. Although Tuttle is attentive to the king's rhetoric, edicts, and other laws, she admits they had little or no impact on the French birthrate. In other words, Tuttle does not provide an understanding of ordinary subjects' views on marriage, sexuality, and reproduction, only what the ruling classes expected of them.
>
> This book provides helpful historical context on the evolution of elite ideologies, but demonstrates that scholars still know very little about the views of French peasants during this period. Given my research interests, it makes me wonder how and why they resisted the king's will, and with what consequence.

WORKSHEET

Drawing on Your Intuition

Part 1: Paraphrase the Thesis		
Secondary Source:	*Conceiving the Old Regime* by Leslie Tuttle	
Thesis Paraphrase	Marriage and the family became salient social and political categories to French rulers and administrators much longer ago than we previously thought.	
Part 2: Record Your Intuitions		
	What I agree with:	**What I'm skeptical of:**
Intuitive Reactions	Tuttle is appropriately attentive to the king's rhetoric, edicts, and other laws (e.g., how the king offered tax breaks to fathers of twelve or more children).	Although Tuttle is attentive to the king's rhetoric, edicts, and other laws, she admits they had little or no impact on the French birthrate.
Part 3: Bring Critical Scrutiny to Bear on the Text *and* Your Intuitive Reactions		
	With-the-grain (WTG) analysis	**Against-the-grain (ATG) analysis**
Analytical Responses	Tuttle shows that the French monarchy began to engage in population experiments which incentivized marriage and heterosexuality as the basis for a stable, reproductive order. ↓	Tuttle does not provide an understanding of ordinary subjects' views on marriage, sexuality, and reproduction, only what the ruling classes expected of them. ↓

Part 4: Combine Your WTG and ATG Analyses and Add a Reflection to Aid with Your Research Project	
Annotated Bibliographic Entry	Tuttle studies emerging pronatalist (or pro-birth) thought in seventeenth-century France. She argues that marriage and the family became salient social and political categories to rulers and administrators much longer ago than we previously thought. Starting with Louis XIV's 1666 Marriage Edict, the French monarchy began to engage in population experiments which incentivized marriage and heterosexuality as the basis for a stable, reproductive order. For example, the king offered tax breaks to fathers of twelve or more children. Although Tuttle is attentive to the king's rhetoric, edicts, and other laws, she admits they had little or no impact on the French birthrate. In other words, Tuttle does not provide an understanding of ordinary subjects' views on marriage, sexuality, and reproduction, only what the ruling classes expected of them. This book provides helpful historical context on the evolution of elite ideologies, but demonstrates that scholars still know very little about the views of French peasants during this period. Given my research interests, it makes me wonder how and why they resisted the king's will, and with what consequence.
Part 5. Build out Scholarly Connections	
Related Scholarly Sources 1. Desan, *The Family on Trial* 2. Cage, "Celibacy is a Social Crime"	**In 1-2 sentences, describe the relationship between these two sources:**

Epistolary Experiments

Lindsay Reckson

Encourage students to shake off the formalities of academic prose and experiment with crafting arguments for an immediate audience.

Writing Focus: *thesis, motive, analysis, style*
Teacher Preparation: *low*
Student Preparation: *high*
Estimated Time: *80 minutes*
General Discipline: *humanities*

EXERCISE

Prep Work: Before class, ask students to read examples of epistolary criticism that model lively, informal, and sustained intellectual dialogue. The goal is to demonstrate that scholarship and friendship can be acts of shared curiosity, and to showcase analytical writing that engages a direct and immediate audience. I recommend selecting texts that combine scholarly and interpersonal care as a way of emphasizing that community is central—not incidental—to our intellectual work. For example, in "Most Affectionately Yours," scholars Tara Bynum and Alexis Pauline Gumbs write to and with one another for *The Feminist Wire* about the friendship between enslaved poet Phillis Wheatley and Obour Tanner, exploring how letter writing sustains Black women's friendship and freedom under surveillance. Gloria Anzaldua's "Speaking in Tongues: A Letter to 3rd World Woman Writers" uses the epistolary form to theorize writing as a space of collective survival. *Dear Television*, a forum published by the *Los Angeles Review of Books*, features scholars writing to one another about the cultural and communal work that television performs. Prior to class, also ask students to select a primary object of study that is familiar to them from an earlier week on the syllabus (a poem, a prose piece, an image, an artwork, a film) and bring it to class with them.

Step One: (10 minutes) Begin with a brief guided discussion of epistolary criticism that draws out the key points you want students to have in mind as they start their own experiments with the form. Ask students: What feels most exciting or productive to you about this form of criticism? What feels possible here that might not be possible in more conventional scholarly prose?

Step Two: (10 minutes) Next, have the students return to their object of study, decide where they will focus their analysis, and jot down some notes. Smaller is better here; encourage students to select a few lines of poetry, a short paragraph of prose, a portion of an image or artwork, a short film clip. In this step, the goal is simply to write down as many observations as possible, not to parse, judge, or categorize. Ask students: What are the details that make this thing what it is? Why do these details matter to you? And why might they matter to others?

Step Three: (20 minutes) Group students in pairs, set a timer for twenty minutes, and ask them to write brief letters (roughly five hundred words) to one another about their observations. Each writer might begin with a single word that seems crucial to their chosen text and spin out its possibilities; or they might start with why they felt compelled to write about this particular artwork, photograph, or film still. Encourage students to embrace informality and invite an exchange. These letters can and should ask questions, express delight or frustration, describe the details that fascinate and why. Remind students that polished prose is not the goal here—this is an experiment in writing to an immediate audience (in this case, someone sitting right next to you who will be answering very shortly).

Step Four: (25 minutes) In this step, invite pairs to read and respond to one another's messages, taking up the invitation to engage their classmate's ideas and highlighting what they found exciting in them. Emphasize the need for a real response, one that recognizes and affirms what the original message is aiming at and builds on it in some way. Ask students: what did your classmate's letter allow you to understand differently about the text or image? What are some questions that it opened up for you? Since their correspondence in essence becomes a jointly produced analysis, ensure that students have complete records of the exchanges to reference if they'll be going on to write individually authored papers on the topic.

Step Five: (15 minutes) In this final step, encourage students to reflect on what they learned in the process of writing directly to a peer. Invite them to share favorite moments from their exchanges with the class, and ask: What fresh analytical insights did you gain by corresponding with your classmate? What did you learn from the experience of informal peer exchange that might be helpful when it comes to writing your way into a scholarly conversation?

REFLECTIONS

The letter form demonstrates that writing and analysis are, fundamentally, acts of shared curiosity and care. Over and over, I have witnessed student writing transformed by the simple yet profound addition of an immediate addressee. Rather than trying to produce something that looks and sounds like a successful academic essay, students almost invariably shift their focus to the hard, messy, and joyful work of communicating: to sharing, on their own terms, what they observe and why it matters. Their letters are funny, irreverent, self-reflexive—full of the personality that academic writing in its less inspiring forms can sometimes suppress. Released from the pressure of formal prose, students also pay attention in new ways, learning to understand a text or image through the perspectives of their peers, to account for multiple (sometimes conflicting) interpretations, and thereby to deepen their own analyses.

Writing directly to a peer enables students to take risks, giving them space to be more playful and exploratory in their thinking and writing. While students are occasionally unnerved by the prospect of throwing off their hard-earned fluency in the conventions of the academic essay, they also report feeling challenged and empowered to write from a place of real intellectual curiosity. One student observed, for example, that through this experiment they felt "liberated" to make a "braver claim," while still "remaining grounded by the text." Students often reflect that writing to someone they know (even a little bit) makes the argument matter more—it makes it personal. In this sense, the epistolary form helps students develop a stronger understanding of motive, a compelling reason for why we should pay attention to something in a particular way. Asking students to describe the tone of their letters (wistful? conspiratorial? ebullient?) also helps them recognize the importance of style as it frames the reader's entry into the writer's intellectual world.

Instructors have several options for ensuring students produce and maintain a record of their in-class correspondence. They could write their letters as an email exchange, compose them in a shared Google Doc, or pass a Word document back and forth, making sure both participants have a saved copy afterward. Or they could (even!) handwrite their letters, taking photos of them afterward. Whatever mechanism you choose, the key is that students retain access to the primary source they've created, so they can draw on (and cite) it later as needed.

Try experimenting with timing and format. Rather than two longer sessions, for example, you might break it up into three or more short exchanges to emphasize the loose, improvisational form of this writing. You might position student pairs on opposite sides of the room and have them send emails or DMs to each other in class (messaging can be a great way to release students from the pressure of drafting formal prose). As a follow-up to this exercise, I often ask students to revise their in-class writing into full drafts that extend their analysis of a creative text. In some cases, students might retain the epistolary form, continuing their exchange with a classmate over a set period of time or a set number of letters with the goal of developing their argument through scholarly dialogue. Alternatively, students might keep the core ideas they developed through the exchange and revise them into a single-authored essay, with citations to mark where a classmate's contributions shaped their thinking.

The exercise works particularly well when asking students to tackle questions of address and authority. By inserting an "I" into their academic writing, and reflecting on the shift, students often develop important insight on scholarly voice, situated knowledge, and disciplinary norms. Many students reflect that this exercise helped them unpack their assumptions about academic writing and learn to practice it on their own terms. Endlessly adaptable, an alternative version of the exercise can help students grapple with a difficult theoretical text: rather than writing to a peer, students write directly to a theorist ("Dear bell hooks," for example), engaging the theorist's ideas and narrating how those ideas helped expand the student's understanding of a text or other object of study. This version of the exercise is especially useful for helping advanced students shift from *applying* theory to engaging in dialogue *with* theory, authorizing them to be in conversation with a theorist whose ideas they admire.

Most importantly, the epistolary form helps students realize that writing is always a conversation, and that we need scholarly community—and friendship—to clarify and extend our thinking. The exercise insists that we treat the work of others with attention and care, building invaluable community and trust in the classroom. It also leads to stronger citation practices. When students revise their exchanges into single-authored essays, I encourage them to mark where the exchange influenced the direction of their analysis, and to cite and acknowledge their peers in the footnotes, alongside their scholarly sources. Foregrounding scholarly dialogue means students are better able to recognize and name the way others' ideas have shaped their thinking, and to make that explicit in their writing. The results are often beautiful. The epistolary experiment reminds us that even when we are writing alone, we are never actually writing alone.

Click to Reply

Christopher M. Kurpiewski

Develop concrete strategies for productive conversation by engaging in forums sometimes notorious for just the opposite: online discussion threads.

Writing Focus: *ethos, motive, evidence, analysis*
Teacher Preparation: *low*
Student Preparation: *medium*
Estimated Time: *60 minutes*
General Disciplines: *humanities, social sciences, sciences*

EXERCISE

Prep Work: Go online to Reddit (or another discussion-based, social media site) and select a popular discussion thread about a topic or news item that's relevant to an academic reading you've assigned for this class. The ideal thread for this exercise invites genuine discussion but demonstrates a mix of generous and ungenerous responses. Bear in mind, given the genre, that you'll have troves of mean-spiritedness to select from. Calibrate your choice of thread according to how much you expect your students to tolerate the presence of trolls. In particular, online discussion forums can raise sensitive issues of race, class, gender, and sexuality, which, on the one hand, can be useful opportunities for productive analysis, and on the other, may also require an investment of time and careful facilitation to manage effectively. The example thread I use in class is quite friendly and supportive, and I've included sample comments and discussion notes with my reflections at the end.

For homework, have students read the assigned academic text and the discussion thread. Ask them to identify at least one detail in the academic text that feels relevant to the discussion thread. In the discussion thread itself, have students highlight different moments from the conversation a) where they feel persuaded, b) where they feel ready to debate, and c) where they feel like the conversation gets cut short or sabotaged. Ask them to take notes about what they notice in terms of tone and substance across these different moments.

Step One: (10 minutes) Ask students to take out their annotated version of the discussion thread. Place them in pairs and have them work together to identify particular comments that fit into each of the categories listed below. They should expect some disagreement about particular choices. When deciding, they should characterize any differences in language they observed between moments when they felt persuaded or open to debate, and moments when they felt the conversation had reached a dead end.

1. Comments that add value
2. Comments that are both productive and problematic
3. Comments that are problematic but not yet trollsome
4. Comments that are trollsome

Step Two: (15 minutes) Reconvene and lead a full class discussion about the students' choices, inviting them to reflect on the rhetorical moves that seem to invite debate and extend the conversation versus those that stifle nuance or shut the conversation down. This can also be an opportunity for students to reflect on their personal limits for when to remove themselves from a conversation that's become circular or unproductive, aggressive, or otherwise toxic. You may find the following questions useful to guide discussion:

- How do writers persuade you that they have a question worth asking or an insight worth taking into account?
- What was different about the language and delivery of these comments compared to those that made you feel less engaged?
- Identify a comment that made you ask a question of your own. What about the comment brought this question to mind?
- Identify a comment that's trying to deliver a conclusion, whether warranted or not. How does the writer attempt to establish authority? How effective is the attempt?
- For comments that are problematic but not yet trollsome, why were they so? How could the writer revise to make their comment more helpful?
- For comments that are trollsome, what separates them from the merely problematic? (We'll revisit this question in step five.)
- What different intentions seem to underwrite different categories of comments? While one can never prove intention, students might have good reason to suspect varying motives behind the contributions.

Step Three: (10 minutes) Back in pairs, have students choose a moment in the discussion thread where their assigned academic reading has some useful application. Have them collaborate on a potential response—in a hundred words or less—that draws explicitly on the reading, invites further debate, and keeps the conversation going. No trolling.

Step Four: (10 minutes) When they're ready, have each pair present their intervention to the class. Discuss strengths and areas for improvement, reflecting back on the previous discussion. Let the class vote on the best intervention and award the "Wisest Posters" a prize.

Step Five: (10 minutes) Having practiced productive interventions, move to consider their opposite (all too common online). Note that in earlier steps we never defined "troll"—how would students do so? What are some of the *trolliest* rhetorical moves that separate a troll from merely a bad responder, let alone a good digital citizen? How should we respond, if at all, to trolls when we encounter them? How should our practices differ across contexts or platforms? Does the presence of a moderator change how we think about our own responsibilities?

Step Six: (5 minutes) Conclude by asking students to take a step back to consider how they might use their analysis of the digital environment to articulate an ethics of conversation in the "real world" of their academic interactions with each other and with their sources. Invite them to propose specific strategies for sustaining a generous and productive ethos in their classroom discussions and essay writing. (They might identify already named strategies in action, or draw on the academic article for additional models.) Collect the strategies on the board so students leave class with a useful reference guide to ethical scholarship.

REFLECTIONS

I developed this exercise in response to students feeling intimidated at the prospect of responding to a scholarly text in class or on the page. And while it's true I want to teach my students new strategies for engaging scholarship, it's also true that they already know something about the differences between generative and dead-end discussions. This lesson attempts to build on their social-media savvy to help them over the hurdle.

The structure of "Click to Reply" facilitates critique, and by keeping the focus on ethos, language, and audience, the sequencing helps students assess and revise their own practices for motivating an issue and supporting a claim with evidence. I chose Reddit because it can be a surprisingly generous, at times even thoughtful community; topics range from human evolution to climate change, and from the economy of tariffs to the authenticity of vinyl records. Drafting responses to the Reddit thread also provides low-stakes practice responding to critical terms and assumptions, giving students the opportunity to translate strategies for taking a stand while still inviting further debate.

During class discussions, my students tend to gravitate toward generous comments, taking expressions of gratitude by the original poster as a measure of a comment's persuasiveness. In contrast, they identify commonplace remarks and cues as weaker forms of rhetoric, especially compared to comments that are more specific in their thinking or that synthesize new viewpoints for consideration. Frankly, I wasn't expecting that. Rather than veer away from comments that presented ambiguity, students reported feeling more engaged by posts that complicated or drew distinctions between key terms. They were identifying motive in the wild, then recognizing the persuasive impact of relevant examples and specific explanations. When sometimes students mistook interpretations for facts, it became an opportunity for us to wrestle with the meaning of "proof" and with qualifiers like "correct," "incorrect," "right," and "wrong." One student summarized her takeaway: "Being specific and leaving out judgments is how we take [our readers] seriously." And as they learned to calibrate their

Reddit responses, I witnessed my students beginning to take themselves seriously as critical writers.

For my class, we analyze the responses to Reddit user Mikjall22 in the subreddit r/Genealogy who says he is "36% Irish" and is "trying to figure out . . . a good tattoo and spirituality," unsure whether he should identify more as "germanic/Norse [*sic*]" or "Celtic." (As of this writing, the full archived thread is available at https://www.reddit.com/r/Genealogy/comments/cb2j59/.) Here are excerpts from the thread that my students have tended to reference in the course of our discussion, organized according to the broader categories, with brief insights that have emerged from analyzing them:

1. Comments that add value

[THEPINEAPPLEMAN:] *There are theories that the Celts never invaded/migrated to Ireland. It's called Celtoskeptism. It's up for debate whether or not the pre-Roman Britons were Celts. Others say "Celtic" is just a culture, not a people group.*

[GRIBBSJ:] *I would recommend looking at the specific regions where your ancestors are from if you want to connect with them spiritually or culturally. If your [sic] interested in ancient Irish ancestry specifically, start your research with groups around those areas.*

Discussion Notes: I emphasize the persuasiveness of specificity when students are intrigued by new details or when a comment draws a critical distinction between key terms. Later in the thread "thepineappleman" synthesizes news reports about recent archaeological finds, and students remarked how persuaded they were by his effective combination of quotation, paraphrase, and summary.

2. Comments that are both productive and problematic

[GRIBBSJ:] *You're asking a complicated question, it would be more accurate to say "Celtic" is a cultural identity. We may attribute DNA to certain groups of people, but that tells us nothing about individual or collective cultural identity.*

[HELLA_CIOUS:] *To quote T. W. Rolleston's classic work Celtic Myths and Legends, "A Celt is anyone who considers themselves a Celt." Basically if you're Irish and you consider Irish Celtic, you're a Celt.*

[STRIXTHEOWL:] *I do know that a fair bit of Norse symbolism is being co-opted by far right neo-nazis [sic] as well, so yeah, choose carefully.*

Discussion Notes: The first two posts helpfully let us ask what it means to be Celtic by distinguishing genetic from cultural identity, but then also make rhetorical moves that may discourage further discussion. The first introduces a relevant distinction, but in so doing seems to undermine the validity of the initial question without offering the original poster a way to make use of this new information. The second cites Rolleston as a "classic" source with a contribution to that question, but wrongly assumes it carries decisive, conversation-ending authority on the matter. Here my students picked up on the use of the word "basically," which led to the realization that the comment lacked sufficient detail to allow them to respond substantively. From there, we were able to begin identifying commonplace remarks and distinguish them from stronger evidence-based claims. The final commenter isn't wrong. But the admonition comes out of the blue, at once escalating the stakes and perhaps attempting to give the final word on the original poster's choice of tattoo. The comment is a chance to use Godwin's Law ("as an online discussion grows longer, the probability of a comparison involving Nazis or Hitler approaches one") as an opportunity to discuss the dangers of casual historical analogy, and informal fallacies like the slippery slope more generally.

The Reddit thread I use for class is perhaps unusually generous, which keeps us from directly engaging with the *trollier* end of the rhetorical spectrum. That being said, I have strategies in mind for when we do come across committed trolls. The examples below by the user "ckurpiewski" are completely fabricated, but they can help illustrate how I discuss problematic and mean-spirited contributions with students.

3. Problematic but not yet trollsome

[MIKJALL22:] *I guess nothing is 100% . . .*

[RITE2:] *. . . tbh that sounds very generic and edgy for a tattoo, but hey, your decision.*

[CKURPIEWSKI:] *It's amazing that 40 is the optimal scale value of a 7 x 11 isosceles triangle, which the ancients understood when they built the pyramids at Giza. And I think the Mayans knew it too. Math is our shared inheritance.*

Discussion Notes: These commenters aren't *trollsome*, but platitudes, value judgments, and off-topic claims rarely contribute or extend the conversation; if anything, they tend to shut it down or send it off on wild tangents unhelpful to the original discussion. When asked to respond to one of these comments, students realize they can only counter with their own opinion or otherwise acknowledge a dead-end in the conversation. It further clarifies the distinction between editorial and arguable claims.

4. Trollsome

[CKURPIEWSKI:] *"germanic/Norse"or "Celtic" . . . you don't even know if you're from Asgard or Boston, but you're ready to put a tattoo about it on your body? What an idiot. Go buy yourself some Lucky Charms and give thanks to Odin.*

[CKURPIEWSKI:] *The actual Celts were heroic warriors, you're just some wannabe! What are you going to do—build a fort and fight the Romans from your mom's basement?!*

Discussion Notes: I expect students will quickly categorize comments like these as unhelpful, but reflecting on why can help generate more specific discussions about ethos. For example, comments like these are opportunities to talk about deflection and the ad hominem fallacy, differences between value judgments and assessing evidence, and when—or if—it's worthwhile to engage someone's position. It's also a chance for students to consider how to process and/or respond when a stranger throws shade their way. We can ask how comments like these reflect on the writer, and how pathos compares with ethos when entering scholarly conversations.

Don't Forget Your Backpack

Leslie Ribovich

Equip students with a primary source backpack as they set out to make their mark in the scholarly terrain.

Writing Focus: *motive, analysis, evidence, sources*
Teacher Preparation: *high*
Student Preparation: *none*
Estimated Time: *80 minutes*
General Disciplines: *humanities, social sciences, sciences*

EXERCISE

Prep Work: Bring: 1) a thematically relevant primary source (such as copies of a graph and/or a short clip from a television series), 2) note cards, 3) "backpacks," one per small group—brown paper lunch bags work well (you need not be skilled in arts and crafts to run this activity!), 4) short summaries of three or four scholarly sources, and 5) a sample trail map of your choice—for example, the Pinelands National Reserve Batona Trail, available online.

Step One: (15 minutes) Distribute or show copies of your primary source, along with two notecards per person. After students read/watch the source, ask them to brainstorm two observations about what strikes them as interesting, puzzling, contradictory, or otherwise important. Each observation should be written on a notecard. Collect and randomize the notecards, sneakily putting them in the backpacks (which you have hidden under the table or behind a podium) while students go on to step two. This creates an air of mystery—where did the notecards go?

Step Two: (20 minutes) Now distribute the scholarly source summaries and have students read two of them aloud. (It will likely be most helpful if you work through the two most conceptually complicated examples at this stage.) Lead a short discussion establishing what the core arguments of both texts are and what a scholarly conversation between the sources might sound like. What shared topics or themes are they interested in? Where do they likely disagree? What key concepts and terms are in play?

Put students in small groups and task them with talking through the remaining sources to find the core arguments and how those core arguments speak to each other. Then share the sample trail map and explain the second part of their task: to represent the relationship among the authors' arguments visually as camps in a landscape. Encourage students to lean into the metaphor as far as possible. Are there clear paths or navigable rivers between authors with compatible arguments? Are there downed trees blocking trails or roving wolf packs making the territory between some authors treacherous? Is there uncharted territory and what might be found there? What broader academic debate is the map adjacent to or embedded in? Have each group draw their map on the board—or make their map available for others to see in some way.

The trail map metaphor is an adaptation of the scholarly ballroom metaphor that Mark Gaipa uses to such excellent effect in his 2004 article for the journal *Pedagogy*, "Breaking into the Conversation: How Students Can Acquire Authority for Their Writing," where he describes the benefits of helping students visualize the scholarly conversation—and their place within it—through cartoon sketches.

Step Three: (10 minutes) Moderate a discussion in which students share and compare their maps collectively as a class. This provides an opportunity to clear up any fundamental misunderstandings of the sources and explore the legitimate range in interpretation. If they wish, allow groups to revise their maps in light of the conversation since the richer the landscape, the more effective the next step will be.

Step Four: (5 minutes) Time for the big reveal! Pull the backpacks out from under the desk and distribute one to each group. A snazzy picture of a colorful backpack on a slide can also add to the effect. Each backpack should include roughly twice the number of primary source observations as there are members in the group. Explain that when we enter a scholarly conversation, we become one of the scholars navigating the trail map, and we must come prepared with our research to have a conversation that challenges, complements, or revises the existing conversation. While scholars may spend years gathering and sifting through evidence, for this class, our analysis of the primary source allows us to contribute to the conversation.

Step Five: (20 minutes) Back in the same groups, have students pull notecards from the backpack. Invite them to discuss which observations—ultimately arriving at one per student—seem most promising. What looks different about the observations now that they've read the scholarly summaries and made the trail map? What can they do with the observations to make their own mark on the map? In other words, how would their analysis of their observation possibly change the landscape of the debate in some substantive way? It can be helpful to model a sample intervention on the map before having the groups start their work.

Each student is then responsible for drawing in their own intervention on the group's map. Students might, for example, build a new camp, mark new trails (sensitive to which trees might fall in the process), release or weed out an invasive species, establish a joint research base camp, construct a bridge over a rock fall—and they need to be prepared to explain the underlying logic of their intervention.

Step Six: (10 minutes) Reconvene and have each group share the one or two interventions on their map they feel turned out to be most significant/most promising as the starting point for an essay. Emphasize that there is no one right way to do this, but rather the backpack empowers them to make their own claims through visualization.

REFLECTIONS

When students first encounter the prospect of original research, they often ask how they can enter a scholarly conversation given that the other scholars are experts who have spent years gathering research. This exercise gives you a framework to respond to that question, while honoring their valid concerns. The backpack and trail map metaphors emphasize that students earn their way into the conversation by combining original analysis of primary source material with an awareness of the existing scholarly landscape.

I developed the exercise the first time I taught a first-year writing seminar on mass incarceration. In draft conferences, I saw that students were confused about the differences between scholarly and primary sources. I found myself repeating that the key was in how students used the sources. In each conference, I ended up drawing stick figures with a backpack. I asked students what they were bringing to the conversation about media representation and wrote their responses—in this case, observations about *Orange is the New Black*—in the backpack. They were able to articulate their original questions and claims much more clearly following these conferences.

In later semesters, I foregrounded the backpack metaphor with this exercise when introducing students to a curated scholarly conversation about the mental health consequences of incarceration for individuals, family members, and whole communities. In sorting through the accompanying primary evidence, students often noticed that incarcerated women experience higher rates of mental illness than incarcerated men. With that observation in mind, students wondered if women in communities with high incarceration rates experience higher instances of mental illness than men. They quickly developed a research question that arose from evidence and pointed toward a promising project.

The fun of the exercise is in the reveal of the backpack. Students tend to think that learning about the serious task of academic research with a makeshift backpack constructed from a paper lunch bag is pretty silly. I embrace the silliness. For instance, after we do the backpack exercise, I leave the backpacks on display in my office to spark students' imaginations as they write their own papers. Once, weeks after we had done the exercise in class, a student came in for a meeting about a draft that wasn't making an original claim, but instead delivering information, report-style. We were having a conversation about one of the draft's paragraphs when the student suddenly said, "Backpack!" "Backpack?" I asked, forgetting the paper bags behind me. "We wear the backpack—it just clicked! The primary source goes in the backpack and then we go to the scholarly conversation wearing the backpack. I get what we're doing now." To prompt such moments, I have also made individual backpacks for each student, so that they can practice the exercise with their own material. Students joke about their cool new accessories. Or, if there is time in class, students can craft their own backpacks.

I've found that the backpack provides a useful visual metaphor that transfers to other assignments. Early in one semester, I had a student struggling to get from the sources provided to an original argument. She wanted to make an argument about the purpose of prisons as it related to mental health, but only one of the sources offered a definition; the others just provided data. The exercise helped her see that her contribution would come in part from analyzing the sources' implicit assumptions about the purpose of prisons—for instance, as seen in the data they collected, what methodology they used, and so on. This was the material that belonged in her backpack. Even with this breakthrough, it was still a reach for her to bring the analysis of each individual source to a cohesive thesis, but it was a start. The payoff really emerged in a later paper, when she wanted to write about the environmental toxicity of a particular prison where there was no direct evidence about that prison. The student looked to sources that were not specifically about that prison—in particular an environmental mapping tool—and effectively constructed an original question and argument by bringing indirect evidence in the backpack and offering original analysis. The skills learned in the backpack exercise tend to reappear throughout the semester and in papers with different disciplinary bents.

Synthesizing Science

Loren B. Byrne

Students engage in the work of scientists by summarizing research articles, collaboratively writing synthetic abstracts, and proposing questions for further inquiry.

Writing Focus: *sources, motive, analysis*
Teacher Preparation: *medium*
Student Preparation: *high*
Estimated Time: *50 minutes*
General Discipline: *sciences*

EXERCISE

Prep Work: Identify a topic (general or narrow) amenable to having students locate, read, summarize, present, and synthesize peer-reviewed articles. A controversial topic or one that can be analyzed from diverse perspectives works particularly well because many articles will be needed to understand it in a holistic way. (In my courses, I have used natural selection, food webs, water pollution, amphibian declines, green roofs, and the effects of earthworms on soil.) The exercise's general structure is a modification of the "jigsaw" technique, as described at www.jigsaw.org.

For homework, ask each student to find a peer-reviewed article relevant to the focal topic. Beginning students may need additional help to find and assess scholarly articles, such as a lesson about how to use library databases or other search engines. Have each student email you a properly formatted bibliographic reference of the article for approval. This allows you to ensure that everyone has a relevant, useful, and unique article (though uniqueness matters less in large classes if students will present the same article in separate groups). Emphasizing proper formatting reinforces the professional practice of paying attention to details when preparing reference lists. Be sure to assign this search-and-approval step well before the class meeting because students may need to find an alternative article if their first choice is taken or inappropriate for the exercise.

Before class, have students prepare short presentations about their articles, focusing on the research question, a brief summary of methods and results, the conclusion, and the broader scientific or social significance. Share strategies with students in advance about how to read scientific articles (for example, encourage them to identify the one essential point from each section). Reassure less-experienced students that research articles can be difficult for even professional scientists; and that it's okay not to understand all the technical terms or details, especially of methods and statistics. To facilitate presentations, ask students to prepare formal notes or slides (see below). Finally, to guide students' in-class work, create a handout with prompts, like the "Worksheet Prompts" from step four below.

Step One: (5 minutes) Introduce the exercise by emphasizing how synthesizing "the literature" is essential to the work of scientists. In this context, synthesis refers to the process of bringing together information from different articles to generate emergent insights. Share upfront with students the purpose of the exercise: their presentations will enable them to gain a more holistic understanding of the topic, generate connections among the results of different studies, and ask better questions for future research. Note that professional scientists complete these essential tasks when writing grant proposals and manuscripts.

Step Two: (30 minutes) The format and time allotted for student presentations are flexible—a function of class size, meeting duration, and instructor preferences. In smaller classes (ten students or fewer), have each student present to the whole class for three to five minutes, either informally without handouts or more formally with one or two summary slides. In larger classes (more than ten students), consider creating small groups of four to six in which students present only to their fellow group members. To ensure sustained attention during the presentations and to prepare for synthesis work, ask students to record summative notes about, and in-text citations for, the presented articles (worksheet prompt 1 below).

Step Three: (15 minutes) In pairs (or in small presentation groups), have students discuss and integrate information from across the articles to draft a synthetic abstract (prompt 2 below). If your students are unfamiliar with synthetic abstracts, you might consider providing them with a one-paragraph model on a different topic. Remind them of the importance of proper attribution, which dictates the inclusion of properly formatted in-text citations in this paragraph. Reconvene the class to compare main points from their abstracts and discuss missed or underemphasized relationships and synthetic insights.

Step Four: (15–20 minutes, optional) If time permits—or for homework—have students respond to prompts 3–6, which ask them to brainstorm and generatively write about follow-up questions, hypotheses, future research, and personal reflections, all inspired by the set of articles. In the same or next class, students can share some of their ideas, which can facilitate further discussions about synthesizing science.

REFLECTIONS

Many students do not realize how important reviewing the literature and writing effectively are to the work of scientists (both are absent from simple models of "the scientific method"). They often find themselves challenged by the tasks of conducting rigorous literature searches, reading and synthesizing multiple articles, and writing in the science genre. Repeated practice of these tasks, including with peers, can help improve students' abilities and confidence. When using this exercise, I emphasize that "this is what real scientists do" and that it is not "busy work." Further, the exercise reflects the collaborative nature of contemporary science, which requires skills for interpersonal communication and co-creation of synthesized knowledge through presentations, discussion, and writing.

I have found the exercise to be pedagogically valuable both because it is easily modified (for varied topics, it can be shortened or extended) and because it helps introduce variety into a series of lecture-heavy class days. It can be used in many course contexts, from introductory through advanced; from narrowly focused through broadly interdisciplinary; in lecture, laboratory, and seminar formats; and with enrollments of many sizes. A variety of follow-up assignments could be used: students might draw concept maps to illustrate connections across and locate gaps within the literature; extend their review with a more targeted search of articles; prepare an annotated bibliography; or write a formal literature review paper.

In one particularly successful iteration, I used the exercise in an introductory biology lab in which students worked in pairs to choose and present an article about the ecology and evolution of cardinals. As part of the lesson, I introduced the idea of the literature and walked students through the search process, subsequently providing guidance and approving articles for presentations as they searched during class time. Because this was some students' first time presenting an article, I gave them an explicit outline requiring five slides—for 1) introduction, 2) question and hypothesis, 3) methods, 4) results, and 5) conclusion—which reduced their anxiety. To emphasize that giving and accepting constructive, peer-review comments are essential parts of science, these students were asked to offer immediate oral feedback on each other's presentations. The approach worked extremely well with high levels of engagement from many students; in part, I think this was helped by my explicit creation of a safe space, making it clear that all students would be equally critiqued because everyone (including me) can improve their communication skills. After the presentations, most students were able successfully to complete the worksheet and seemed to enjoy the process of critical reflection and asking follow-up questions. For a few, the exercise generated valuable just-in-time teaching moments, such as discussing how to do synthesis when one student admitted that she didn't understand what was expected.

Another option, if you are emphasizing course content over research skills, is to choose the articles yourself, or to use non-peer-reviewed texts (newspaper and magazine articles, or websites). I used these approaches in an introduction to a sustainability studies course, with many nonscience students, to explore the topic of lawn and garden ecology and management. By simplifying the exercise, I found that students were readily able to achieve the desired synthesis goals, which may not have been possible if they became overwhelmed by the unfamiliar tasks of locating and reading science articles. This variation can also be used to emphasize the need to evaluate the quality and reliability of popular press articles and websites (for example, websites authored by lawn chemical companies).

In summary, I have found that this exercise accomplishes several learning goals at once. It fosters rewarding student-generated discussions and connections (many of which I would not have included in a lecture). It helps students recognize the importance of reviewing the literature and of collaboration as essential parts of "doing science." Perhaps most importantly, it creates dynamic learner-centered classrooms in which students improve both their synthesizing and scientific writing skills.

HANDOUT

Synthesizing Science Worksheet

1. Lit Review & Summary: Record a summative take-home message (2–3 sentences) and in-text citation (for example, author and year format) for each presented article.
2. Synthesizing Science: What can be learned from this group of articles? Write a synthetic abstract (one paragraph) that identifies connections among the articles. What are the similarities and differences across the studies? How does the information from each relate to the others? What insights emerge from bringing them together that would be missed with just one article? Include properly formatted in-text citations to identify the sources for each sentence.
3. New Questions: Using the presented articles as inspiration, write three follow-up questions to guide future research about the topic.
4. Hypothesis Formation: Choose one of the questions and write an (alternative) hypothesis about expected results that you predict to find with additional research. Why do you expect those findings?
5. Hypothesis Testing: What could be done to investigate your hypotheses? Describe a field experiment or observational study that could be conducted to test your hypothesis. Identify as many essential methodological details as you can.
6. Reflection: Take a moment to reflect on what you've learned. What new insights have you gained about the topic and value of reading and synthesizing peer-reviewed literature as a part of scientific research? Be as specific as you can.

Puzzling Out Structure with a Jigsaw

Marcus Johnson

Unpack the structural logic of research articles with an in-class jigsaw puzzle.

Writing Focus: *structure, conventions*
Teacher Preparation: *medium to high*
Student Preparation: *none*
Estimated Time: *60 minutes*
General Disciplines: *sciences and social sciences*

EXERCISE

Prep Work: Select a text that follows a standard structure within your discipline. In the case of the empirical political science research articles with which I work, for example, the elements typically include introduction, literature review, argument, methods, results, and conclusion, and these elements are explicitly signaled with subheadings. (In the case of the sciences, they might be: abstract, introduction, methods, results, discussion, conclusion.) There may be differences in emphasis among the sections or in the details of the subheadings, which can reveal the valuable flexibility that inheres within the traditional baseline structure.

Create a handout that consists of bolded subheadings corresponding to the main sections of the paper's structure along with one or two brief excerpts (two to four sentences each) representative of the work that section performs in the overall argument. Your excerpt for the introduction, for example, might be the statement of the author's research question. One of my preferred articles for the exercise is "Race, Resources and Representation: Evidence from Brazilian Politicians," by Natalia Bueno and Thad Dunning. It can also be productive to use one of your own articles since that allows you to speak firsthand to your structural choices. That is the context in which I created the sample handout below, which you are welcome to use for the exercise or as a model to create your own.

Note that the sample handout's bold subheadings correspond to the article's essential structural elements—not, in all cases, to the subheadings that appear explicitly in the published article. This will provide an important opportunity for discussion at the end of the exercise.

Your class will be working in small groups, so make enough copies of the jigsaw handout that each group will have one. Cut each copy into pieces to create the puzzle, making sure to separate the subheadings from their associated excerpts. You will end up with subheading pieces (six if you're using the sample handout) as well as individual pieces for each excerpt from the scholarly text (ten if you're using the sample). Be sure to prepare a complete set of puzzle pieces for each group with the pieces pre-scrambled.

Step One: (10 minutes) Get students situated in their small groups and distribute the scrambled puzzle pieces. Explain the task: They'll be doing an essay jigsaw puzzle with a couple of advanced twists. First of all, they have only a handful of pieces to lay out, not the entire essay, so they should leave gaps where they think missing pieces should go. Second, there's no picture of the finished whole to look at as they work—they are intuiting what they can from what they have. Their mission is to match each excerpt to the subheading to which it seems to belong, and then to place the sections in what seems to them the most logical order.

If you enjoy a good competition, have a desirable prize ready for the first group to finish. Especially if it's a race, students may be tempted to act first and think later, so give them fair warning that they'll have to explain *why* they made their choices in the next step.

As they get to work, give students a tip to get them started: each excerpt belongs to only one subheading, but a subheading may have more than one excerpt associated with it. Circulate among the groups to offer encouragement and answer questions, but the point is to let them struggle at this stage as they infer what they can from the limited information in front of them.

Step Two: (15 minutes) Once students complete the puzzle, ask for a group to volunteer to talk through their choices for the class. Check in with other groups to see if they have different solutions to propose with alternative rationales and lead a discussion in which students reflect on the logic of how they determined that a given excerpt was associated with a particular subheading, and what sequence made the most sense. For example, you might ask: What were some of the key terms and clues that you used to decipher the components that belonged in the introduction, literature review, argument . . . etc.? In a more general sense, how would you distinguish the function(s) of each section? How are the different components of the paper structure interrelated? What happens if you rearrange the order of the paper sections? See how close the class can come to consensus about the order of the puzzle pieces in anticipation of the big reveal in step three.

Step Three: (20 minutes) Provide digital copies of the full-length article to each student, allowing ten minutes or so for them to locate the pre-highlighted excerpts and familiarize themselves with how the puzzle pieces fit into the surrounding argument. As an alternative, you could guide students through the process of using the library's online database to locate the article, although this may add more time to the overall activity. Then have students reconvene in their small groups to discuss the following questions, which you might put on the board for reference or distribute as a handout:

1. What surprises, if any, did you discover in comparing your completed puzzle to the sequence of excerpts as they appear in the article itself?
2. How do the subheadings on the handout map onto the subheadings in the article itself? Is it a one-to-one match? If not, what might account for the variation?

3. How would you sum up the key ingredients of a paper's introduction? What do you see as the key ingredients of a conclusion, and how does that final section relate back to the introduction?
4. What about the middle sections of the article? What distinguishes them from each other, and how do they build on each other?

Step Four: (15 minutes) With the same bold headings that appear on the jigsaw puzzle handout already written on the board, reconvene the full group. The goal of this final step is to crowdsource an inductive set of general criteria for the individual sections and the overall structural logic of a social science paper. Taking notes on the board as the conversation unfolds, collect the insights that students volunteer from their small group discussions and field questions along the way. The ultimate takeaway: to show that structural conventions are neither arbitrary nor inflexible. They are helpful guideposts for writers and readers alike, once they gain a bit of familiarity with the field.

REFLECTIONS

I first used this exercise in an undergraduate writing course as I introduced the research essay unit. We had spent the first half of the semester on shorter papers, working to move past the constraints—and reassuring familiarity—of the five-paragraph essay as students started to build more complex analytical arguments. As they faced the longest paper of the term, they were anxious all over again about letting go of the reliable structure of the five-paragraph essay. With the jigsaw exercise, they experienced for themselves how papers that might seem at first overwhelmingly long and complicated are undergirded by structural order and integrity. It also provided students with a useful model for structuring their papers—including the value of using subheadings—and a handy tool for testing the structural stability of their own or one another's drafts: can you create a handout version of the draft that distills each section into a two-to-four-sentence summary and makes clear how it builds on the previous section?

After the exercise's big reveal in step three, students will often comment that "I actually liked the way I organized the puzzle pieces better than their order in the real article." This is a welcome reminder that while conventional writing structures are often second nature to instructors, especially when we assign work from within our own disciplines, these "obvious" conventions are anything but to our students. There is a tightrope to walk here. On the one hand, we want students to recognize and understand the disciplinary conventions of essay structure. On the other hand, this knowledge can become an invitation to break with convention (appropriately) to bring their own voice and agency into their writing.

Students may not readily pick up on hints that the decontextualized excerpts offer to decode where they belong in the article. For example, a phrase like "I control for" or descriptions of what the researcher *does* would suggest the excerpt belongs in the "methods" section, whereas a recommendation for the direction of future research likely comes from the conclusion. It's worth pointing out these clues that expert readers can identify, and it also provides an opportunity to emphasize that students need to be attentive to explicit signposting moves in their own writing.

I have modified the exercise for an introductory political science course during the first or second week of the semester to orient students to the different places in an article where they can find the central components of the scientific method (question, hypotheses, methods, findings, analysis) and the fleshed-out statement of the author's argument and assumptions. This is essential for teaching effective note-taking strategies for a twenty page (or more) article or chapter packed with interesting but overwhelming details that may distract novice students from the main reason you assigned it—its underlying argument.

If you worry that your students may struggle with the exercise, you can simplify the puzzle by limiting the excerpts to one per subheading. That allows them to rely on a process of elimination as they settle on their sequencing.

The activity can also be adapted for a deeper dive into essay structure. For example, instead of doing a jigsaw of an entire article, you might select just one section, put each paragraph on a separate jigsaw piece and then have students discuss the function of each paragraph as they put them in a logical order. A jigsaw puzzle version of the introduction, for example, can give students a finer-grained understanding of what elements need to be included and how to arrange them for their readers. A jigsaw of the paper's literature review can help them learn to organize a scholarly conversation and lay out starting assumptions, and so on.

HANDOUT

SAMPLE JIGSAW

(to be cut up before distributing)

Excerpted from Marcus Johnson, "Electoral Discrimination: The Relationship between Skin Color and Vote Buying in Latin America," *World Politics* 72, no. 1 (2020): 80–120.

Introduction

Centuries of colonialism, nation-building, and migration created culturally and phenotypically diverse citizens in Latin America within a robust system of pigmentocracy—that is, stratification by skin color. Skin color remains the principal predictor of ethnoracial group membership and status in the region, yet relatively little is known about the electoral salience of racial stratification.

Through a closer examination of the predictive power of skin color, this article uncovers independent and persistent effects of racial discrimination on Afro-Latin and indigenous electoral mobilization. I focus on a particular manifestation of electoral discrimination: vote buying.

Literature Review

Skin color is strongly associated with individual well-being and social status and perceptions of discrimination. Skin color is an important predictor of wealth and educational attainment for indigenous people, as it is for Afro-descendants across much of the region.

Matthew Cawvey and colleagues find that alongside perceived discrimination, Latin Americans with darker skin report being solicited more frequently to pay bribes than people with lighter skin tones. In a field experiment of traffic policing in Mexico City, Brian Fried, Paul Lagunes, and Atheendar Venkataramani find the police are more likely to solicit bribes from drivers whose clothing, car, and skin tone together signal that they are lower class because the officers perceive that these drivers are less able to exact legal retribution against corrupt policing.

Argument

The central claim of this argument is that in ethnoracially stratified societies, where candidates and parties tend to manipulate electoral processes and outcomes, electoral discrimination is likely to occur through two interrelated processes: 1) the overlap of ascription and race-neutral targeting criteria (disproportionate impact), and 2) differential treatment based on stereotypes of descent-based attributes (differential treatment). The two forms of electoral discrimination are not mutually exclusive, but each form is likely to predominate under different circumstances.

Methods

I construct my primary independent variable using the interviewer's classification of the respondents' skin color. The original variable in the data set ranges from one (the lightest category) to eleven (the darkest category). Following Damarys Canache and associates, I standardize the original variable at the regional level.

To account for voters' level of reciprocity, I control for *interpersonal trust*, a measure of whether the respondent believes that people in his or her community are generally trustworthy. *Interpersonal trust* takes values from 0 to 3.

Results

On average, 15 percent of Brazilians with dark skin tone report vote buying compared with 11.3 percent of Brazilians with light skin tone, a difference of 3.7 percentage points. Of this total difference, 37 percent (1.4 percentage points) can be explained by average differentials in race-neutral covariates across light- and dark-skinned voters. Moreover, 77 percent of the total explained difference (1.1 percentage points) is due to the wealth gap. In other words, the higher rates of poverty for dark-skinned Brazilians explain approximately 30 percent of the total skin-color gap in vote buying.

Conclusion

Further research should investigate alternative manifestations of electoral discrimination, such as ballot stuffing, turnout suppression, and onerous voter registration requirements.

I operationalize ethnoracial traits narrowly in this article, focusing on skin color. A more general version of the electoral discrimination should apply where sticky, visible traits provide cues for subaltern group membership and political elites neglect the interests of subaltern groups. The broader reality of racial stratification outside of the region should make this article's argument and findings of general interest to scholars of race and ethnic politics.

The Data Never Speaks for Itself

Peter G. Johannessen

Students discover that standards of good writing still apply when writing about quantitative evidence.

Writing Focus: *evidence, analysis, conventions, orienting*
Teacher Preparation: *medium*
Student Preparation: *none*
Estimated Time: *60 minutes*
General Disciplines: *social sciences, sciences*

EXERCISE

Prep Work: Before class, find an academic article with a statistical analysis and prepare a handout with only the article's abstract. In addition, bring two versions of the methodology and analysis sections: the original one and an abbreviated "bad" one that you've created by stripping out key information. This bad version should be primarily descriptive: remove details about why the author chose the methods they did, what the limitations of that approach are, or how the results can be interpreted. Print enough copies of both versions (and the abstract) for all students and bring highlighters to class.

Choose your reading based on course context, taking care to select the right article for the occasion. In writing courses or lower-level social science courses, I recommend using a brief, well-written article that tests a single hypothesis with a simple method. This keeps the focus on the writing and prevents students from getting bogged down in irrelevant details. In upper-level courses where students have more disciplinary experience, I recommend choosing an article with a clear research question that uses methods that are closer to the edge of students' understanding. This allows you to make the point that even complicated quantitative methods can be explained in ways that are legible to people who are interested in the field but who are not necessarily experts in a given quantitative technique. In my own field of political science, some leading journals publish focused articles that can work well for this purpose (e.g., "short articles" in the *Journal of Politics* and "research notes" in the *American Political Science Review*). Articles with tables or graphs are encouraged, but not absolutely necessary.

When editing the selection for the activity, be sure to leave in the *what* of the method, but omit much of the *why*. For instance, you can make sure the selection contains answers to questions one and two on part one of the "Writing with Numbers" worksheet (included below), but remove the parts that address questions three and four.

Step One: (15 minutes) Pass out copies of the abstract and give students a moment to read it. Then pass out the bad (abbreviated) handout and have students work in small groups to fill out part one of the "Writing with Numbers" worksheet. By working in groups, they can support each other as they struggle to understand the poorly written (due to sabotage!) analysis. They are welcome to reference the abstract for help when it comes to identifying hypothesis.

Step Two: (20 minutes) Come back together as a class to go over students' responses to the worksheet questions. The discussion will immediately unearth the difficulties students had answering them. Empathize with students and note that their confusion should decrease their confidence in the authors' findings. Even if students are not themselves experts, their inability to understand the broad outlines of the author's intentions is a sign of problems in the text itself.

Use students' frustration to prompt a conversation about the types of information that would help them understand the analysis. Write their ideas on the board. Students might express confusion about what authors are doing (*method*), why they are doing it (*motive*), and *orienting* readers to the connection between the results (*evidence*) and the broader argument (*thesis*). After collecting these ideas, explain that the missing types of information are exactly what they would need to see not only in this article, but in *any* article. Now is the time for the big reveal: as it turns out, this particular article actually *did* include the features they were looking for.

Step Three: (15 minutes) Pull the rabbit out of the hat and provide students with the original document, which they can use to revise their answers on part one of the "Writing with Numbers" worksheet. Then, have students complete part two, which requires them to use different color highlighters to identify different elements of "A Writing Lexicon" in the text.

Step Four: (10 minutes) Have students come back together as a class to discuss how their answers have changed. They might still be confused about the details of the methods used in the paper, but they should have a better sense of *why* the authors used that method (and of its limitations). Use any lingering confusion to emphasize that disciplinary expertise is required to fully understand and evaluate complex methods, but that strong writers enable readers to understand motive, thesis, and the purpose of their analysis even when that disciplinary expertise is absent. Readers can be confident in a paper even when they can't follow all the complexities as long as the authors anticipate what readers need to interpret their analysis and its implications.

REFLECTIONS

Students often have an ambivalent relationship with statistical evidence (and you might too!). They are fascinated by the seeming certitude that numbers provide, but also intimidated by them. When reading, this mix of emotions can lead students to accept writers' claims without digging into the details; and when writing, it can lead students to believe that graphs and tables are self-explanatory, requiring no elaboration.

The goal of this exercise is for students to learn how the elements of good writing apply to quantitative analyses. This simple exercise has two main payoffs: First, it helps students become better readers of quantitative research, so that they don't skip over the details of an analysis and blindly accept authors' claims about the strength of evidence. This exercise forces students to grapple with a poorly explained analysis by identifying what is missing in the text. By pushing students to acknowledge their confusion and pinpoint the source of that confusion, this activity helps them become more critical consumers of quantitative writing. And second, it pushes students to be more careful in their own writing because it articulates the constituent parts of a convincing quantitative analysis.

When teaching this exercise, I vary my emphasis depending on my audience. For instance, in a class of first years planning to go into quantitative disciplines, my students were oddly convinced that they didn't need to know how to write well. More than once, I heard the phrase "the data speaks for itself." This exercise often (but not always!) convinces them that this isn't the case. It also has the positive spillover effect of increasing their engagement in the course going forward. For this reason, it can be useful to put it relatively early in a semester.

I have also used the exercise to demystify quantitative analysis for students who have had less exposure to it. I emphasize that quantitative evidence should be treated the same way as qualitative evidence: good writing in any analysis involves justifying choices and linking evidence to arguments. This realization has two payoffs. First, when students see similarities across quantitative and qualitative analyses, it reduces their anxiety when they encounter quantitative research. Many of my students note that the exercise gives them the confidence to approach quantitative articles with a healthy amount of skepticism. Students find it liberating to realize that their confusion can arise from poor writing, not just their own difficulty understanding quantitative techniques. And second, it helps students' writing because it forces them to deploy quantitative evidence with the same rigor that they use when employing qualitative evidence.

Be particularly mindful about keeping students engaged through the first steps of the exercise, as its initial steps are designed to frustrate students, but not so much that they give up. In my classes, for example, I often hear comments like: "I don't understand what this table/graph means," or "I don't know what the authors are doing here," or simply, "This is so confusing." I have found it helpful to walk around and intervene with a dose of empathy, humor, and substantive help when pairs seem like they are flagging.

Depending on your course content, it can also be useful to combine this activity with one involving students' drafts. If students are working on a paper that involves a quantitative analysis, you can include a mini-draft workshop in which students complete part 2 of the worksheet on their own papers (or one of their peers' papers). This additional element can help them see shortcomings in their own discussion of quantitative evidence.

HANDOUTS

Writing with Numbers (Part 1)

Take some time to read the methodology and analysis sections of the provided paper. Then, answer the following questions:

1. Which hypotheses does the author test in the analysis?
2. Which method does the author use to test these hypotheses?
3. Why does the author use that method? (Are alternate approaches considered?)
4. What are the author's findings and how substantively important are they?
5. Based on these answers, how confident are you in the author's findings?

Writing with Numbers (Part 2)

Look over the original version of the analysis. You will notice that it is significantly easier to understand, but it is okay if you still have lingering questions! Even professional academics are often confronted with methods and terms with which they are not familiar. To help pinpoint the types of rhetorical moves the author is making, highlight sections of the text using different colors.

Color #1 (_______)—***Methodological Motive*:** The challenge a writer faces in testing a hypothesis, along with the reasoning for selecting a particular method, rather than an alternative, to conduct that test.

Color #2 (_______)—***Empirical Methodology*:** The author's technique for analyzing the data in light of that challenge.

Color #3 (_______)—***Empirical Analysis*:** The author's description and discussion of the results.

Color #4 (_______)—***Implications*:** The author's explanation of how those results support the paper's argument (and fit within our broader knowledge).

After you finish, take a moment to think about what is *not* in the analysis. Are there certain decisions that are not justified in the text? Why might that be?

From Graphs to Questions

Alexander K. Davis

Kickstart a research unit with a deep dive into visual data.

Writing Focus: *sources, motive, analysis*
Teacher Preparation: *high*
Student Preparation: *none*
Estimated Time: *65 minutes*
General Disciplines: *humanities, social sciences, sciences*

EXERCISE

Prep Work: Curate a bank of data visualizations (e.g., graphs, charts, tables) with the needs of your course and your students in mind. (For suggestions about how to populate your visual archive, see the "Reflections" section below.) Print each individual visualization on a separate page as large as possible.

Before class begins, distribute the visualizations around your classroom space, with one visualization at each cluster of desks, corner of a seminar table, and so on. Another option is to tape each visualization to the wall around the room's perimeter.

Step One: (15 minutes) As students enter the classroom, invite them to peruse the data visualizations placed or posted around the room. Encourage them to choose a seat by the visualization that interests them most.

Once students are settled, have them each pull out a piece of blank paper and a pen. Their first task is to spend four minutes examining and jotting down notes about all the individual elements that make up their chosen visualization. (Remind them that captions count as part of the picture!)

At this stage, they should focus on details, identifying and describing as many particular visual choices and specific empirical ingredients as possible.

When the first four minutes are up, offer a new focus for their note-taking. This time the goal is to step back and consider the bigger picture, identifying and describing the visualization's overall takeaway message to viewers—or, in a word, its argument. As they wrap up, encourage students to make note of anything in the visual argument they find surprising, notable, or otherwise curiosity-provoking.

Step Two: (10 minutes) Break students into small groups—ideally, with other students who have explored the same visualization—to discuss their observations. (Three students per group works best; if you have larger groups, you may need to adjust the time both here and in step four.) Give students about three minutes collectively to discuss details, about two minutes to come to a consensus about the visualization's argument, and about five minutes to share their reactions to that argument as they understand it.

Step Three: (10 minutes) Step back to situate the exercise within its broader intellectual context and explain that today's dive into visual data is not only an opportunity to explore interesting findings from professional research publications or to practice dissecting published charts, graphs, and related figures. It's also an opportunity to learn skills and strategies for one of the first and most important steps of the research process: asking a truly worthwhile question.

Now it's time to convert the observations that students developed in step two into the form of questions. Invite them to flip over the page of notes and take a fresh look at their favorite visualization (If any students are dissatisfied with their initial choice, let them move on to a different one.)

Their job for the next five minutes is to follow their curiosity, jotting down as many questions as they can about the visualization itself, as well as the *causes* and/or *consequences* of the pattern(s) depicted.

Step Four: (15 minutes) Have students switch to new groups—ideally, with students who have explored different visualizations in steps one through three. (Three students per group again works best.) Once they're settled, ask students to rotate their question sheets one seat to the left or right within their groups. Give them three minutes to review the barrage of questions on the sheet now in front of them and write as many new questions as they can in response *to* the barrage of questions already present on their group member's sheet. Emphasize that students should now *only* be posing new questions in dialogue with their group member's initial interrogative thoughts, not posing new questions based on the original visualization.

Repeat the cycle until each sheet has returned to its original owner. With each new iteration, instruct students to respond to *all* the thinking recorded on the page, not the original visualization and not just the initial barrage of questions.

Step Five: (15 minutes) Ask students to review all the accumulated questions on their returned sheets, underlining the questions that excite them the most. Among those, they should also add a star to the question(s) most likely to require research to answer—because, for instance, the answers are not obvious and would require some kind of new data collection and analysis to untangle fully.

Finally, invite students to envision a future in which their next task is to hone, finalize, and begin to answer their favorite question. Reflecting on the notations they've just done, students should take a new blank page and craft a freshly revised version of their working research question, one that both excites them personally and opens the door to novel empirical research.

Below that question, have them outline a brief research agenda. What steps would they need to take to strengthen and refine the question itself? What sorts of existing data would they need to locate and what new data would they need to collect to work toward an answer? What method(s) would be most useful for obtaining and/or analyzing those data?

If you wish and time allows, students can exchange their agendas with a peer and suggest additions or refinements to the plan—or they can segue into a brief, full-class discussion of takeaway lessons learned from each step of the exercise.

REFLECTIONS

"From Graphs to Questions" allows students to discover possible research interests in much the same way that professional social science projects do: in dialogue with empirical evidence about social trends, patterns, and relationships. It links valuable strategies for apprehending visual data (e.g., looking at the same graph multiple times to understand it as thoroughly as possible) with fundamental writing practices (e.g., it takes several rounds of revision to generate the strongest ideas possible). Most importantly, it demystifies the often-intimidating step of brainstorming possible research questions at the outset of a new project—as attested to by many students over the years who have left class at the conclusion of this exercise saying, "I didn't realize I could develop a real research question just from following my interests" or "I thought a good research question had to be big to make a real contribution, but better questions are actually smaller."

A key strength of the exercise inheres in its ability to accommodate a broad array of other learning goals for students—depending on the choices made in the initial, behind-the-scenes curation of the visual archive.

To curate that bank effectively, first consider two key variables:

1. Are your students more *novice* or *experienced* researchers? Graphs from the Pew Research Center or a public-facing academic blog like *Contexts* would be most appropriate for kicking off a research unit in an introductory or lower-level survey course, while charts copied from recent peer-reviewed publications—or pulled directly from your own research output in R or Stata—are far more sensible for students with stronger research (and/or quantitative) backgrounds.
2. Does your course target a more *niche* or *generalist* audience? For a small seminar organized around a special topic, it's worthwhile to seek out visualizations that dovetail closely with your course readings and assignments. For a true introductory course or required research methods course, however, the more topics you can cover with your bank, the better.

Beyond that, however, the sky is truly the limit. For instance, if you wish to underscore the importance of questioning cultural norms or prestigious government documents whose accuracy is often taken for granted (a common goal in many social science courses), selecting graphs that are misleading, rest on problematic assumptions, and/or conflict with expert information contained in a course reading would be an excellent strategy—and you could rework the note-taking and small-group conversation prompts in steps one and two to force a more critical approach to visual interpretation. Or, if you want students to emerge from the exercise less intimidated by the complex data visualizations they might encounter in the peer-reviewed literature, visuals that are clear and compelling yet challenging to dissect at first glance would be the way to go. (In the words of one student after grappling with a *Nature* publication: "I might not know anything about ammonia formation, but I totally get this graph!") It would also be quite easy to lay the groundwork for a lesson on *creating* effective data visualizations through this exercise by ensuring that a wide variety of visualization types are represented in your archive.

That flexibility can be extended further to other disciplines and pedagogical settings, even those that emphasize humanistic and qualitative forms of evidence. One of my colleagues in art history has students proceed through the note-taking, conversing, and revising sequence outlined here, but locates step one at the entrance to the university's on-campus art museum—so that students can use a physical gallery of oil paintings as their visual archive. Another variation would be to mix and match source types, as I often do in my own multidisciplinary, first-year seminar. When confronted with a hodgepodge of figures from recent issues of *Nature*, scans of personal papers from nineteenth-century Supreme Court justices, photographs of MoMA's sculpture collection, statistical snippets from World Health Organization fact sheets, TikTok links, and architectural blueprints from our campus's oldest buildings, students are able to discover for themselves what kinds of research questions tend to emerge from certain kinds of empirical evidence.

And that discovery, in turn, does far more than kickstart their final research papers. It also allows them to learn firsthand why scholars in different academic fields tend to gravitate toward different kinds of research questions—an experiential lesson that empowers students early in their academic training more successfully to navigate the rest of the liberal arts curriculum and settle on an academic major in the years to follow. Indeed, as one student commented memorably in their end-of-term course reflection, "The one thing I'll never forget from our seminar is the question barrage activity, because that was when I really understood that the most important ingredient in excellent academic research is *my* interests and *my* curiosities. Why did I ever think I should be writing about anything else?"

REVISING

Yes. We, too, sometimes turned in first drafts and got respectable grades. But think of what those papers *could* have become had we really revised. That's the pitch we make to our own students when we introduce the idea of radical revision—a capacious understanding of the process in which every element of a first draft is on the table for rethinking and rewriting, from motive, thesis, and structure to evidence, analysis, and beyond. It's the stage of revision before proofreading. And it's a mode of revision that requires students to let go of superficial approaches like swapping in fancy thesaurus words or playing with format and font choices to meet page-count requirements. Now is the moment for sharing successive essay drafts demonstrating the leaps in persuasiveness, clarity, nuance, and analytical rigor that can be achieved by investing at least as much work in the revision stage as the original draft. Now is the moment to teach students how to go panning for gold in their drafts, seeking the flash of insight or the compelling question that emerges where least planned or expected. And now, most of all, is the moment when readers need to be present and plentiful, when students need feedback not only from you as their instructor, but from each other. This section begins with a brief guide to the indispensable practice at the heart of any writing classroom: the draft workshop, from which a roadmap for revision emerges. Next, you'll find exercises in which students learn to test their thesis statement, clarify their contribution to the scholarly conversation, respond thoughtfully to counterarguments, deepen their analysis, and streamline their sentences, along with other strategies for diagnosing and revising their drafts.

THE DRAFT WORKSHOP AND VARIATIONS

The Draft Workshop

Speedback

The Editorial Board

The Draft Workshop

Amanda Irwin Wilkins and Keith Shaw

The draft workshop is *the* fundamental, flexible tool for teaching writing. It can also be one of the most fun. On the surface, it is simply a facilitated conversation among students about a draft written by one of their classmates with the aim of producing a revision strategy. But it is also a construction site for a classroom community embodying an ethos of honest, generous feedback, and a training field for students to become stronger critical readers and writers. The draft workshop is where we, as instructors, most try to render ourselves obsolete, over time slowly handing over responsibility for substantive feedback to the class as the students develop the intellectual muscles to handle it. The draft workshop does not necessarily require advance planning: it can be dropped into a class nearly anytime, for any reason, to good effect, so long as you have writing in need of revision and students ready to talk about it. Here is the full forty-minute classic edition of the draft workshop, followed by thirteen of its infinite variations.

EXERCISE

Prep Work: Select a student draft for the workshop and distribute it to your class with reasonable lead time. There are many approaches to determining which draft will be workshopped in a given class: ask for a volunteer, designate a student in advance of the deadline, or quickly skim the papers when they are submitted to select a draft that has usefully representative strengths and weaknesses. Ask students (save the writer) to read the draft closely and compose a response letter addressed to the author with four components:

1. A quick *summary* of what they see as the draft's motive and thesis.
2. A specific reflection, with evidence from the text, on one important *strength* of the draft (often with reference to a high-order element from "A Writing Lexicon," e.g., thesis, motive, analysis, structure).
3. A specific reflection, with evidence from the text, on one important *weakness* of the draft.
4. Specific *ideas* for how to address the weakness (identified in #3) through revision.

The letter should be about a single-spaced page long and students should bring two hard copies to class on the day of the workshop, along with the draft itself. At the end of class, one copy of the letter goes to the author and the other to you. Be sure to closely read the draft yourself to develop your own sense of its strengths and weaknesses.

Step One: (2 minutes) Open the workshop by asking the writer to share *briefly*—emphasis on *briefly*—what he or she is attempting to argue in the draft and then identify one or two hopes for revision and for the discussion to follow.

Step Two: (10 minutes) Open the floor by asking students to identify strengths of the draft as you record their findings on the board. Contributions must be specific; encourage students to "show us in the text." They should also identify the precise way(s) the identified strength improves the essay (making the thesis more persuasive, introducing complicated evidence in a clear way, deftly addressing a counterargument, and so on). Try to spend at least a quarter of the time you allot to the workshop here, and resist overeager attempts to pivot to weaknesses.

Step Three: (25 minutes) Once a critical mass of strengths is on the table, move on to areas in need of revision, or what Richard Martin so aptly calls "strengths-in-the-making." Students should again show evidence from the text itself and explain why, in their view, the specific weakness they identify problematically affects the entire essay. As you record these findings, encourage students to suggest revision strategies to address the concerns, ideally fielding multiple possible approaches for each issue (these will often be mutually exclusive, and that's fine). The majority of your workshop time will be spent here.

Step Four: (3 minutes) Before the workshop wraps up, pause to consider what has been said and what your copious notes on the board may suggest for next steps. Take a few minutes to talk through what the most important priorities for revision should be. The writer will not be able to address everything, and there will often be competing strategies for revision. Highlight the three or four *most important* things for the writer to focus on. Do *not* skip this step; be sure to leave yourself enough time. Close by thanking the writer for sharing their work, and the rest of the class for their considered feedback.

SOME ADVICE FOR RUNNING THE DRAFT WORKSHOP

As simple as the steps above may be, the draft workshop is actually quite challenging to teach well, particularly early in the semester when students are still getting acclimated to the class and to each other. In time, as a product of early investment on your part, the draft workshop eventually runs itself. But you have to get it there. Below, we revisit each of the four steps to provide some advice we hope proves useful, whether you plan to use the workshop model just once or to make it a recurring feature of your course.

Step One: Early in the semester, or in your class's first workshop, the position of being in the "hot seat" can be uncomfortable. Even students who appear relaxed or non-defensive can get unnerved the moment they realize their work is about to go under the microscope. This discomfort may manifest as a desire simply to keep talking when you hand them the floor at the beginning of the workshop, either by preemptively defending themselves from every attack they can think of, or by proclaiming their draft worthless and apologizing for wasting everyone's time. In either case, kindly but firmly cut off the monologue and trust that step two will help mitigate the fear.

We don't recommend making any general rules that limit the author's ability to speak. You will occasionally need to manage an over-talker, but the risks of telling authors to stay silent while their work is discussed are substantially greater. They miss out on the opportunity to clarify their thinking in dialogue with their readers, and even the thickest-skinned among them may end the workshop feeling exposed and disempowered. A draft workshop should be a rigorous and challenging discussion with the author as full participant, not as passive—or aghast—spectator. Another important way to involve the author respectfully is to have students address all their comments and questions about the draft explicitly to the writer. For example, "I thought the paragraph at the bottom of page two was awesome because you really show me there the problem your essay is trying to solve." Or: "I was wondering if you could say more about the point you bring up on page five? It seems like X evidence from the book might contradict that?"

Students will be tempted to start referring to the writer in the third person and addressing their comments to you, the instructor, since you're the one standing at the board and facilitating the conversation. Redirecting students to engage directly with the author, and reframing their contributions only if necessary, is a crucial part of your job.

Step Two: Some students are inclined to view this step as an inefficient "buttering up" of the author before the real work of devastating criticism begins. That's the case only if it's done badly. The opening step of appreciation should be just as rigorous, efficient, and real as the work of rigorous, efficient, and compassionate criticism that follows. It's important for the author to see genuine accomplishments in a draft, not only to encourage confidence for the revision ahead, but also to hedge against reverse revision. If we don't explicitly identify the strengths and show the author *in the text* where and how their draft is working well, it's liable to disappear in the course of revision when addressing the weaknesses to be discussed in step three. Moreover, it is often news to the author that the strengths are in fact strong. Novice writers, or even experienced writers lost in the weeds, sometimes need an outsider to point out what is particularly successful.

Even seasoned workshoppers may get impatient with this step. For instance, to force a segue to the paper's weaknesses their contribution may begin with the construction, "I really like X, but . . ." A more welcome version of this move is, "I really like X, and you could make it even better by . . ." (which you should feel free to pursue in detail). While you don't need to identify every last thing a draft does well, or hold the conversation here longer than is productive, be sure to resist moves that prematurely highlight weaknesses, making that transition only when you're ready.

You may sometimes find it nerve-racking to hear students offer praise for an aspect of the draft that actually still needs a lot of work—perhaps especially, "I think you have a really good thesis." Resist the temptation to leap in immediately and contradict. Instead, that's precisely the moment to ask the student who is commenting to point to where they see the thesis coming through most clearly in the text of the draft. Keep taking notes on the board. And be patient. In most cases, the early praise for the thesis will be balanced out and usefully complicated as soon as step three comes around (or even sooner). In the rare cases where students don't circle around to bring up questions or critiques of the thesis on their own, it's important to prompt them before the workshop ends. If rule one is "don't freak out" or "let them figure it out," then rule two is "don't leave them in the dark at the end."

Step Three: The key to this step is linking the identification of a weakness to a revision strategy. This rule forces students to think constructively and take responsibility for considering how they themselves might respond to problems they uncover. It's the difference between an exercise in evaluation and an exercise in collaboration. It's also a built-in trap for classroom alpha dogs: they're welcome to propose sophisticated criticism, but then they also need to accept the work of helping their classmate find an escape hatch.

The structure of the conversation nudges the substance of contributions toward generosity, but by itself does nothing to guarantee a professional tone. Tone can be difficult for students to calibrate early, either because they don't know how or because they don't want to. An ethos of compassionate, honest criticism is not a mode that all students will naturally inhabit, and you will need to do the work of modeling it for them. One useful approach is to encourage students to frame concerns as a function of their experience as a reader, which keeps the focus on the text and not the writer. The difference between "You're confusing at the top of page three when you_____" and "I become confused at the top of page three when the draft moves to_____" may seem minor, but the shift from "you" to "I" or "the draft" can make a world of difference in how willingly writers hear and respond to feedback.

Be prepared to intercept frustrated, mocking, or otherwise insensitive criticism immediately and reframe it the way you want it to be heard. Normally, the simple act of publicly translating a student's contribution is enough to make the tonal point clear. But be ready to intervene more directly if necessary, especially if the criticism *is* about the author rather than the draft. While uncomfortable for everyone, doing so protects the writer, preserves the values of the course and the workshop, and demonstrates to the rest of the class that they can trust you to protect *them* when it's their turn to share their work. While you might find yourself performing acts of "translation" quite frequently, especially early in a semester, the need for more direct intervention is usually rare. Just as the quality of student feedback improves over time, so does the tenor of their contributions and their willingness to police each other's tone.

At the other end of the spectrum, some students are so worried about hurting their peers' feelings or appearing confrontational that they simply refuse to provide honest criticism at all. These students will clam up during step three and, if forced to make contributions, will offer vague generalities that dodge the real issues. It can help to ask students to share what they wrote in their response letter. Usually, when they discover they haven't made an enemy of the author, this concern goes away.

You'll want to use a relatively light hand when intervening on the substance of critical suggestions, but you should still do so when you find a contribution to be completely off base. Most of the time, you can invite further dialogue about the point and other students will build the case against it for you. At other times, it's wise to make a polite show of skepticism while leaving it up to the author to decide what to do.

Step Four: By now, the author has received a barrage of feedback, and whether or not they've taken careful notes, whatever revision plan may exist in their head will be forgotten by their next class unless you take a moment to highlight the most important priorities the class has identified for revision. This step allows the author to register the major takeaways, and even if they aren't yet sure *how* they will address these priorities, at least they will have a clear sense of where they should focus. It's usually the case that a rough consensus emerges on what the revision priorities should be, even if there's some disagreement about which priority is the most important. You should feel free to tilt the scales toward what you see as the best use of the writer's time.

VARIATIONS ON THE DRAFT WORKSHOP

With special thanks to Raphael Allison, who compiled an early version of workshop variations.

Dress rehearsal: Before the first real draft workshop of the semester, have the class practice the workshopping steps using a sample student paper. Following this dress rehearsal, invite students to collaborate on generating a list of criteria for what kind of feedback is most useful to receive on a draft. You can refer back to and refine this list throughout the semester.

Thought-lines: Prior to the workshop, divide students into twos and assign each pair a paragraph in the draft to summarize in a single sentence. Put these sentences on the board and then lead a discussion regarding the paper's line of argument, or "thought-line."

Thesis spot-checks: Invite students to rewrite from memory the thesis of the paper being workshopped. Before discussing, ask each student to read their version of the thesis to the class. Break the class into groups of three or four and have each group refine or complicate the paper's thesis. Regroup and compare definitions, testing them against what the writer thought their thesis was.

Workshop smaller elements: Workshop titles, abstracts, openers, figures, and tables for all papers in the class. Circulate the papers themselves prior to the workshop or prepare dedicated handouts for the smaller items—all the titles in one document, all the abstracts in another. Then workshop your way through the "little" or "last-minute" pieces that are often overlooked in a draft but still carry great weight.

Writer-run workshop: Have students run their own draft workshops, following these two rules: 1) the writer begins by asking what the class finds promising or exciting about the draft; and 2) the writer only asks questions unless they are responding to a question posed by one of their readers (to ensure that the author maintains a guiding voice in the discussion without overtaking it).

Student moderator: For the later workshops when the class has become skilled at workshopping, choose a student moderator to lead the workshop. Resist the urge to jump in. Let them know they're in charge.

Small-scale peer response guides: Assign students to groups of two or three and, for homework, have each group circulate and read all drafts from their group and write response letters ahead of time. In class, convene the groups and provide them with a "response guide" handout of questions to discuss about each draft, encouraging them to draw on their response letters during their conversation. (Tip: focus the handout on issues common to all papers.)

Advisory councils: As the workshop begins, break students into three advisory councils, each charged with a different element from "A Writing Lexicon." For example, the first might focus on thesis, the second on sources, and the third on structure. Allow time for these councils briefly to confer. Reconvene when they are ready to offer the draft writer advice.

Highlight general applicability: Have all students bring copies of their drafts to the day's workshop. At appropriate moments during the class as a student's draft is being workshopped, pause and ask the other students to consider how their own papers might be developed or revised in terms of whatever issue is being discussed. To wrap up, invite volunteers to share what they learned from the workshop that gave them an idea for improving their draft.

Choose drafts strategically: When choosing two drafts to workshop together in a given class session or week, you might pair them thematically or select those that share similar weaknesses to revise.

You might also workshop the draft of a student whose early draft is strong but who tends to perceive their own writing as weak. This does double duty by building the student's confidence while providing a strong model for other students in the class. The method can also be reversed: workshop the problematic draft of an overconfident student to help them acknowledge and address its weaknesses.

Return to sources: Ask students to bring to class all readings or sources that pertain to the writing assignment. In the midst of or near the end of the workshop, have the class locate passages in these sources that might help enrich—or complicate—the writer's argument.

Forensic sketch artist: For research paper drafts, invite students to swap *only* their works cited pages with a partner. Ask them each to imagine what kind of an argument the other might be constructing on the basis of the sources alone.

Then have them compare the sketch of the "suspect" to the author's actual intention for the paper, identifying other source types that might usefully help fill in the picture.

Parallel workshops: Run two parallel workshops in separate rooms, shuttling between them. While the whole class will have read two students' drafts beforehand, each group will discuss only the one they've been assigned to workshop. After thirty minutes or so, have the class reconvene in full to debrief about the generalizable lessons they have identified through the experience.

Speedback

Aditi Sriram

An all-hands-on-deck peer review exercise to help students strengthen their drafts and their feedback skills.

Writing Focus: *any*
Teacher Preparation: *medium*
Student Preparation: *medium*
Estimated Time: *80 minutes*
General Disciplines: *humanities, social sciences, sciences*

EXERCISE

Prep Work: Prepare copies of the "Speedback" handout (see sample below) or be prepared to project it on a screen at the front of the classroom. You will also need the opening paragraph of a sample essay with which to model the "Speedback" technique in step two. The opening paragraph can be from an actual student paper (though not from your current class), or it can be pure invention; the students won't be reading the full essay.

Students will need substantive drafts, even if unfinished and unpolished, in digital form. They will also need their laptops, which should be fully charged, as the activity requires them to work on one another's devices for nearly a full class period. (It's also helpful if students extend the idle time before their screen locks.) Before class, ask students to create a fresh copy of their most recent essay draft, so their peers can annotate without risk to the original. This can be done in Microsoft Word or Google Docs—any platform that allows users to leave comments in the margin, manipulate font, and has a "track changes" feature. Also instruct students to type the essay prompt at the top of the copy of their draft.

If sharing laptops isn't feasible, have students bring a hard copy of their draft to class instead, with the margins set wide to allow for marginal annotations. With hard copies, you'll also need a supply of different colored pens for each round of the activity.

Step One: (5 minutes) Have students open the fresh copy of their drafts on their laptops. All other windows should be closed except for the draft document. Then preview the mechanics of the exercise: the technology will stay in place, while the students move from chair to chair, meeting a new laptop every few minutes, reading one portion of the essay on that laptop, and reacting to it.

Step Two: (10 minutes) Distribute the opening paragraph of the sample essay and project the opening stage of the "Speedback" sequence for the class:

> 1st Editor
>
> **Read:** ONLY the first paragraph.
>
> **Reflect and Suggest:** How effectively does the first sentence serve as an opener to draw you in? What's working well, and how might it be improved? Is there another line in the same paragraph that might be a stronger opener? Add your comment(s) to the margin of the draft.
>
> **Sign and Save:** Include your name with your comment. Save your document before you go!

Invite a student to read the paragraph out loud. Then facilitate a brief discussion about the effectiveness of the opener. Solicit reactions from the class and create a comment that distills them. Add the comment to the margin of the sample so that everyone sees the annotation being created. Close by reminding students what they've just demonstrated: that whether or not they are familiar with an essay's topic or research material, they can provide crucial feedback by being a systematic, engaged reader. This work isn't simply altruistic; providing feedback to other writers is a crucial way to improve their own writing.

Step Three: (5 minutes) Have each student move to a new laptop. Once they settle in, instruct them to conduct the "1st Editor" stage on the draft before them.

Step Four: (45 minutes) Invite students to move to the next laptop. Proceed through as many more "Speedback" editor stages as you have time for, allotting five to ten minutes per stage (depending on its complexity), and having students move to a new laptop each time. To keep things moving, consider calling time (a one-minute warning) before students move to the next laptop. Regularly remind students to save the work on the laptop they are in front of and to include their name with their comment, so that the essay author can follow up with them later, as needed.

Step Five: (15 minutes) Have the students return to their own laptops and review the comments their classmates have offered. Remind them that, as the author of their paper, it is ultimately up to them to weigh all feedback and accept, modify, or reject it as they see fit. In cases where they don't understand a piece of feedback, encourage them to seek clarification from its author. And in cases where they instinctively resist a piece of feedback, encourage them first to take a step back before rejecting it to imagine why it might have some validity. They may or may not be persuaded in the end, but feedback deserves a fair hearing and a reasoned response. Have students choose three to five annotations and respond with reflective notes of their own about how they plan to address the feedback in the revision process—or why they don't think it warrants incorporation. If time runs out, students can complete their reflective notes for homework.

REFLECTIONS

The goals and benefits of "Speedback" for students are many: to become comfortable sharing their work; to practice giving feedback; to get used to receiving feedback (and figuring out how to act on it); and to experience *reading* student work, rather than just writing it and submitting it without considering their work as something that others read.

The fast-paced, round-robin approach encourages students to work with quick, focused attention. They don't need to craft beautiful or eloquent comments; rather, they are developing and sharpening their diagnostic skills, and building their overall appreciation for the possibility of revision. It's important to emphasize that the feedback should lean toward annotation, rather than extensive editing. Practicing the first prompt from the handout together as a class is crucial because it will show the students how they can react to their peers' work without writing over it or accidentally creating a document with blurry authorship.

Depending on the nature of the essay assignment, which aspects of the "Lexicon" you want the students to focus on, and how much of the paper the students have written already, you can customize the most meaningful prompts for your in-class exercise. The activity can be as long as eighty minutes, or as short as twenty, depending on what you hope to achieve, and it lends itself well to either the entire class working together or in smaller groups of three or four.

I find this exercise most beneficial when students have time for guided reflection on the feedback that they have received. Part of that happens in step five, but more can follow in a subsequent class discussion for which students prepare with some informal reflective writing. For example, you might prompt them to summarize the macro and micro revisions they chose to make following the "Speedback" session, reflecting on how they decided which suggestions to implement (and which didn't feel right), what they learned from offering feedback to their peers, and how that experience influenced their approach to their own papers.

HANDOUT

1ST EDITOR

Read: ONLY the first paragraph.

Reflect and Suggest: How effectively does the first sentence serve as an opener to draw you in? What's working well, and how might it be improved? Is there another line in the same paragraph that might be a stronger opener? Add your comment(s) to the margin of the draft.

Sign and Save: Include your name with your comment. Save the document before you go!

2ND EDITOR

Read: ONLY the first and second paragraph.

Reflect and Suggest: What questions do you have of the essay so far? What do you identify as the motive and thesis, if they appear? Do you have the right amount of orienting information to follow the argument so far? How is the writer building your trust? Add your comment(s) to the margin of the draft.

Sign and Save: Include your name with your comment. Save the document before you go!

3RD EDITOR

Read: The first two pages of the essay, and highlight or underline any key terms. You may go further if time allows.

Reflect and Suggest: Identify what appear to be emerging as the key terms of the paper. Where do you see these concepts introduced and defined, or where do you see missed opportunities for such definitions? What kind of relationship does the thesis establish among the key concepts in play? Add your comment(s) to the margin of the draft.

Sign and Save: Include your name with your comment. Save the document before you go!

4TH EDITOR

Read: The first two pages of the essay, and highlight or underline any uses of a source (summary, paraphrase, or quotation). You may go further if time allows.

Reflect and Suggest: What function does each appearance of a source serve in the argument (e.g., orienting information, object of analysis, establishing the scholarly conversation, defining a key term)? Note these functions with a tag in the margin, along with your assessment of how effectively the source is being used for its intended purpose. Add your comment(s) to the margin of the draft.

Sign and Save: Include your name with your comment. Save the document before you go!

5TH EDITOR

Read: The first two pages of the essay, for the transitions between each paragraph (i.e., last sentence of one paragraph paired with the first sentence of the next). You may go further if time allows.

Reflect and Suggest: Pick two transitions to examine in detail, and leave a comment for each in which you describe your understanding of how the transition works. Is it continuing an idea, complicating an argument, starting a new thought? Does the transition clearly advance the essay's progression? If it doesn't, what might you do differently? Add your comment(s) to the margin of the draft.

Sign and Save: Include your name with your comment. Save the document before you go!

6TH EDITOR

Read: The first two pages of the essay (or further if time allows).

Reflect and Suggest: Highlight what you identify as the thesis statement in the introduction. Then highlight references back to the thesis statement that appear in subsequent paragraphs. Suggest any clarifying questions you have about the thesis statement itself, and comment on moments later in the essay where you clearly glimpse (or lose sight of) that guiding argument. Add your comment(s) to the margin of the draft.

Sign and Save: Include your name with your comment. Save the document before you go!

7TH EDITOR

Read: The first two pages of the essay (or further if time allows).

Reflect and Suggest: Choose a paragraph on each page and look for variation in sentence length, as well as in punctuation. Leave a comment in which you identify sentences that might be clearer if shortened or combined. Would a sentence improve with a comma, a semicolon, em-dashes—or a full stop? Add your comment(s) to the margin of the draft.

Sign and Save: Include your name with your comment. Save the document before you go!

8TH EDITOR

Read: The first two paragraphs and the last two paragraphs of the whole essay.

Reflect and Suggest: Based solely on the few paragraphs you have read, leave a comment in which you list the paper's key terms and summarize its overarching argument. Your expectations based on the introduction and conclusion will help the author track how well they have set up and structured their essay. Add your comment(s) to the margin of the draft.

Sign and Save: Include your name with your comment. Save the document before you go!

9TH EDITOR

Read: The third and fourth pages of the essay, or further if time allows.

Reflect and Suggest: Locate each moment the essay incorporates a source. Note any that would benefit from a clearer signal phrase introducing it, as well as any citations that appear incomplete or problematic. Add your comment(s) to the margin of the draft.

Sign & Save: Include your name with your comment. Save the document before you go!

10TH EDITOR

Read: The first two pages of the essay.

Reflect and Suggest: Find your favorite sentence, phrase, or even a particular word choice. Leave a comment in which you elaborate on why you find it so compelling, and what you yourself as a writer have learned from the example. Add your comment(s) to the margin of the draft.

Sign and Save: Include your name with your comment. Save the document before you go!

The Editorial Board

David L. Lindauer

Turn advanced students into disciplinary practitioners by handing over the reins of the draft workshop.

Writing Focus: *any*
Teacher Preparation: *low*
Student Preparation: *medium*
Estimated Time: *80 minutes*
General Disciplines: *humanities, social sciences, sciences*

EXERCISE

Prep Work: Two students pre-circulate drafts of relatively short op-eds (five hundred to eight hundred words). Everyone in the class should read the drafts and come prepared to discuss them as an editorial board. Be sure to preview for students in advance how the editorial board will operate, as described in the steps below.

Step One: (5 minutes) At the beginning of class, randomly determine the order in which the op-eds will be workshopped. Then, for each one, name from the pool of students who did not submit that week an editor-in-chief and also a reporting editor. Explain that all other students are members of the editorial board. Together, the editors-in-chief, the reporting editors, and the members of the editorial board will discuss each submission "behind closed doors" for fifteen minutes per op-ed. The editor-in-chief's role is to moderate discussion, to solicit and prioritize comments from members of the board on the strengths and weaknesses of the draft, and to facilitate feedback once the authors are back in the room. The editor-in-chief also keeps track of the time. The reporting editor participates fully as a member of the editorial board and takes notes on the discussion. The board should discuss the quality of the op-ed's argument as well as its exposition. Does the op-ed have an opinion and is it one supported by reasoning and an appropriate appeal to data and evidence? Will a lay reader understand the logic presented and find it persuasive? Will the intended audience want to read the op-ed to its conclusion?

Step Two: (15 minutes) Leave the room with the author of the first op-ed but not before reminding the editorial board to summon you and the author back into the room when they conclude their deliberation. The editor-in-chief organizes the subsequent conversation, summarizing the board's discussion and, if they choose, calls on individual board members to present specific points. Authors can respond or ask further questions. The reporting editor takes careful notes, in anticipation of providing the author, later in the day, with a written summary of the board's comments and of its conversation with them.

When you leave the room with the author, do not discuss their op-ed. Offering your opinion prior to the editorial board's presentation can undercut the legitimacy of the peer review. Reassure them that they will receive your written comments later. You could use this time for an individual conversation about their work in the class more broadly or strategies for handling the potentially contradictory feedback that emerges from a wider readership. Because students usually are tense in anticipation of this more formal review by their classmates, you may find it helpful to calm them down by finding other things to discuss, like prospects for the Boston Red Sox season.

Step Three: (20 minutes) Once back in the classroom, withhold remarks you may want to make or questions you may be tempted to raise until after the editorial board's conversation with the author. Should students turn to you to resolve disagreements, try to resist. Time permitting, if the editorial board overlooked a central argument that the op-ed got wrong or missed, you might wish to raise the issue. But it is best to let the class take ownership of the day's meeting and exert its control over the discussion independently of your input.

Step Four: (35 minutes) Repeat steps two and three for the next op-ed with a new editor-in-chief and reporting editor. Again, leave the room with the author and wait for the editorial board to call you back in.

Step Five: (5 minutes) As class concludes, remind the reporting editors to review their notes and send them to the author by the end of the day.

REFLECTIONS

I use the editorial board approach to student workshopping in my course Economic Journalism. The primary motivation behind Economic Journalism is to get senior economics majors to think like economists. One way to do this is to get them to write about economics for a general audience rather than to complete yet another problem set or research paper. Writing about an economic issue requires a different set of reasoning skills than solving mathematical problems or undertaking empirical exercises. That said, engaging in public rather than academic writing requires students from any discipline to abandon jargon they may not fully understand and to provide the nonspecialist with a context for why their work matters. Adopted by the Calderwood Seminars in Public Writing, "The Editorial Board" has proved adaptable across disciplines, including biology, psychology, history, literature, music, and the environmental sciences.

Writing op-eds became a means for my students, especially the seniors, to take stock of what they learned as economics majors. The exercise offers them the opportunity to discover their voices as fledgling economists, inviting them to translate work from their field into language a parent, or a friend from a different major, might understand. Explaining to a nonexpert concepts that may have taken the writer years to grasp fully requires a deep understanding of one's field and an appreciation of one's audience—training that should be part of any liberal arts education. As one recent student put it, "This semester has made it clear that the true mark of understanding is to be able to explain something so that it makes sense to others."

"The Editorial Board" provides a change of pace from the more conventional draft workshop discussions. To be successful, the exercise requires that students regularly engage in in-class workshopping and become accustomed to giving and receiving criticism from their peers. Workshopping of student writing takes place every week of my thirteen-week seminar. In the early weeks, the class gains experience critiquing the work of their classmates but also observes, and hopefully learns from, the range of comments and the type of feedback I provide. I only employ "The Editorial Board" after the halfway point in the semester, and typically use it for two class meetings. I have found that this activity works best when the instructor cedes full control to the board. My students frequently cite the editorial board sessions as the best discussions of the semester. One student characterized them less as criticism than as "crowdsourcing" solutions to problems in her writing. Participants feel empowered and professional.

In keeping with the theme of empowerment, I tend to provide the editorial board with few instructions. I randomly assign the order in which students review the op-eds rather than sequence them from weakest to strongest. I do not cherry-pick who will serve first as editor-in chief, nor do I provide any guidance on questions authors might pose to the board. Across many years of education, our students have listened and watched us; hopefully, they have learned something from these observations. It is time to loosen the reins. "The Editorial Board" is a moment to let students figure things out on their own. In my class, they get to repeat this experience multiple times. They don't need to be told what to do; figuring it out is important in its own right.

Some faculty are adamantly opposed to peer editing and peer review, arguing that students just give each other bad advice. This happens. But even when it does, it is valuable for student writers to weigh the range of feedback they receive and make considered judgments about what advice to follow. If we don't give our students, especially our seniors, the opportunity to learn how to give and receive criticism, when do we expect they will acquire these skills? You'll find they are awkward at first but get better with practice. With the instructor out of the room, students rise enthusiastically to the occasion, knowing the editorial board is putting responsibility for coherence and quality where it belongs: with them. More than once after class a student has told me, "You should have heard what we said when you guys weren't in the room." While I don't know what the board said behind closed doors, I do know when it is doing its job. When, in their discussion with the authors, the editorial board raises the same points about an op-ed that I have written on the drafts, I know that they are thinking like professionals.

DIAGNOSING DRAFTS

Project Falcon

Keith Shaw

An argument clinic cleverly disguised as a James Bond covert op.

Writing Focus: *thesis, motive*
Teacher Preparation: *low*
Student Preparation: *low*
Estimated Time: *60 minutes*
General Disciplines: *humanities, social sciences, sciences*

EXERCISE

Prep Work: Students need to have advanced far enough in a writing assignment to have a tentative thesis. Having a working draft or partial draft is helpful, but unnecessary.

Step One: (10 minutes) Frame the workshop by asking students what they take to be the qualities of academic writing that's worth reading. They quickly identify thesis and motive-ish ideas without using the terms. "An idea that seems unlikely but turns out to be true." "It makes me think about the topic in a way I haven't before." Once we're there, ask them:

1. What do you think makes for a good thesis?
2. How have you been taught to make and defend one?
3. How have you been taught to choose a thesis in the first place?

They often have good answers for the first question, and high school answers for the second and third. This is useful; it's an opportunity to show how scholarship works differently, but be sure to respect what they've learned from their high school answers.

Step Two: (5 minutes) Ask students to take out their drafts and distill their tentative thesis down to a sentence or two. While students are writing, draw a 2 x 2 table on the board, labeled like Table 7, which asks whether the thesis falls into four categories.

Table 7 ("Project Falcon")

Is the thesis:	
Arguable?	Interesting?
Manageable?	Important?

Introduce The Four Questions as a useful test for the potential quality of an argument. "Arguable" and "manageable" are (mostly) thesis-level questions, and "interesting" and "important" are (mostly) motive-level questions. If students can look at their tentative arguments and answer "yes" to each of the questions, they're probably in good shape. If they're forced to answer "no" to any of them, it's worth taking time to think about how to adjust or reframe the argument to flip the answer to a "yes."

Step Three: (15 minutes) Ask for a volunteer willing to have their tentative argument workshopped. Talk through each question to see if the answer is "yes" for all of them. When, inevitably, the answer for one or more is "no," discuss as a class how the author might revise the thesis, or the scope of the thesis, to rectify this. It's crucial to model the discussion of the workshop as a full class before moving to the next step, since it gives you the opportunity to define/refine what each question really means:

Arguable: This criterion lets you rule out theses that are obviously true or obviously false, and push for theses that are counterintuitive but defensible. You may be able to use theses from your course readings as good (or bad) examples.

Manageable: Students often lack the experience to judge how much work, in terms of time or page count, it takes to defend a given thesis. They're especially likely to be too ambitious, and you'll often find yourself encouraging them to narrow the scope of their projects.

Interesting and important: It is useful to separate these components of motive. In both cases, you'll need to explain how what's interesting and important to an academic or specialist audience is different from what's interesting to the general public. Opportunities for jokes abound.

Step Four: (15 minutes) Divide the class into small groups. Instruct students to workshop the thesis statement of everyone in their group, and brainstorm ways to flip any "no" answer to a "yes." Where appropriate, invite students to revise their thesis on the spot to account for useful feedback. If they get stumped on a particular argument, ask them to remember the concern and we'll field it at the end. If you have extra time, ask students to sketch out how revisions to their thesis should affect their essays' structure, or the evidence they should reexamine.

Step Five: (15 minutes) Reconvene as a class and field any remaining difficulties. It's worth spending a few minutes bringing attention to some recurring categories of problems. When using "Project Falcon" with inexperienced writers on early assignments, the following are all common:

- The thesis statement couldn't adequately be defended in the page count permitted by the assignment.
- It couldn't adequately be defended by the evidence the student possesses, usually due to overgeneralizing.
- It lacks richness because of a lack of engagement with the evidence. (You can't confirm this until you see the essay, but it's a common drafting mistake for some writers.)

- It ignores or misrepresents a crucial implication or consequence.
- It undersells or oversells its significance or doesn't register why the argument matters at all.

REFLECTIONS

"Project Falcon" is designed to show that scholarly writing is about argument rather than description, that the argument one can most easily defend usually isn't the argument one should make, and that an argument must be meaningful to a reader to be worth making. It's particularly useful at the beginning of a semester as early practice for peer feedback. Since it employs *tentative* arguments, students don't have enough at stake to get defensive. It's also an opportunity to make any necessary "good citizenship" interventions about how students should talk to one another before they workshop completed drafts. Better still, it helps break thesis and motive down into easy test questions students can reliably ask and answer. My students employ The Four Questions throughout the semester without prompting, and so the exercise appears to be sticky. As a result, I get fewer drafts with totally unworkable theses, which makes the revision strategies I develop with my students more achievable in scope.

Plenty of variations are possible:

- In a draft workshop, ask students to distill the writer's thesis, and talk through their answers to The Four Questions before moving to specific strengths and weaknesses.
- Use the exercise on a subclaim nested in the thesis, rather than the thesis itself. This sometimes reveals that a subclaim is more trouble than it's worth because it isn't easily manageable, isn't especially important, or both. But sometimes students learn that the subclaim is what they care most about and make it the new thesis, narrowing the scope (and therefore the manageability) of the whole project. (This use follows up nicely with "Tying Down Your Thought Balloons.")
- For more sophisticated writers and/or more advanced revisions, use "Project Falcon" as a heuristic rather than a checklist. Rather than answering "yes" or "no" to each question, ask students how their arguments might become more arguable or better motivated. Even if the argument is manageable, can it be pared down without hurting the thesis, or can it explore the evidence in more nuanced detail without becoming bogged down?

You might be wondering why this exercise is called "Project Falcon." It could be called "The Four Questions," but that would be boring. It's more exciting to put "Project Falcon" on a syllabus, and refuse to answer conscientious students' questions about what we're doing that day. Yes, teaching is about transparency and trust. But small mysteries make class more fun and make this exercise more memorable.

Charting Your Contribution

Jonathan Niles-Weed

Explore how new arguments fit into—and build on—the existing literature, for students writing original papers in mathematics and the sciences.

Writing Focus: *sources, thesis, motive*
Teacher Preparation: *medium*
Student Preparation: *high*
Estimated Time: *50 minutes*
General Disciplines: *sciences, social sciences, humanities*

EXERCISE

Prep Work: Students should have already established (by laboratory experiments, mathematical proofs, or otherwise) the results that they plan to write about, and they should be prepared to describe those results in detail. Request that they bring along at least three sources on which their work builds. Ask for a volunteer to share with you in advance their three selected sources, to be workshopped by the group. Make enough copies of these three sources for everyone to look at during class.

Step One: (10 minutes) Ask students to discuss how they go about assessing the impact of a paper that has appeared in a journal in their discipline. Try to get students to be precise about which parts of the paper they look at first. Encourage students to recognize that it is often possible to figure out the importance of scholarship by focusing on just one part of a paper. (For instance, in the quantitative disciplines, students will often say that a single graph or table is enough to encapsulate a work's primary impact.) As a consensus forms, write down examples on the board. Use the volunteer's set of three sources as a common text to help anchor the discussion.

Step Two: (5 minutes) Have students write briefly on their own about each of the volunteer's sources, describing in informal terms the key contribution of each source. Encourage them to try to boil these down to a single sentence or two: "Miller et al. improved the technique developed by Zhang to make it more precise," or "The authors developed a new analysis technique and applied it to existing data." Remind students if they get stuck that the hot spots they generated in step one (listed on the board) are great places to start looking for a paper's intervention.

Step Three: (10 minutes) Reconvene and ask the student volunteer to take the lead on describing each source's contribution to the literature, with the rest of the class joining in to offer refinements based on their own assessments.

Table 8 ("Charting Your Contribution")

	Experimental Technique	Analysis method	Theoretical framework
Smith et al. (2011)	New mixture improved efficiency by over 40 percent		
Xu & Val (2009)			New model 10 times more accurate when compared to past data
Wang (2013)		New classification method yielded 10 percent fewer false positives	Unified Xu & Val model with earlier predictions

As a class, help the student volunteer make a chart representing this information on the board. (A completed example appears in Table 8.) First, group the contributions the student has identified into two or three broad categories—these will serve as the columns in the table. Next, give each source a row, and indicate each source's contribution in the appropriate column.

It's likely that it will take a little back-and-forth to come up with labels for the columns, and you should plan to revise them as you consider each source. (Some sources, like Wang in Table 8, may ultimately appear in more than one column.) Take time along the way to model how students might perform this assessment themselves.

Step Four: (10 minutes) Have students individually complete steps two and three on their respective sources, starting with the process of summarizing each source's contribution (step two), and ending with the creation of their own chart (step three), which may or may not use the same column headings as the example chart on the board. Circulate among the students and answer questions as they arise—and have the student who volunteered circulate as well to serve as a peer sounding board. Before moving on, ask if anyone happened to discover, while summarizing their sources, a new contribution category. Add any new column headings to the board as they arise.

Step Five: (5 minutes) Tell the students that the remainder of the exercise will be dedicated to helping them fit their own work into the charts they created in step four. Remind them that just as they've assessed how each of their sources makes a contribution to the field, future researchers will ask the same question about their project.

Ask students to add a row to their tables labeled "my work." In each column, the students should indicate whether and how they innovate over the existing literature. Of course, it's fine if their work doesn't contribute in each column. If they can't fill in a contribution in any column, encourage them to add a column that does capture their contribution and to reassess the rest of the sources along that axis.

Step Six: (10 minutes) Reconvene and invite students to describe the main contributions of their work, using the categories they've defined and discovered in their charts. Encourage them to "tell the story" of their contribution, showing how it fits in with the contributions made by sources in the past. In this final wrap-up step, emphasize to the students that, by building a chart, they are in essence building a *motive*. The chart makes it clear what gap in the literature their work fills. Explain that, with motive in hand, they will find it much easier to write a convincing and clear literature review structured around the questions that their new work addresses.

REFLECTIONS

This exercise aims to address two questions that every beginning writer in the sciences has. The first feels practical: how do I write a literature review? The second feels fraught with a whole different level and kind of anxiety: how do I make my work stand out? By showing how the two questions are best addressed in tandem, the exercise makes the whole enterprise less fraught and mysterious, and students finish with a better sense of how to articulate succinctly the way their work improves on the prior state of knowledge.

The practical technique of building a chart distills the essence of the literature review and makes it less likely that students will get lost in descriptive prose. But ultimately the psychological benefit of the exercise may be most important of all. "Making a contribution" sounds like a big task for a student, especially one who is new to the discipline. Many students think good papers have to be revolutionary in all respects—better data, better analysis, better conclusions. I have found that breaking down other papers' contributions by using this exercise helps my students feel that "making a contribution" is a smaller and more manageable job, and that their own work can contribute in small but significant ways to the scholarly community.

I developed this exercise with science and mathematics students in mind, but the basic structure can work across the disciplines. History, literature, and philosophy sources, for example, also make contributions in different ways along different axes. For instance, history papers may innovate by bringing to light new primary sources; applying a novel lens to a time period, person, or event; or making a new comparison or connection. Philosophy papers may likewise bring new sources or theoretical frameworks to bear, describe a new philosophical puzzle or problem, or propose a new solution to a problem raised by an earlier thinker. A literature paper could offer unique close readings or thematic analyses.

"Charting Your Contribution" works in different disciplinary contexts, but it also shines in *multi*disciplinary settings, including, for example, a summer research mentorship program that paired graduate students across the humanities, social sciences, and sciences with undergraduate research mentees. While the graduate students brought substantive expertise in their disciplines, they lacked the pedagogical training to teach the research process itself. By naming features common to scholarship in all fields, the exercise helped mentors and mentees alike identify the intended contribution of undergraduate research proposals. As a surprise bonus, the exercise also facilitated better explanations of what kinds of questions different fields ask and how they go about answering them. Amusingly, given the disciplinary source of this exercise, the mentor/mentee pair from mathematics, who had struggled to explain their work to the "outsiders," found that this exercise produced "Ohhhhh! That's what you do!" moments that resonated across the rest of the summer.

The Source Use Proximity Map

Sajan Saini

A mapping exercise to visualize the functions of the sources at play in a research argument.

Writing Focus: *sources, analysis, motive, evidence, orienting*
Teacher Preparation: *medium*
Student Preparation: *low*
Estimated Time: *80 minutes*
General Disciplines: *humanities, social sciences, sciences*

EXERCISE

Prep Work: Assign a scholarly reading that models a wide variety of primary and secondary source uses. For your own reference, draft a "Proximity Map" describing the reading (see map details and sample below) and select a few examples of source use that might be especially helpful to highlight.

Step One: (15 minutes) Frame the purpose of the exercise as establishing the surprising range of roles that sources can play in an argument. Then invite students to see what they can discover themselves by investigating the assigned reading. In pairs or small groups, have students select a passage that uses a source in an impressive way and decide on a label that describes the type of work the source does ("provides evidence," "establishes context," etc.). After a few minutes, ask each team to comment briefly on their source and label for their contributing move. Keep a running list on the board of labels the students come up with.

Step Two: (10 minutes) Lead a discussion that consolidates the student contributions into four categories or compass points. (You could do more or fewer, but four is the ideal number, as you will see in the next step.) While the exact source functions you come up with may vary depending on the text, you may land on something like this:

1. Provides evidence for analysis
2. Helps frame the scholarly debate and/or motivating question
3. Presents a useful theory, or analytical tools, concepts, or key terms
4. Provides orienting context or background

The exact breakdown of these functions can vary, as long as they're all genuinely distinct and useful. By naming four, or at least more than two, you'll inevitably complicate the common but also confusing and often unhelpful distinction between "primary" and "secondary" sources. Students sometimes get lost down a rabbit hole trying to identify which of these two categories a source belongs to, whereas the more crucial intellectual work of this step is successfully to describe the function a source is serving in an argument.

Step Three: (10 minutes) Time to map the text's ambitious source use! Write the author's last name for the reading in the center of the board and encircle it. Then explain the two-step logic they will use for mapping. First, pick a cardinal *direction* representing contribution types one through four (north for one, east for two, and so on) and divide the map into four quadrants. Second, in the appropriate quadrant, gauge a *distance* representing the source's contribution to the core argument: the closer to the center, the more the source matters. After selecting an appropriate spot, write the source name there and connect it with a straight line to the reading at the center. See the included sample proximity map at the end of this exercise.

Now model two sources from the text so students can see how the map works. Ideally use two different source functions; choose one that belongs close to the center and another drifting toward the edge of the map.

Step Four: (20 minutes) Back in their groups, give students a minute or two to decide where to map their source(s) from step one. Then have them select and map two other sources of their choice. Next, have a volunteer come up to the board to map one source and explain the reasoning. See if other groups mapped the same source in a different way, and lead a short discussion aiming for a consensus about where the source properly belongs. Note that a single source might provide multiple functions, and in that case it's useful to map the source multiple times in different directions.

Repeat the process with other groups until you've mapped all or nearly all of the important sources in the text. If students miss a key source, be sure to point it out and get it on the map.

Step Five: (20 minutes) Now demonstrate how this process can be used as a diagnostic tool, not only for assigned readings, but for students' own work-in-progress. In all likelihood, the map your class has created boasts a relatively uniform spread in terms of the directions the sources inhabit. It is also likely to feature a range of distances; if anything, the map may skew toward sources lying closer to the center, because students properly recognize them as being more important. But not all scholarly writing—particularly drafts—will have these characteristics. Ask students, in their groups, to consider what it would mean if different essays map out in the following ways:

1. Most sources are clustered in the direction of evidence to be analyzed.
2. Most sources are clustered in the direction of providing orienting context or background.
3. Sources are clustered toward establishing a scholarly debate and/or motivating question, but one finds little in the way of evidence.
4. Sources are uniformly spread in all directions, but nearly all of them are at distant edges of the map.

Reconvene to discuss the scenarios. Essay 1 likely indicates a lack of engagement with the scholarship that would help motivate the analysis. Essay 2 might feel like a report, operating at a superficial level that doesn't develop analysis or argument. Essay 3 reviews and may intelligently engage the relevant scholarship but struggles to contribute something new in the absence of an object of analysis. Essay 4 might diligently hunt down a wide range of sources serving different functions but fails to zero in on the "core" sources—those that should be close to center—from which the writer will develop a thesis.

This discussion highlights the proximity map's role as an at-a-glance survey of how a particular argument engages with relevant sources.

Step Six: (5 minutes) Ask students to begin composing a similar map-in-progress for their research papers, and to bring the completed version with them to their next office meeting with you.

REFLECTIONS

This exercise works best in a research paper's drafting stage, as students strive to assemble initial sources and a nascent argument. The ideal assigned reading is a scholarly essay in which a diversity of sources serves a range of functions (object of analysis, orienting context, theoretical lens, key term definition, etc.). I use a piece by Scott Bukatman called "X-Bodies: The Torment of the Mutant Superhero." This 1994 essay is a tour de force example of source use from varied disciplines and writing genres by a media scholar self-consciously struggling with his disciplinary authority in the then-emerging field of comics studies. It's a terrific essay for teaching students how to map sources that appear in research papers, including their own.

Proximity maps underscore how writing is a practiced craft that may rely on multimodal techniques—such as visualizing a paper's source contributions—to draft and revise a nuanced essay. Academic writing breakthroughs occur with diligent effort to refine every paragraph's focus and function in a well-tested argument. But to get there, these maps offer an initial diagnostic to assess whether a writer's research process has cast a wide enough net and sufficiently analyzed its sources.

I've found in my classes that the use of proximity maps can alleviate students' anxieties about assembling thoughtful, long-form arguments. Bukatman makes a sprawling, multi-staged argument, but once you've helped students map a couple of the author's source uses in step three, they are generally quick to see that the research process in the model essay is just a more practiced version of the work they'll do in their research essays.

With source mapping, students have an opportunity to x-ray a source to see the bones of its argument: how a writer positions novel claims against researched sources. Students sometimes ask in the closing discussion if Bukatman's thesis could rely on *fewer* sources, which leads to the recognition that the motive of the author's project was to *legitimize* comics studies by sustaining a conversation with a large body of scholarship. I find that, while students are impressed

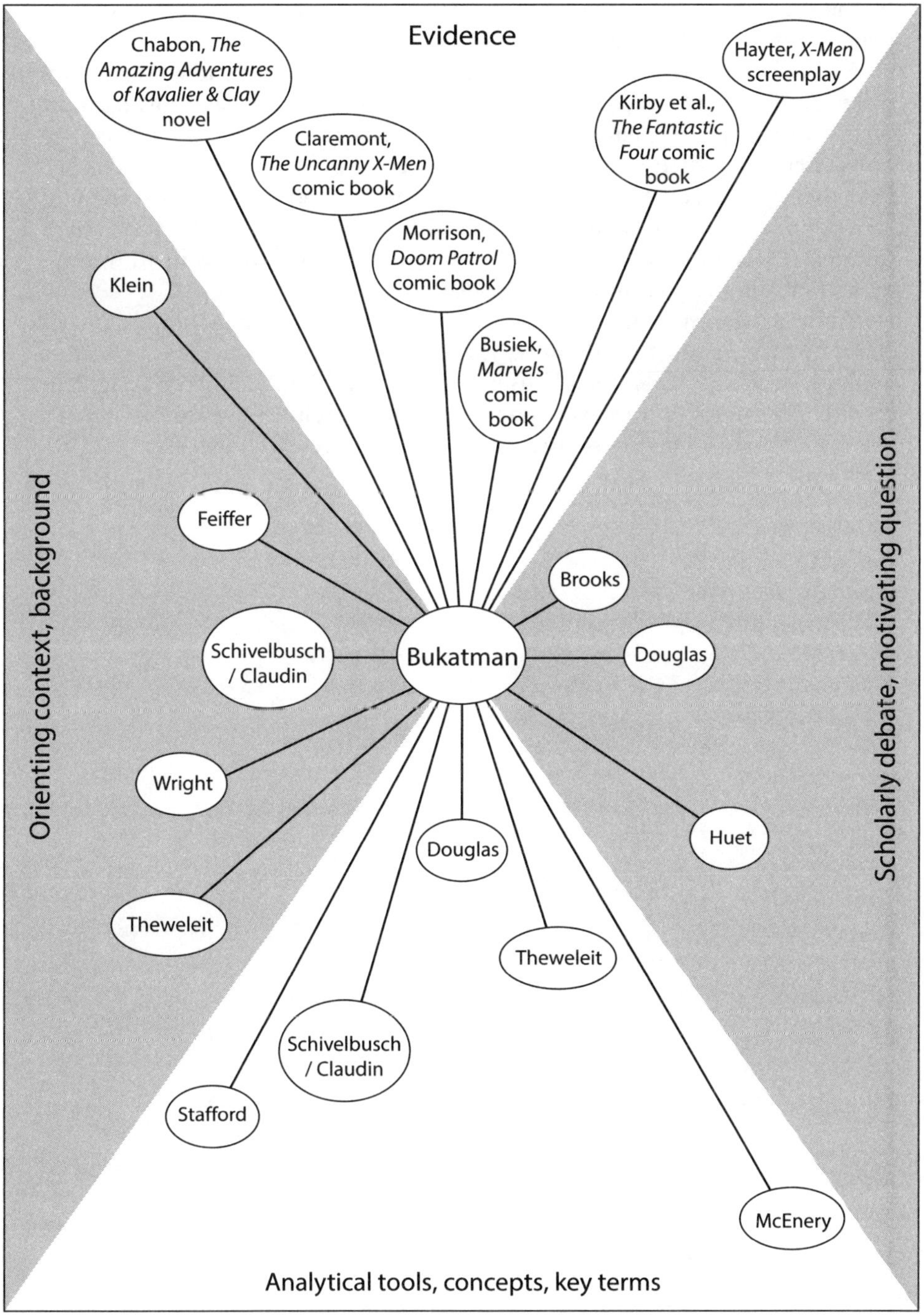
Evidence
Chabon, The Amazing Adventures of Kavalier & Clay novel
Claremont, The Uncanny X-Men comic book
Morrison, Doom Patrol comic book
Busiek, Marvels comic book
Kirby et al., The Fantastic Four comic book
Hayter, X-Men screenplay
Orienting context, background
Klein
Feiffer
Schivelbusch / Claudin
Wright
Theweleit
Bukatman
Scholarly debate, motivating question
Brooks
Douglas
Huet
Douglas
Theweleit
Schivelbusch / Claudin
Stafford
McEnery
Analytical tools, concepts, key terms

by the example of an in-depth case study of source use, during their own research process most remain hesitant to attempt such an extended analysis.

As a result, I ask students to bring a proximity map to review research-in-progress in our first office meeting for the research essay. In a follow-up draft review, I structure office meetings as mini workshops with three students, since cross-referencing their maps leads to illuminating discussion. In these sessions I've observed students identify gaps in source use or undervalued sources—and spot promising primary sources for a case study—by literally *pointing* to sources on their colleague's map and asking, "Where did that show up in your argument?" or "Should you move this in *closer*?"

While a writer shouldn't blindly rely on a proximity map as an indicator of thesis quality, or as an overly prescriptive assessment of a research process or analysis, it does provide notably useful rule-of-thumb guidelines. Thoughtful research for an essay project isn't just about careful citation and annotation. It's also about drawing pictures—maps—to visualize a research process.

Building Original Arguments

Geneviève A. Creedon

Build with LEGO bricks to help students visualize complex texts and reconceptualize the relationship between thesis and structure.

Writing Focus: *structure, thesis, conventions*
Teacher Preparation: *low*
Student Preparation: *low*
Estimated Time: *50 minutes*
General Disciplines: *humanities, social sciences, sciences*

EXERCISE

Prep Work: You'll need a box of LEGOs with as wide a variety of pieces as possible. Choose two argument-driven readings that students have already discussed together in some depth. I typically use a literary studies or history article alongside a quantitative social science essay. Ideally, the selections will dramatize differences in disciplinary conventions and/or the structural range and complexity of academic writing. Have copies of "A Writing Lexicon" on hand.

Step One: (5 minutes) Ask students what adjectives come to mind when they think of the five-paragraph essay. Building on students' likely answers (helpful, rigid, simple, easy, etc.), acknowledge both the virtues and limitations of the five-paragraph essay. Now, using four LEGO bricks, build for students a LEGO model of a typical five-paragraph essay: three same-shaped bricks representing evidence in support of a descriptive thesis represented by one longer brick (figure 1). Ask students how this structure compares to LEGO structures they've seen or built themselves. Responses typically include "simple," "boring," or "uninteresting," which sets the stage for building more sophisticated structures in service of more complex arguments.

Step Two: (15 minutes) Putting students in small groups, open the box of LEGOs for the class to share and ask each group to build the two sample readings, using "A Writing Lexicon" as their guide. In other words: if these readings were LEGO structures, what would they be? As students are building, encourage them to reflect on why the authors might have structured their texts as they did and how the structures serve the central arguments. Students tend to appreciate having creative license in designating which "Lexicon" terms correspond to which kinds (or colors) of brick. Let them know that in the next step they'll be asked to explain their choices as well as their overall designs in a quick presentation to the rest of the class.

FIG. 1. LEGO model of five-paragraph essay as described in Step One.

Step Three: (20 minutes) Have groups volunteer to share what they came up with for both readings. Ask them to elaborate on how and why they built the essays the way they did and what surprising overlaps or unexpected contrasts they discovered. Students are likely to produce different models of the same pieces of writing, and it's important to draw attention to what we can learn from this. Some might represent motive as the foundation while others might represent evidence or method or sources as the primary ground on which the rest of the essay is built. Though their buildings may emphasize different features, students generally arrive at a shared understanding of the structure and thesis overall, and you want to emphasize that consensus.

Step Four: (10 minutes) Return to the basic five-paragraph LEGO structure and ask students to describe how the LEGO structures they built differ from it. Next, ask *why* their structures differ as they do, encouraging students to look back at the articles themselves to see what qualities of their arguments make them irreducible to the five-paragraph model. Conclude with a discussion about the relationships between evidence, analysis, thesis, and structure, emphasizing the main takeaway: thesis and analysis drive structure, not the other way around.

REFLECTIONS

Students are used to valuing complexity and difficulty in building LEGO sets, from the expert-level Coliseum or Taj Mahal to the humble Volkswagen Bus, in ways that stand in sharp contrast to many students' formulaic views of writing as they begin college. Trained on the five-paragraph model, they are used to writing papers by predetermining a thesis and seeking evidence to "back it up," and they're very good at it. Their understandable attachment to a one-size-fits-all model makes it difficult for them to see how confining it is as they undertake more open-ended inquiry with a broader range of evidence.

When I first used this exercise and asked students how they would build a five-paragraph essay, I got a lot of blank stares in response. Moving into three dimensions can feel like a leap. But visualizing the five-paragraph essay with

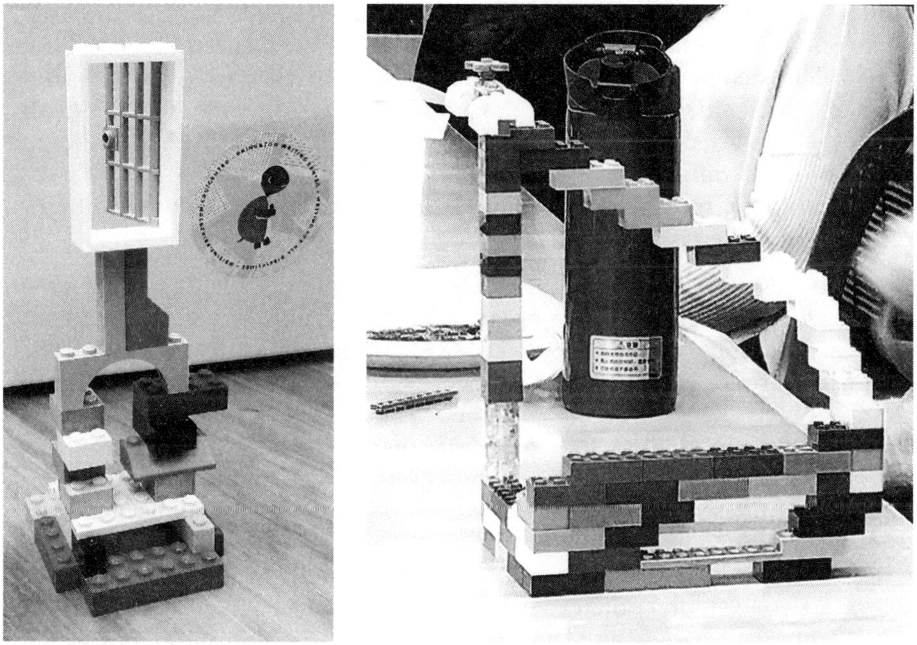

FIG. 2. Snapshots from the classroom: two different student representations of the structure of a scholarly article using LEGOs to render concrete the elements of "A Writing Lexicon".

four LEGO bricks makes the exercise click quickly, and I have yet to encounter a student who finds this representation to be anything but simplistic and dull. When it comes to how to move *beyond* the five-paragraph essay, however, the LEGO metaphor becomes usefully complicated. Many students are used to building complex LEGO structures with step-by-step directions. With academic writing, however, there is no one preset correct structure or building method for the students' individual arguments. But that doesn't mean anything goes. The multiplicity of options is constrained both by disciplinary conventions and by the unique demands for a logical chain of analysis that each thesis requires. To craft that logical chain, authors engage their writing as LEGO-users do when building without a manual. This exercise helps students cultivate that more interesting and complex approach to structure in their own papers.

The two LEGO representations pictured in figure 2 offer sample student responses to Stanton-Chapman et. al., "An Observational Study of Children's Behaviors Across Two Playgrounds." The article brings together arguments about playground design and gender and children's play by offering a new data-driven perspective. In the example on the left, students described their build as representing a bridge between two scholarly conversations that opens a door to the different method. In the example on the right, students built the tall tower in the back left to represent the essay's new evidence and used the primarily blue bricks in the foreground to represent previous scholarly interpretations. Meticulous step-by-step analysis brought the existing scholarship together with the new data to define a fresh peak and direction. After building one or two pieces of published scholarship, students have a sense of what they're aiming for at its most sophisticated.

The utility of the LEGO metaphor naturally lends itself to a number of variations on the exercise that focus on students' own work:

- In class or office hours, ask students to produce a LEGO freeze-frame structure of their work-in-progress. This offers an easy self-diagnostic for identifying missing pieces—the absence of sources, a clear research question or motive, analysis—in student drafts. Asking them to envision tangibly their own structure gives them a bird's-eye perspective, and thereby makes it more likely that *they* rather that *you* will identify the problems to address. For example, if a student seems to be building from a preexisting thesis, or is offering claims without evidence, it's immediately visible.
- In a more elaborate variation, ask students to build their drafts-in-progress at two (or more) different stages in their writing or research process. By comparing earlier with later versions, students are able to track their own progress through a particular project. Moreover, they learn to articulate the different stages and the intellectual work those entail, from initial curiosity and discovery to the cultivation of a motivated thesis to the clearest and most persuasive presentation of that argument with its audience in mind. For writing in the disciplines, this version also highlights what analytical practices go into the early stages and the conventions of argument and presentation that are expected in polished scholarly work.

After running the basic exercise once, incorporating short bursts of LEGO play is a fun respite from words, and a shift in medium that offers a generative metaphorical arena for problem-solving.

Losing Your Keys

Tim Haupt

Students appreciate the value of key terms by losing track of them first.

Writing Focus: *key terms*
Teacher Preparation: *low*
Student Preparation: *low*
Estimated Time: *65 minutes*
General Disciplines: *humanities, social sciences, sciences*

EXERCISE

Prep Work: Bring copies of a short paragraph laden with meaningful but underdefined key terms. (A densely written text from any discipline will do, though I favor an excerpt from the Declaration of Independence or Karl Marx's brief "Theses on Feuerbach.") Ask students to bring drafts-in-progress of whatever assignment they are working on.

Step One (15 minutes): Begin with an especially "meta" opener: ask students to provide a key term definition of the phrase "key terms" (without reference to "A Writing Lexicon"). It doesn't need to be fancy; something like "a text's key terms are its most important concepts" is all you need to get moving.

Divide your class into small groups and present them with your excerpt. Here's mine (or Jefferson's):

> "We hold these truths to be self-evident, that all men are created equal, that they are endowed by their Creator with certain, unalienable Rights, that among these are Life, Liberty, and the pursuit of Happiness."

Ask each group to make a list of the passage's key terms and to be ready to justify their choices. Reconvene to discuss as a class. The ultimate goal is to select the *three most important* key terms, but begin by nudging them along with complicating questions:

- Can a key term be a phrase or does it have to be a single word? If it can be a phrase, where would we draw the line?
- How about words that have (perhaps) less intentional significance (such as "we" or "men")? How does it change our perception of the point of the passage if we include or exclude them as key terms?
- Should key terms always be nouns? How should we factor in the adjectives (such as the "self-evident" "truths" and "unalienable Rights")?

Wrap up this discussion by asking your class to revisit their definition of "key terms." Are there any additional general principles that we can conclude about key terms?

Step Two (20 minutes): Have each small group rewrite the passage without using its key terms, and without simply replacing them with new, synonymous key terms. In other words, their task is to write out more fully and explicitly what they think each key term means rather than just replace it with an alternative. Students may find it helpful to dig around in a dictionary or thesaurus to open up possible meanings of the key terms, and that's fine, but you'll likely need to circulate among the groups to push them toward sufficient definition. When everyone is finished, either have them post their rewrites on a common Google Doc or write them on the board.

You'll end up with a range of examples, which highlight the unexpected complexity of each seemingly straightforward key term. (See below for a sample of my students' revision of the Declaration of Independence excerpt.)

Read the samples aloud and ask your students what they notice in the contrast between rewrites. Highlight some tensions or ambiguities inherent in the key terms. For example, does *self-evident* mean that everyone *already* knows it or just that everyone *can* know it. If everyone *can* know it, is it possible nevertheless to misrecognize or deny the "truth"? Do they still need some kind of teacher or authority to help them recognize it as a "truth"? And so on. The dual aims are: 1) to unsettle students' assumption that key terms can speak for themselves without significant, additional discussion, and 2) to demonstrate that different definitions of key terms lead to very different interpretations of the text.

Step Three (10 minutes): Have students turn to their own drafts and ask them to locate a paragraph, probably relatively early in the body of their essay, where they are introducing and defining one or more key terms. The most consequential paragraph is likely to be one where they are establishing a theoretical framework, which grounds subsequent analysis and discussion. Once they've selected a paragraph, have them highlight the three most important key terms.

Next, have students share their chosen paragraph with a partner via a Google Doc or email. (You could also have them print out a hard copy of their paragraph ahead of time.) Students should now rewrite their partner's paragraph in the same way they did with the Declaration. They must delete the key terms without simply substituting synonyms; the point is to express more fully and explicitly what they think each of the key terms really means.

Step Four (10 minutes): Have partners return the paragraphs they've rewritten. Once everyone has read their own rewritten paragraph, ask the partners to discuss the following questions:

For the rewriter:

- Which aspects of the rewrite were most challenging? Why?
- Which key terms were most clear in their meaning and which were most ambiguous? Why?

- What further advice would you offer your partner for revising the paragraph so the key terms are clarified or used more effectively?

For the original author:

- Did the rewrite successfully capture your intended meaning for each key term? Does the new paragraph *say* what you *meant*?

Step Five (10 minutes): Reconvene the full class and ask students for examples of particularly noteworthy or effective rewrites. Once you've discussed a successful example or three, abstract general principles together for using key terms effectively. Write these on the board as a final takeaway that students can use after class to start revising their use of key terms in the paragraph they've been discussing, or to make a plan for using these key terms more effectively throughout their essay.

REFLECTIONS

This exercise plays on the only somewhat corny metaphor of *keys*, those handy little objects that open doors without ever revealing the secret of how exactly they do what they do. Like keys, key terms open doors that connect our work to existing scholarship; they can also reveal meaning that would otherwise remain locked within a primary source. And they accomplish this work as if by magic: simply writing the word often seems sufficient to achieve the effect.

But the magic is an illusion; a careless key term *looks* like it's doing work, but unless it's consciously curated for a specific, intended purpose, the term produces meaning the author didn't intend, confuses a reader, and undermines an argument. The writer becomes the sorcerer's apprentice. That's what makes key terms tricky to use effectively. It's easy to take them for granted and assume that they are doing everything that we imagine them to do without much or any explicit thought on our part. When this happens, writing can become clunky and laden with jargon. A surprising solution is to lose your keys—if only for a moment—because sometimes it's difficult to see or experience the significance of something until it's gone. This exercise will help students see more clearly how and why their key terms work in the context of their arguments, which will, in turn, help them to use key terms more effectively. (For another approach to defining key terms, you can also try "Cloudy Key Terms.")

I use this writing exercise late in the semester after students have submitted a draft of their independent research project. A common problem with these projects—and the reason why I developed this exercise in the first place—was that students weren't sufficiently integrating more theoretically driven sources into their writing. They knew that such sources could help them launch their analysis, but working with sources that weren't already discussed or unpacked in class turned out to be challenging. They too often left the sources to speak for themselves and insufficiently analyzed tricky concepts.

That's why the excerpt from the Declaration of Independence works so well. (For two other exercises that make use of the Declaration as a sample text, see

"Declaring Your Independence" and "You Can't Have Everything.") First, it's *loaded* with key terms, so there's no objectively correct response. My students underline so many different words and phrases in step one that deciding what should count as a key term—and which key terms are the *most key*—always produces lively discussion. We typically narrow a capacious list of contenders—"We," "truths," "self-evident," "men," "equal," "Creator," "unalienable rights," "Life, Liberty, and the pursuit of Happiness"—to these three: "self-evident," "equal," "rights." My students usually decide that a key term can be a phrase, but it has to function as a coherent unit. If you can define the components of the phrase in isolation, you're dealing with multiple key terms. They also tend to conclude that the significance or point of a passage depends to a certain extent on which terms are taken to be *key* terms, and that the meaning of the passage varies greatly with different interpretations of the key terms. If it doesn't, they probably weren't really key terms.

Second, many of the seemingly straightforward key terms in the Declaration turn out to be unexpectedly complex, as made clear in this sample rewrite from step two in one of my classes:

> We hold these truths to be **knowable to all without needing someone to tell you about it**, that all men are created **such that no one is given unfair advantage over others at birth**, that they are endowed by their Creator with certain, unalienable **possessions, which aren't so much things as they are opportunities**, that among these are Life, Liberty, and the pursuit of Happiness.

Whatever excerpt you choose, it should help your students abstract a set of general principles for using key terms as a capstone to the exercise. Here, for example, is a list of principles my students put together in one of our recent classes:

- Define key terms fully and explicitly as a first order of business.
- Use key terms in a way that prevents misinterpretation or ambiguity.
- Don't overburden a paragraph with too many new key terms because it will be impossible to define each adequately.
- Jargon may sound impressive at first glance, but it doesn't really accomplish anything substantial or worthwhile.

Reactions to the task in steps three and four have been interesting. On the one hand, students have been more excited about revising their peers' essays than their own. On the other, they have also expressed surprise or confusion about what emerges. "We aren't supposed to keep the rewritten paragraphs in our revision, are we?" one student asked when confronted with his partner's revision. It's the dream of every inexperienced writer to move swiftly from a draft to a "final" essay by working on word choice and the flow of the prose. Yet this exercise produces awkward formulations, which reveal ambiguity rather than tidy it up—and that's a great opportunity to remind students that revision isn't a one-way, linear path. Sometimes you have to go backward or sideways or in circles before you can make a breakthrough. And a breakthrough generally involves substantially developing your understanding of your sources or your argument about them.

For upper-level seminars, I switch out the sample text with an exemplary source from the disciplines. In anthropology, for instance, I want a passage in which a theoretical insight or construct is being challenged via a discussion of the density and complexity of ethnographic evidence. One could also streamline the exercise by skipping the first step and giving your students the example passage with a set of key terms already highlighted. Or if you have more time, you could have them reconsider and revise their own work in class as an additional, final step. Given that the exercise is also a workshop on paraphrasing, you could use its first half to explore the relationship between key terms and integrating sources. Instead of using student drafts in step three, you might have everyone choose a passage from a scholarly source that's of use to them in an essay they're just starting to draft. The exercise in that case would be to develop a close reading of a passage's key terms in order to use them or critique them.

You Can't Have Everything

Keith Shaw

Refine a draft essay's structure by mapping and prioritizing the different components of its argument.

Writing Focus: *structure, thesis, analysis*
Teacher Preparation: *low*
Student Preparation: *low*
Estimated time: *50 minutes*
General Disciplines: *humanities, social sciences, sciences*

EXERCISE

Prep Work: Students bring a copy (electronic is fine) of a draft in progress. Bring hard copies of an argument-driven reading they have seen before, ideally one they have already dissected in some detail, and that has *some* analytic complexity but not *too* much. I use the Declaration of Independence because I'm a history and politics nerd, and because my students have already been subjected to the "Declaring Your Independence" exercise from earlier in this collection.

Step One: (5 minutes) Working in groups, ask students to identify the thesis, and then a half-dozen analytical claims that support the thesis. There should be a mix of *major* claims that are central to the argument, but then also a few *minor* claims. For the Declaration, they'll write something like:

Thesis: We're breaking up with Great Britain, and we're justified in doing so. (It's not us, it's you.)

Major claims:

1. All men have rights.
2. When the state routinely violates your rights, you gain the right to rebel.
3. We tried to warn Great Britain we were mad, but they didn't listen.

Minor claims:

4. Britain is bringing our people overseas for trial.
5. And they're harassing us with a horde of imperial bureaucrats.
6. *And* they're bringing foreign mercenaries to North America.

Step Two: (10 minutes) Still in groups, students should assign two different scores to each claim:

First, how *important* is the claim to the overall argument? In other words, in the absence of this claim, how persuasive would the thesis be? Score this on a scale of one to four:

1. *Necessary*: An absolute requirement; the thesis is automatically unintelligible or unpersuasive in its absence.
2. *Valuable*: A key claim without which the thesis would be difficult to sustain.
3. *Helpful*: A useful supporting claim, or an analytical link between other claims, but one the writer could live without.
4. *Unhelpful*: A claim that actually isn't supporting the thesis, perhaps because it's a tangent or overtly undermines the central argument.

Second, how much work, or *investment*, measured roughly in page count, should it take to introduce, substantiate, and show the importance of each claim? Note that how much space it *should* take may be quite different from how much space it *does* take in the sample. (This distinction matters greatly with the Declaration.) Score this on a scale of A to D:

A. *Heavy*: A serious commitment of space and resources; a third or more of the essay might be devoted to deploying just this analysis.
B. *Substantial*: Probably measured in pages even in a short paper, but not an investment that dominates the entire essay.
C. *Minor*: Likely measured in paragraphs or even sentences.
D. *Trivial*: The reader might be expected to accept the claim as an assumption, or as "self-evident" (which, again, matters in the Declaration).

While they work, draw Table 9 on the board, with only the row and column labels for now, which will allow you to map each claim's two-part score.

Table 9 ("You Can't Have Everything")

Investment Importance	A	B	C	D
1	All Men Have Rights	Right to Rebel, [Airing of Grievances]		
2			We *Told* You	
3			Overseas Trials, Bureaucrats, Foreign Mercs	
4				

Students evaluating the Declaration using the example claims above might score it as follows, though there will be some natural variation:

1. All men have rights: *Importance:* 1; *Investment:* A
2. If the state routinely violates rights, you have the right to rebel: 1B
3. We tried to warn GB we were getting mad, but they didn't listen: 2C
4. GB is bringing our people overseas for trial: 3C
5. And they're harassing us with a horde of imperial bureaucrats: 3C
6. *And* they're bringing foreign mercenaries to North America: 3C

Step Three: (10 minutes) Reconvene, have the student groups volunteer their claims with their scores, and write shorthand versions ("Right to rebel," "We *told* you," etc.) in the proper square on the table. Give space for students to disagree about the proper scoring of particular claims; in a sufficiently complex writing sample, their scores will likely differ. Then lead a discussion about what the distribution of scores tells us about what the author needs to accomplish, and how well he or she did in fact accomplish their aims. Does the author shortchange a key bit of analysis, or overemphasize a claim that turns out not to matter much at all? Where might the author have cut to buy space for more significant claims?

Step Four: (10 minutes) Now ask students to repeat the process individually for their own drafts: identify their claims, score them with the same system, and see what they find. While it was useful to limit the number of claims in the sample essay, have students extract as many entries as possible (since that's how they'll find their 3s and 4s).

Step Five: (10 minutes) When they're done, lead a conversation about how one should interpret the sixteen possible scores, or what one should take from patterns in their resulting tables.

SOME USEFUL TAKEAWAYS:

- The top left (1A, 1B, 2A): "1" claims definitionally require whatever attention they need, and "2" claims typically should be preserved. However, if writers have several claims in this range, it may be a sign of a manageability problem, and they might consider reducing the scope of the project through revision.
- The top right (1C, 1D): If many or all of the "1" claims fall into this range, it may signal an arguability problem. In that case, the thesis may rely on "analysis" that is too easy to establish, and so it might be persuasive but underwhelming or undermotivated.
- 2B, 2C, 2D: Most claims worth keeping, beyond the single most important claim of the essay, probably fall into this range. Lots of 2Bs quickly become a manageability problem.
- 3C, 3D, *maybe* 3B: These claims *could* merit mention in the essay, but may better appear as substantive footnotes.
- The bottom-left (3A, *probably* 3B, 4-anything): The Danger Zone. Buy yourself some space and your reader some time!

Step Six: (5 minutes) Before wrapping up, have students draft a structural revision strategy to cut, condense, or bolster the claims in their drafts.

REFLECTIONS

This exercise addresses a recurring frustration my students face in introductory writing courses. Entering the term often having written nothing longer than a few pages, students assigned a five- or six-page essay think they confront an infinity of space that couldn't possibly be filled. But they quickly discover that the suggested page count was there for a reason, and a strong argument *easily* fills it. The scope challenge then abruptly shifts in the direction of paring down. Curiously, this phenomenon recurs with *each* assignment, no matter the quality of my Manageability Rant at the introduction of each new, slightly longer essay. Once students undertake a substantial research assignment, inattention to scope leads to sprawling drafts that writers struggle to corral. It's at this point, when morale is low and concrete revision priorities are needed, that I use this exercise.

While the key takeaway is also the most obvious one to the instructor—life and papers are short, so make smart decisions—some of the better spontaneous conversations I have had about the research process emerged from this exercise. In generalizing from their own projects, students can see how what seemed like a relatively simple line of inquiry triggers a decision tree with endless branches. A lifetime *could* be spent discussing suicide bombers, AI, or Cuban architecture, but what *will* you say? Once you have more or less settled on your thesis, how do you determine your priorities and allocate time and word count?

The Declaration of Independence, being short, rich, and incorporating some noteworthy structural choices, is a great writing sample for this exercise. Students latch on to Jefferson's claim that "all men have rights" is *self-evident*, meaning it's an assertion he won't even bother to defend. But that assertion is actually a necessary premise for the entire argument that follows—that's why it's a "1." The Declaration may get away with it because Jefferson thinks his relevant audience already agrees, but *arguing* that is a serious challenge—indeed, one of the great challenges of political theory as a field. Jefferson treats the claim as a 1D, a truly necessary claim but one dispensed with quickly. To do it right in the context of an academic essay requires a more serious investment of time, space, and resources. It *should* be a 1A.

The "minor" claims students assess usually come from the Declaration's seemingly endless twenty-seven-point list of charges, which serve as evidence weighing whether Great Britain has routinely violated the Americans' rights (spoiler alert: they have). Each claim taken *individually* supports the thesis, but each is both unnecessary and perhaps insufficient to trigger the colonists' right to rebel. But neither do they take much argument to substantiate, hence the run of 3Cs (and sometimes 3Ds). Taken *together*, however, students realize the twenty-seven charges add up to something that is indeed necessary to the argument and deserving of real investment. In discussion, I ask students to combine the whole list into a single claim—"airing of grievances"—and they usually assign it a 1B. Students notice, though, that *Jefferson* seems to treat the list as a 1A when, in fact, he could probably establish British culpability with many fewer pieces of evidence. While the rhetorical pile-on has an emotive effect, curating a handful of the most serious bits of evidence would do the job just as well. When students notice that Jefferson could have trimmed back the "airing of grievances" to buy space for the critical but shortchanged "all men have rights" claim, I feel my work is done. The point is not to rewrite the sample piece but to establish that the scoring system gives us insight into how space *should* be allocated to argue a thesis efficiently.

In a recent use of this exercise, an engineering student approved of the "trendline" from the top left (1A) to the bottom right (4D) of the table for the Declaration. She thought it an especially good thing that the bottom left was vacant, as that zone is "inefficient," and hypothesized that good argument-driven writing would share these qualities. Pushing the idea further, another student wondered if any piece of writing with the opposite tendency (claims scattered from bottom left to top right) would automatically be unpersuasive. This was the perfect setup to transition to the students' essays, since they were motivated to have a "Jefferson line."

Once students know how to use the table, it's a useful homework assignment for future drafts-in-progress, or for mapping their peer's writing prior to a draft workshop to help ground the discussion.

PRACTICING REVISION

Stages of Historical Analysis

Tying Down Your Thought Balloons

Replying to Real Objections

Source Function BINGO

The Rhetoric of Source Use

Students Surf Internet in Class! You'll Never Believe How This Instructor Used It to Teach Writing!

Wrecking a Sentence

Disciplining Sentences

Stages of Historical Analysis

Christopher W. Close

Teach students a deep analysis of historical sources that goes beyond superficial observation to produce complex arguments.

Writing Focus: *analysis*
Teacher Preparation: *medium*
Student Preparation: *none*
Estimated Time: *30 minutes*
General Discipline: *humanities, social sciences*

EXERCISE

Prep Work: Make copies of the accompanying "Stages of Analysis" handout, unless you wish to compile your own version reflecting the themes of your course. Advice on this process appears in the "Reflections" section below. The exercise works best when students have read several primary and secondary sources and are in the process of composing or revising a paper. If you have more than thirty minutes to devote to this exercise, you might encourage students to bring their own drafts and allow time for them to apply what they've learned about analysis.

Step One: (5 minutes) Open by discussing the importance of continually analyzing one's sources throughout the writing process, whether brainstorming an argument, drafting a paper, or refining a thesis. The goal is to enable students to model their process of analysis on the steps employed by a practicing scholar.

Step Two: (5 minutes) Distribute the handout and explain how it works. Though it is a single document, the shifting formats signal a series of draft stages with increasing analytical sophistication. Statements in regular font are from stage one, underlined text is added in stage two, italicized text is added in stage three, and bold text is added in stage four, the final revision. Strikethroughs signal text that has been discarded in the revision process. Explain that the aim of the exercise is to read these five stages sequentially, identify what analysis has been done, what has changed from previous drafts, and what should happen to improve the analysis in the next revision.

Step Three: (3 minutes) Have a volunteer read the first stage. Then lead a discussion asking students to evaluate the quality of the analysis. It won't take much nudging for them to realize that the analysis is incomplete.

Step Four: (15 minutes) Select different volunteers to read the remaining stages and be ready to help interpret the formatting to ensure each stage is read correctly. After each reading, lead a discussion on what has changed and improved, what the writer did with evidence to produce the improvement, and where there remain opportunities for continued revision.

Be sure to draw attention to the substantial change in the main claim of the paragraph as a result of the deep dive into the evidence. While stage one merely introduces evidence, leaving it to speak for itself, the later stages do more sophisticated analytical work. Stage two expands upon and interprets the evidence. Stage three introduces secondary sources to contextualize the scholarly debate about the meaning of the primary source. Stage four finally plays off the evidence to lead the writer to their (or as it happens in this case, my) own conclusion.

Step Five: (2 minutes) Because good analysis entails substantial revision, encourage students to keep the stages of this exercise in mind as they wrestle with evidence. If you have extra time in class and students have drafts in progress, this is a good opportunity for them to deepen their own analysis using what they've learned.

REFLECTIONS

By analysis, scholars mean the interpretation of source evidence in pursuit of an original claim. Many students have difficulty understanding what instructors mean by analysis, even after the term is defined for them. Instructors may also struggle to teach analysis since it feels like second nature. These dynamics contribute to underdeveloped analysis in student papers and confusion about what instructors mean when they ask for "more complete" analysis or push students to "go deeper." This exercise demystifies the process by demonstrating how a practicing scholar analyzes sources in progressive stages, thereby empowering students to incorporate new techniques into their own writing.

In history courses, I've found this exercise particularly useful in teaching the necessity of using multiple pieces of evidence, and demonstrating the connections between them, to support historical arguments. Breaking this process into individual steps allows students easily to see the shortcomings in the earlier stages where multiple pieces of evidence are either not present or not related to each other in a clear fashion. The different stages show how to avoid simplistic or superficial readings of evidence, avoid selection bias in source use, and help students become more attuned to complexity as a historical concept. Used to this end, the stages can motivate students to think as historians in ways that carry over to reading comprehension and class discussions. Finally, while the exercise shows students the importance of establishing context for their evidence, it also illustrates how the author's analytical voice must remain present in order for the reader to understand how the evidence supports a claim of causality or change over time.

The right handout is the crucial piece of prep work. Though you are free to use the one provided, the exact number of stages, and the way the different stages are defined, may differ according to your pedagogical needs. It is easiest and most effective to use something you have written yourself, which allows you to reflect for your students on how you constructed a particular piece of analysis and offer an insider's perspective on the strategies at play in moving from one stage to the next. Students are usually excited to read something their instructor wrote, especially when they have the opportunity to see drafts that show how you encountered challenges similar to what they confront in their own writing. It makes the scaffolding of the stages seem more real and achievable, while modeling what you see as the bullseye for their own analysis. While created for use in a history course, the techniques of this exercise are transferable to any disciplinary setting and can be adapted to fit the needs of any subject matter.

When creating your own handout, format it as a series of nested stages with titles, so students benefit from a concrete language for identifying and remedying issues of analysis. The stages should show an increasingly complex engagement with evidence, progressing from the obvious and superficial to deeper analytical work in service of an argument. In this way, the handout models how to move from merely reporting on source content to demonstrating the meaning of evidence for their claims. From my experience in class, students will retroactively realize that their analysis stalled in stage two or stage three on previous assignments, and they now see why that was problematic. In my senior history research seminar, a student who had struggled with analysis all semester declared during the exercise, "I finally get it! I finally understand what your comments about deeper analysis meant!" Her analysis on the final paper, which focused on eighteenth-century female pirate trials, improved dramatically. On the draft, she had left whole sections of evidence where the female pirates on trial claimed to be pregnant unanalyzed, which missed a golden opportunity to make a claim about gender expectations in the trials. On the final revision, she deftly interpreted these passages and connected them directly to her claim about the ability of female pirates to adopt male or female identities based on their specific needs. While not all students experience such epiphanies, most improve their ability to identify insufficient analysis after doing the exercise, even if they haven't fully transitioned into applying the lessons to their own writing yet.

In teaching this exercise, I've been struck by students' ability to identify the incomplete analysis at each stage, but they often struggle to explain precisely *why* it is problematic. In that sense, student engagement with the handout at first mirrors the analytical difficulties the exercise is designed to address. I've found it useful to ask them what more they as readers would like to know about the writer's thinking at each stage of the process. This helps them imagine the audience for their own papers and gives them practice deepening their observations.

Beyond the benefits during class time, I have also found that naming the different stages of analysis doubles as a useful language for commenting on papers, pinpointing for students how far their analysis has progressed and what they still need to do to engage their evidence fully.

HANDOUT

Stages of Historical Analysis[1]

Key

Normal = First stage of analysis
Underlined = Added at second stage
Italics = Added at third stage
Bold = Added at fourth stage
~~Strikethrough~~ = Insufficient conclusions deleted at next stage

What was the nature of the relationship between the imperial cities Augsburg and Donauwörth? Donauwörth had a long history of orienting its religiopolitical policies toward the example of Augsburg. During the 1530s, Augsburg played a particularly important role as a proxy for Donauwörth's interests at regional and imperial diets. The exact nature of their relationship on the eve of Donauwörth's introduction of the Reformation emerges from two instances of intercity correspondence in 1537–38. In January 1537, shortly before Augsburg's abolition of the Latin mass, Donauwörth's council wrote its neighbor for guidance in initiating a "reformation of our statutes, old customs, and traditions. . . . Since we and our forefathers have emulated the statutes and ordinances of the praiseworthy city Augsburg in such affairs," Donauwörth hoped Augsburg would send a copy of its statute books to assist the council.[2] Augsburg's magistrates agreed to help Donauwörth, "which we wish to show good neighborliness."[3] ~~Good neighborliness, therefore, was the basis of their relationship.~~ For Donauwörth's council, the logical first step in reforming its statute books was to seek advice from its larger neighbor. It hoped to secure Augsburg's support, in the process obtaining external models to guide and legitimize its own magisterial initiatives. ~~The norm of good neighborliness guided this process.~~

Conversely, Augsburg's council wished to display "good neighborliness" to Donauwörth. This emphasis on neighborliness appears throughout sixteenth-century urban correspondence, underscoring the significance of regional relationships among imperial cities. Indeed, its frequent use as a social norm has led several scholars to examine how neighborliness operated in different contexts. Rolf Kiessling has described the importance of the neighborhood for the interaction of imperial cities with surrounding polities,[4] while Pascale Sutter has asserted that neighborhoods played a central role in regulating relations among burghers in the late medieval period.[5] In the context of the urban Reformation, Emily Fisher Gray has argued that within individual communities, "good neighborliness" served "as a standard on which the two competing confessions could negotiate the practical challenges of physical proximity."[6] ~~*Thus, good neighborliness shaped the relationship between Augsburg and Donauwörth in fundamental ways.*~~ **This could occur on the regional level as well, as the in-**

vocations of neighborliness in Augsburg's correspondence with Catholic Bavaria and the bishop of Augsburg imply. Between imperial cities, however, good neighborliness was not limited to matters of religious reform or confessional conflict. Rather, it signified the importance of regional support networks to the introduction of any type of reform, religious or secular. On the intercity level, good neighborliness served less "as a principle of [confessional] coexistence"[7] than as an acknowledgement of the interdependencies that linked cities together. Neighborliness was a complicated norm that could mean different things in different contexts. For Augsburg's council, good neighborliness meant it had a responsibility to aid Donauwörth both in its statute reform and in later times of religious need. Good neighborliness, therefore, could both enable different confessions to live together and encourage polities to agitate for the introduction of their confession in neighboring communities.

NOTES

1. Adapted from Christopher W. Close, *The Negotiated Reformation* (New York: Cambridge University Press, 2009), 111–13.
2. StadtA A, RA 571, January 13, 1537.
3. StadtA A, RA 571, January 18, 1537.
4. Rolf Kiessling, "Die 'Nachbarschaft' und die 'Regionalisierung' der Politik," in *Europa 1500*, edited by W. Eberhard and F. Seibt (Stuttgart: Klett-Cotta, 1986), 262–78.
5. Pascale Sutter, *Von Guten und Bösen Nachbarn: Nachbarschaft als Beziehungsform im spätmittelalterlichen Zürich* (Zürich: Chronos, 2002).
6. Emily Fisher Gray, "Good Neighbors: Architecture and Confession in Augsburg's Lutheran Church of Holy Cross 1525–1661" (PhD diss., University of Pennsylvania, 2004), 13.
7. Gray, "Good Neighbors," 39.

Tying Down Your Thought Balloons

Soo La Kim

Understand paragraphs as a unit of thought and how the sentences in a body paragraph function to support a claim.

Writing Focus: *analysis, evidence, structure*
Teacher Preparation: *low*
Student Preparation: *low*
Estimated Time: *60 minutes*
General Disciplines: *humanities, social sciences, sciences*

EXERCISE

Prep Work: Identify one or more examples of effective body paragraphs that have clear claims supported by analysis of evidence. (One sample obviously takes less time, but you open a number of options by having students look at two.) They may be samples from professional writing, from student writing, or both. They may be from a single discipline or multiple disciplines. Make copies and bring in enough highlighters in three distinct colors for pairs of students to share (pink/yellow/green). In the absence of highlighters, students can simply underline, circle, and so on. Ask students to bring in a hard copy of at least three or four pages of their drafts-in-progress to work on in class.

Step One: (15 minutes) Introduce the idea of different kinds of sentences within a body paragraph that serve distinct functions, working together to give that paragraph a clear focus within the larger argument. Ask students to come up with the various functions of sentences they might find in a paragraph of academic writing. Loosely group their answers on the board using the three broad categories I introduce below.

Students may come up with answers like "factual sentences," "sentences that back up what you want to say," "introductory sentences," "concluding sentences," "assertions," "questions," and so on. Nudge them toward the differences between sentences that claim, sentences that analyze, and sentences that use evidence. Depending on the paragraph's function, the proportions of these sentences will vary. Strong body paragraphs have all three, and some sentences in themselves serve double duty. But you will want to land here:

- **Claim: a statement derived from analysis that serves as the thesis of the paragraph, and supports in some way the thesis of the essay as a whole.** The claim sentence in a paragraph is what needs to be defended; what you're trying to persuade your readers of (i.e., it's not *obvious* that this is the case); a statement that is arguable, and thus needs to be argued for. The claim may often serve as the topic sentence of a paragraph, but they are not necessarily the same thing.

- **Analysis: evaluation of the evidence; interpretation of what something means, suggests, implies.** Analysis sentences connect claims to evidence, they explain what the evidence shows, why it's important, and so on. It's through analysis that we can sense the writer's presence as a reasoning individual who is in control of the argument. The precise nature of the analysis will be determined by the method employed, which in turn depends on the research question and disciplinary framework.
- **Evidence: the "stuff" the author curates from sources for the purpose of analysis.** Evidence includes your object of study—whether quantitative data, primary text, historical document, visual representation, mathematical puzzle—and the scholarly perspectives your essay contends with in some way.

While it's important to define the three categories, the key is recognizing the relationships between them. This is accomplished through high art . . . I sketch the following analogy (poorly!) on the board: a balloon (claim) tied to a rock (evidence) with string (analysis). You don't need to explain the metaphor in detail now, but it serves as a useful heuristic for students to think through the relationships among the three categories.

Step Two: (15 minutes) Distribute the highlighters! In pairs, have students identify the three types of sentences in the sample paragraphs by marking claims in pink, analysis in yellow, and evidence in green.

Reconvene and invite the students to discuss their observations about the sample(s). Be sure to emphasize that the writers, whatever their discipline, don't just let the evidence sit there; they are *using* the evidence to demonstrate a specific claim.

Step Three: (15 minutes) Ask students to take out their drafts and select the analytical body paragraph they have struggled with the most. They should then exchange drafts with a partner and highlight according to the color coding. When they're done, have partners offer feedback based on what they've discovered about each other's paragraphs and discuss strategies for revision. Give them some prompts:

- Can you identify the claim? (And does the author agree that that's it?)
- How does the analysis tie the claim to the evidence?
- Is the analysis persuasive? Why or why not?
- Is it the right evidence? What other kinds of evidence would better anchor the claim?
- Does the sequencing of claim, analysis, and evidence in the paragraph progress logically and clearly?

Step Four: (10 minutes) Reconvene the group to debrief. Invite everyone to hold up their highlighted paragraphs and ask what they notice or have learned about their paragraphs. Are some paragraphs too airy or rocky? Too much pink or too much green?

Step Five: (5 minutes) Give students a few minutes to revise their paragraphs or sketch out a revision plan. Prompt them to be specific: not "Analyze evidence more on page 5," but "Explain how the quote from source X shows that claim Y is true" or "Find more evidence that suggests that claim A is more persuasive than claim B."

REFLECTIONS

This exercise teaches students to produce more substantial, analytical paragraphs in which they are extracting meaning from their evidence, not simply citing it. When working with scholarly sources, beginning writers tend to let the sources speak for them. The preponderance of "undigested quotes" in a draft seems to say, "well, the experts said it better than I could, so here it is." This exercise emphasizes that the student writer needs to do more with the source material than simply quote or paraphrase it. I rely on the balloon/string/rock analogy because I want students to think in relational terms, to consider how the three different parts of argumentative writing that we're naming should be working together. Too many claims untethered to evidence, and the thought balloon just floats in the air, insubstantial and ungraspable, liable to drift in unexpected directions. Too much evidence left unexplained, and readers will feel like they're wandering around among big lumps of information that just sit there.

Choose your own adventure when it comes to selecting sample paragraphs. You might choose professional or student writing, or combine the two (which implicitly makes the point that your students are part of the scholarly conversation). Using two professional samples from different disciplines underscores different methods of analysis while highlighting the common interplay of claim, analysis, and evidence.

The highlighters are, well, the highlight of the exercise. Students immediately perk up when I bring them out, and I usually have one or two who are *really* excited about highlighters (expect not to get all of them back!). There's something about highlighting that doesn't feel like work, and coloring sentences in bright shades brings a welcome form of productive disruption to the classroom. And then you get to step back and see an interesting pattern revealed about your writing. The pattern isn't always what students expect or want, but that realization itself can motivate students to do the difficult work of revision, of thinking more carefully about how a piece of source material supports their claim and explaining that connection to a reader. Students may well be looking for a formula that determines how much of each color goes in each paragraph, and where. But there's no such formula. So much depends on the paragraph's purpose in the essay, and sometimes on the discipline.

The technique of color coding is a tool to identify and avoid classic problems: excesses of opinion or undigested evidence. It's instructive to see the different ways a paragraph can be lopsided: some paragraphs are all claims, a sea of assertive pink with maybe a piece of green evidence thrown in here and there; others are big chunky blocks of green, with no yellow strands to tether them to the claims they're supposed to be supporting. Some students want to say everything all at once—"I stated my claims here, what more should I say?" But revision means practicing how to sequence ideas and evidence in a way that builds toward a thesis, rather than simply asserting a claim that repeats over several pages. Other students, in seeing big block quotes highlighted in green, will sheepishly admit that they were just trying to fill up the page. Part of what we're teaching with analysis, then, is that "unpacking" or "digesting" evidence is a process that takes time; the final version of the paper is itself evidence of that deliberative thought process.

There is usually some laughter as a shorthand develops in our conversation—"I definitely need more yellow" or "Wow, look at all those claims! Tie those balloons down before they fly away!" or "I've got a giant mound of rocks just sitting there." This shorthand is precisely the lasting payoff of the exercise; it establishes a fun, meaningful framework for students to assess their own drafts and offer feedback to their peers. The balloon analogy is especially valuable when students get stuck. I encourage them to diagram their paragraphs: What's in the thought balloon? What evidence is on the ground? What analytical strings should tie the balloon to the rocks? The visual representation may help students structure the writing they've already produced, and then assess what's still missing and what connections still need to be made. The experience reminds them that we're always writing for readers, and we must attend to what they need to know and how we might guide them through our arguments. In their course evaluations, students cite the activity as a memorable, "eye-opening" one that moved them away from generalizations and toward more focused, purposeful writing.

The balloon/rock language extends in useful ways beyond this exercise. As writers, we "string balloons together" to construct theses from component claims. For readers, how we choose to introduce, defend, and sequence those balloons makes all the difference in whether our argument is understandable and persuasive. Sequences of evidence-analysis-claims are the building blocks of argument, forming the links in a carefully staged chain that defends the overall thesis.

Replying to Real Objections

Amy L. Shuster *and* Roblin Meeks

Introduce students to a more generous mode of disagreement, one that struggles *with* rather than *against* objections.

Writing Focus: *analysis, thesis, ethos*
Teacher Preparation: *low*
Student Preparation: *medium*
Estimated Time: *60 minutes*
General Disciplines: *humanities, social sciences, sciences*

EXERCISE

Prep Work: For homework, assign a text that includes a variety of objections and replies. We often use John Stuart Mill's *On Liberty* (chapter 2), which includes eight counterarguments of varying quality, both in his presentation of the objection and in his reply. (For something much shorter, we have also used Michael Kinsley's 1995 New Yorker essay, "The Intellectual Free Lunch.") Finally, make sure that you can project video and sound from an online source in your classroom.

Step One: (5 minutes) Play "The Argument Clinic" sketch from *Monty Python's Flying Circus*. Several versions are available on YouTube. Michael Palin pays to experience an "argument" with John Cleese. Palin first accidentally wanders into "Abuse," before finding Cleese. He's then disappointed when Cleese continually contradicts rather than argues.

Step Two: (5 minutes) In small groups, ask students to consider the three types of engagement presented in the sketch: abuse, contradiction, and argument. Invite them to identify and describe some examples of each of the categories—either from their own experiences or from public life. How do they differ from one another, and why do the differences matter?

Step Three: (10 minutes) Reconvene and field a few examples from each category, and then develop collective definitions of the three terms. (It may be helpful to log these definitions on the board.) Students may quickly dispense with abuse and contradiction, but be sure to press them to articulate how argument differs from the other two. If useful, refer them back to the sketch. Where, if anywhere, do Palin and Cleese ever *argue*, that is, disagree using substantive claims that treat the pursuit of truth as a shared enterprise? Where do they come close to doing so? How can we describe the differences in the quality of the interaction they have, ranging on a spectrum between abuse and argument? "The Argument Clinic" offers students a surprisingly rich range of examples of what to *avoid*, but they still need examples of what to *do*. And for that, it's time to introduce a distinctive method of argument: "objection/reply," aka counterargument.

Step Four: (10 minutes) Direct students to the assigned reading. Choose one good example of counterargument (we often use "the assumption of infallibility" from Mill), and lead a discussion with your students on the following:

A. Paraphrase the objection and the author's response to the objection.
B. Pinpoint the nature of the objection. Is there an internal inconsistency or other inadequacy in the original argument? Does the original argument leave out some important consideration or relevant example?
C. Evaluate the generosity of the reply. What impact does the author recognize that the objection has on the original argument? For instance, in the reply, does the author qualify or clarify their original claim or add a new element to their original idea (like a finer-grained distinction)? Is the author struggling *with* the objection, or merely struggling *against* it?
D. How persuasive is the reply? Is a better reply available to the author?
E. Finally, note the grammar of the objection and reply. What words, phrases, or sentence structures does the author use to distinguish when they are characterizing their objector's position and when they are developing their own ideas? It may be helpful to list these on the board in side-by-side columns. (You can also do this as part B, if you think your students would benefit from describing the rhetoric of engagement before examining the content of the objection and reply.)

Step Five: (10 minutes) Now divide and conquer: put students back in small groups, assign one remaining objection and its associated reply from the reading to each group, and ask them to repeat the process from step four for their assigned selections. (If you have more groups than objections, you can invite more than one group to work on the same objections.)

Step Six: (20 minutes) Ask groups to report their findings and lead a full class discussion of the generosity and persuasiveness of the replies. Was each objection presented in as strong a light as possible? Do the replies fully address their objections, or miss the point or change the subject unfairly? Do some replies need further refinement? Be sure to attend to the rhetorical moves the students have highlighted, adding any new grammar or bits of language to the columns on the board. Close by linking the discussion to your students' own writing. Remind them that considering objections to their own argument early—and generously—will lead them to a refined, clearer, richer, and ultimately more persuasive thesis.

REFLECTIONS

Students report learning about counterargument in their debate club or from watching TV shows where attorneys jump up during a court proceeding and yell, "Objection!" Such courtroom objections rarely have content, and often are posed in order to stop a position from being developed. Debaters are frequently taught to refer dismissively to their opponent's claims. And in both cases, debaters and attorneys are engaged in a competitive enterprise where the success of one party is predicated upon the other's failure. Given what students bring to the exercise, it's not surprising for them to assume that a confrontational style in a zero-sum game is the height of intellectual engagement. The problem with this stance, of course, is that it defeats the purpose of courting objections in the first place; it shuts down the conversation necessary to discover truth and reach understanding.

This exercise models a generous mode of disagreement. A readiness to acknowledge counterargument is central to cultivating writerly ethos. It encourages teaching counterargument not as a mode of tearing claims down but as a way of building them up. In our view, courting real objections is not merely a way of acknowledging that people can think otherwise, but rather a moment in which one's own position can be deepened, extended, curtailed, and—most importantly—*developed*. (For another approach to treating counterarguments with generosity, see "The Principle of Charity.")

We find that attending to the grammar of objections and replies is crucial to this process. Our students often experience difficulty distinguishing the author's views (and reply) from those of the objector, especially when the objection is represented charitably. But when we encourage them to look at the specific language the author uses, those differences become clearer. When our students look closely at Mill's *On Liberty*, for example, they notice how he relies upon certain rhetorical moves to signal that he is courting an objection, including:

- Use of passive voice (instructors might want to discuss its appropriateness for their class): "The objection likely to be made . . ." and "It is also often argued . . ."
- Creation of a generic name for one's opponents: "the enemies of religious freedom . . . say"
- A stylistic shift in voice: "But what! (it may be asked) . . ."

They also notice how Mill uses bits of language to signal his shift back into his own voice:

- He directly but respectfully remains of a different mind: "I answer . . ." and "I affirm no such thing"
- He attends to the scope of the disagreement: "But those who thus satisfy themselves, do not perceive that . . ."

- He qualifies his original claim in order to show how his objector stands in a "both/and" rather than "either/or" relation with him: "Conceding to this view of the subject the utmost that can be claimed for it . . . even so [my] argument . . . is no way weakened"; and "I acknowledge that . . ."

The point isn't to offer Mill, or anyone else, as models to be mechanically replicated in students' own work. Rather, this exercise aims first to raise for students the rhetorical problem of how to distinguish their own position from that of others, and second and more importantly, to leverage their engagement with other writers to enhance the quality of their own arguments. Indeed, if you have extra time, or as a follow-up lesson, you can invite students to exchange drafts of their own papers-in-progress in advance and sketch out one paragraph with the strongest counterargument they can think of in response to their partner's thesis.

As another variation, you can invite students at the beginning of class to write a brief reflection on where they learned about or experienced objections previously, and why/when posing and responding to objections might be valuable to them. (We sometimes do this before showing "The Argument Clinic.") This can help bring forward some of the (often misguided) assumptions about objections students have.

If your students are like ours, they often struggle with the objection/reply mode of reasoning. They confuse an objection that is taken seriously with the author's own position. If the author winds up not accepting the objection in part or in full, they ask why the objection was posed in the first place instead of being built into the original argument. When they find themselves persuaded by an objection, they think it is sufficient either to "agree to disagree" or say that "the truth lies somewhere in the middle." When instructed to focus on such reasoning in what they are reading or in their own writing, they often treat objections as sources of weakness rather than strength. Moreover, viewing the objection/reply mode of reasoning as inherently or inevitably adversarial may obscure the real value of engaging in it. For example, a speaker's competence might be (falsely) thought to correlate to their aggression. A work "full of hesitations and qualifiers" might be undervalued when, in fact, its caveats reflect an author's deep knowledge of relevant subtleties (see Janice Moulton, "A Paradigm of Philosophy: The Adversary Method").

This exercise uses the humor of Monty Python to help students identify different classes of bad arguments or nonarguments, while the assigned reading provides a window into how scholars pose and respond to real objections with varying success. Together they emphasize the distinct ethos of the best forms of academic discourse: valuing fair-mindedness toward those who disagree and prioritizing the pursuit of truth over winning a debate. After all, responding to real objections is a moral imperative, not just an intellectual one. This exercise teaches technique but also models values, encouraging the development of a sensibility that respects constructive difference and disagreement on the page and in our minds.

Source Function BINGO

Alexander K. Davis

Elevate the structure and source use in students' social-scientific research papers through a surprising tactic: a game of BINGO!

Writing Focus: *sources, structure, conventions*
Teacher Preparation: *low*
Student Preparation: *high*
Estimated Time: *50 minutes*
General Discipline: *social sciences*

EXERCISE

Prep Work: For pre-class reading, assign a model publication from a peer-reviewed journal, one that features elegant and effective secondary source integration. It's also helpful to incentivize careful reading with an "active reading" worksheet asking students to do three things before class: restate the article's motive and thesis in their own words, describe the role each subsection plays in developing the argument, and (most importantly) flag one or two instances of source use in each subsection that they find effective. Students should bring to class both the model text (with the active reading handout, if using) and drafts of their own working research papers. Make copies of the BINGO card (see handout) to be kept in reserve until the second half of the exercise.

Step One: (15 minutes) Frame the workshop: explain that rather than discussing the homework's conceptual content, as is often the case in a social science class, today's session will be devoted to uncovering how published scholarship can serve as an excellent model for their own writing—especially when it comes to integrating *sources* effectively.

To that end, set students to work reviewing the model text's overarching line of argument. Divide students into as many groups as there are subsections of the text. Social science articles often fall into five subsections: introduction, literature review, data and methods, results and analysis, and conclusion. Assign one section to each group. Ask them to grapple with a deceptively simple question: what's the relationship between their subsection and the full paper's motive and thesis?

After a few minutes have passed, invite each group to share their observations. Map their contributions on the board, drawing particular attention to student comments about the complexity of structure and argumentation in their respective subsections.

Step Two: (10 minutes) From there, delve deeper into dissecting the model text—focusing on *source use*. Send students back into their groups and have them interrogate two or three instances of source use in their assigned subsection (which can be the examples they flagged for homework): how do the paper's secondary sources support, extend, complicate, or in some way *add* to each section's contribution to the full paper's line of argument?

After a few minutes have passed, invite each group to share again. Add to the argument map on the board, this time emphasizing how the structural complexity from step one rests on a foundation of diverse and dynamic engagement with other scholars' published ideas.

Step Three: (25 minutes) Next, introduce a more abstract principle: although secondary sources serve many ends within each section of a sociological research paper, they *also* work together toward a common aim. For an introduction, sources Begin an article with a motivating puzzle or problem; for a literature review, they Introduce and orient a reader to the existing scholarly conversation on a paper's topic; for the methods section, they Name strategies for analysis; for that analysis, they Guide a reader's understanding with complicating key terms or concepts; and for a conclusion, they allow an author momentarily to Oppose their analysis with an explicit counterargument. In short: BINGO!

Distribute the BINGO card and ask students to fetch drafts of their research papers. Then, issue them a challenge: they have twenty minutes to complete their BINGO cards. But exhort them to read carefully—this BINGO card requires them to scour their work for the *absence* of each BINGO function. Set a timer and circulate to troubleshoot while students work.

Step Four: (Optional) If there is time remaining, have students debrief with a partner. Or close out the session by asking the class to generate together a list of source-related revision priorities.

REFLECTIONS

Students in social science courses are often quick to point out a published article's limitations or problematic assumptions, but they're typically much less inclined to *believe* in an article's usefulness as much as they *doubt* its conclusions. "Source Function BINGO," then, is actually three lessons woven into one. First, structure: the initial discussion reminds students that *every* subsection of a piece of social science writing should have a dynamic and self-standing line of argument. Second, source use: step two prompts recognition that "the scholarly conversation" should shape *all* sections of a full-length research paper. And third, conventions: the whole lesson shows students how to *read* like a scholar by focusing on the successes and conventions of published scholarship and using those boons as an evaluation scheme for their own writing in the discipline.

Given this tripartite character, each step of the exercise could easily be extended or used in isolation. In step one, for instance, be prepared for students to need a few minutes to tap into the hidden argumentative complexity in each subsection of the model text. Once they identify that secret, expect their small group conversation to crescendo—and know that providing them with sufficient time to map the twists and turns of a line of argument more fully can be wonderfully generative in its own right. Similarly, for students who have assembled an annotated bibliography or who are working with a set of curated sources, step three, in which they play BINGO with their own paper draft, works quite well as a brainstorming exercise. Simply change the questions in the leftmost cell of the BINGO card so that students allocate sources to each of the columns and reflect on why those allocations are best. Just be sure to leave some time at the end for discussion and reflection about any empty columns. It's also worthwhile, time permitting, to have students generate the optional to-do list recommended in step four, a handy resource as they move forward with their research, whether they're planning their next move through library databases or refining a methods section that they've already drafted.

Better yet, BINGO's flexibility makes it a valuable exercise across the undergraduate social science curriculum. Even for senior sociology majors willing to believe that professional sociological writing is, in theory, a worthy model for their own work, the bar set by real peer-reviewed publications can seem too lofty to be attainable. By breaking down the process into digestible steps and a straightforward checklist, though, novice and advanced students alike come to see such emulation as possible—even exciting. First-year students tend to be particularly enthusiastic about learning to do more with sources than "prove" their thesis "right," and juniors and seniors are often grateful for help in taking their source use beyond "sociologists know X and Y but haven't studied Z." Plus, students of all levels benefit from the opportunity to get their raw (and much more imaginative!) thinking into a draft *before* they double back to diversify the source use in their final submissions.

Because of those myriad benefits, the core elements of this exercise could also find a suitable home in other disciplinary settings. For students doing research in the natural sciences, computational sciences, or engineering who might object that "the data" or "the literature" can "speak for themselves," the dissection of published scholarly work from steps one and two can be revelatory. And although the appended BINGO card assumes the five-section format conventional in the social and natural sciences, it's also ripe for adaptation to fields with thematic (or no) subheadings. For example, in my first-year writing seminar, which takes an interpretive rather than positivist stance, I use a BINGO card whose five functions are "Begin with motive," "Illustrate with evidence," "Name a key term," "Guide your reader's attention with orienting," and "Oppose with a counterargument." Students simply evaluate their essays holistically, rather than one separate subsection at a time.

Moreover, as that last adaptation suggests, BINGO is just as beneficial an intervention when students are revising as when they're drafting. When I work with seniors (or graduate students!) crafting literature reviews for a major capstone project, for instance, we collectively generate a BINGO card with five, finer-grained categories: "Begin with a leading theoretical paradigm," "Introduce the literature specific to your topic," "Name a second, complicating literature," "Guide your reader to a new theoretical framework," and "Oppose with a counterargument from a competing perspective." I then invite students to carve apart their draft literature reviews—either physically, with scissors, or digitally, with text boxes in their preferred word processor—and reimagine the structure of their arguments *while* they assess the diversity of their source use. Two revision priorities thus get addressed at once!

But no matter how you adapt the exercise, keeping the BINGO moniker is crucial. The acronym itself has a wonderfully resinous character, and the small element of gamification is irresistible to first-year students and second-semester seniors alike.

HANDOUT

	Begin with **MOTIVE**	**I**ntroduce the literature with **ORIENTING**	**N**ame a **METHODOLOGY**	**G**uide with **KEY TERMS**	**O**ppose with a **COUNTERARGUMENT**
Are there paragraphs / sentences which could benefit from integrating a(n additional) secondary source? If so, where? How exactly would the addition of a(nother) secondary source bolster my intellectual work in that section?					

Handout originally created by Alexander K. Davis, Princeton University, for SOC 300: "Claims and Evidence in Sociology."

The Rhetoric of Source Use

Benjamin D. Weber

An active reading exercise that models rhetorical strategies for crafting complex conversations with sources.

Writing Focus: *sources, orienting*
Teacher Preparation: *medium*
Student Preparation: *none*
Estimated Time: *60 minutes*
General Disciplines: *humanities, social sciences, sciences*

EXERCISE

Prep Work: The instructor should prepare two handouts: 1) "Approaches to Source Use," a selection of brief excerpts from scholarly writing for students to read and rate, and 2) "An Exemplary Model of Source Use," between one and three paragraphs that exemplify excellent source use. (Samples of both handouts follow.) If you have in your back pocket a few model student papers—papers that are themselves suitably scholarly and make good use of sources—these too can work. This exercise presupposes that students have been introduced to the idea of "source use" as an aspect of scholarly writing, and that they understand (notionally, at least) scholarly writing as a conversation among sources.

Step One: (10 minutes) Ask students to take a few moments to reflect in writing about conversations they have recently had. First, have them reflect on an exciting, dynamic, or worthwhile conversation—it doesn't have to be a conversation about academic things; any conversation will do. Then, ask them to reflect on a tedious or uninformative conversation. Lead students in a group discussion about their experiences: what makes a conversation exciting or dull, helpful or not? Once the class has reached broad agreement, likely rating more highly conversations that are vivid, energizing, and focused, pivot on the idea that writing is a conversation among reader, writer, and sources. There must be, in writing as in life, identifiable features that distinguish exciting conversations from dull ones. Frame the exercise as a means to identify those features and to help students craft clear, dynamic, and powerful conversations in their own work.

Step Two: (15 minutes) Divide the class into small groups and distribute the "Approaches to Source Use" handout. Ask each group to read the excerpts and rate each one on a scale of one to ten, where one stands for "least effective" and ten stands for "most effective." As the groups determine their ratings, encourage students to discuss what makes source use effective, especially if they struggle to pinpoint *why* a particular piece of writing works, even though they sense that it does.

Step Three: (10 minutes) Write the ratings on the board as a prompt for a full-class discussion. Do the groups agree? If not, why not? It's fine if the responses vary significantly, as long as you get at the assumptions or priorities behind the ratings. List salient ideas/terms from the group responses on the board, and be attentive to any moment a student struggles to articulate why a particular paragraph is or isn't effective.

Step Four: (10 minutes) Now send students back to the handout, and ask them to underline or highlight words or phrases used in each excerpt to introduce sources and/or to describe ideas. Then invite the class to discuss the impact those words—especially the verbs—have on their perceptions of the piece. This is the moment when the payoff of the exercise becomes apparent, as students see that language really matters: "scholar A says X, and scholar B says Y" is not as effective as "scholar A claims X, while scholar B challenges consensus in arguing Y." The scholarly conversation—and the author's place within it—comes alive through those introductory phrases. (Consider the difference, for example, in the first excerpt on the sample handout, between the source "finding" many allegories and "arguing" for an interpretation. "Find" implies that the symbolism really was there to be discovered, while "argues" introduces a claim with which the author can, and will, disagree.)

Step Five: (10 minutes) Distribute "An Exemplary Model of Source Use," and ask your students to rate the exemplary model. Ideally, it should receive a high rating, but it may not—be prepared for that eventuality. Once again, have students underline or highlight the language the model uses to describe the action of its sources. I do this cooperatively, on a projector in front of the whole class, but PowerPoint as well as traditional paper handouts also work. Doing this exercise with an exemplary source allows the class to expand its inventory of rhetorical moves that do argumentative work through the apparently simple means of introducing sources into the conversation.

Step Six: (5 minutes) Offer a brief "outro" reinforcing two valuable, higher-level lessons: first, form and content aren't separable; readers respond to ideas differently depending on how you introduce them. Second, good writers always shape the conversation, even as they introduce other voices. The words a student uses to introduce sources can lead the reader to position the sources against the student's own ideas, or can draw the reader away from the student's ideas entirely as the sources take over. The scholarly conversation comes alive when the writer's voice is confident and precise—a close attention to introductory phrases fosters both dynamic writing and powerful scholarly ethos.

REFLECTIONS

This exercise helps students who can conceptualize relationships among ideas but frequently lose their own voices as they trace those relationships on the page. While the idea of equipping students with rhetorical templates to introduce sources isn't new (Gerald Graff and Cathy Birkenstein's *They Say, I Say: The Moves That Matter in Academic Writing* does just that), this exercise differs in that it asks students to generate their own rhetorical inventory inductively from pieces of scholarly writing. Since students generate the inventory themselves, they will hopefully remember it better, and it will be appropriate to the specific genre(s) of writing covered by the class.

This plan is easily portable, and can be adapted to emphasize the practice of a particular discipline or common approaches across disciplines, depending on the range of excerpts chosen. Be sure to choose excerpts that model what students should produce, and be ready to explain, perhaps even defend, *why* a particular excerpt is or isn't effective. Though this exercise works well with published sources (indeed, published sources might be most appropriate for an upper-level or graduate class), student writing makes the exercise feel more immediately useful. The sample "Approaches to Source Use" handout below, for example, uses scholarly writing from my own students (anonymously and with permission), and the model in "An Exemplary Model of Source Use" uses an excerpt from a piece published in a journal of student writing. All these pieces have sufficient sources and a sufficiently robust scholarly conversation to offer effective models, but they still follow the familiar format of a student paper.

In these selections, students see how convincingly their peers perform expertise on the page—a discovery that may be daunting at first, but that sets the stage to see how nuances of language reveal nuances of thought. Students realize, then, that the task isn't to "be smarter" than everyone else, but to choose words and phrases that communicate the complexities of their individual perspectives. In a recent version of this exercise, my students found that a neutral verb like "states" or "writes" works well to introduce an orthodox critical position, and pointing out that another scholar (or group of scholars) "agrees" can emphasize critical consensus. Verbs like "disagrees" or "refutes" might signal clear departures from that position, but even verbs like "notices" or "notes," applied to a shared object of study, can signal in a subtle way that one scholar has broken with the pack to do something new and exciting. When asked what would happen if we were to replace all of the verbs in the exemplary model with "writes," my students immediately realized how dull and uninformative the sample piece would become: one remarked that the variety of active verbs made the sources seem like real people with real ideas, while using "writes" throughout would reduce the scholarly conversation to a series of pro forma citations.

HANDOUTS

Approaches to Source Use

#1:

There are, undoubtedly, many ways to find Christian imagery in the Weland panel and the poem. Marijane Osborn, for example, finds many allegories: the birds being strangled "represent the death of the beguiled soul" (Osborn 60), Weland's offer of beer is an allegory for the Devil's temptation of Eve (Osborn 59)—the "terror-king" in the poem thus referring to Weland himself—and the fish being cast upon the mountain refer to Christ and his disciples, the "fishers of men," and the shores of salvation (Osborn 58). While her analysis is thorough, it is slightly over-Christianized. James Lang links the casket to Augustine's commentary on the psalms, specifically in Weland's winged escape (Lang 252)—which is not pictured in the panel. Leslie Webster directly connects Widia, the hero born out of Weland's rape of Beadohild (Nithhad's daughter), to Christ, whose adoration is juxtaposed with the scene (Webster 232)—although there is also no visual or textual reference to Widia in the panel. She also argues that Weland is an "image of deliverance" due to his (again, unseen) wings (Webster 233). These Christian readings are not incorrect and must be taken into account as we examine the panel, but they are simplistic and overlook other potential meanings.

#2:

By looking at right-hand side of the Franks Casket through the lens of art critic and novelist John Berger's essay "Ways of Seeing," one can more effectively come to a realization and understanding of Gudrun and her actions. Berger explains that "men act and women appear" (Berger 47). He further articulates that "men look at women. Women watch themselves being looked at" (Berger 47); they essentially turn themselves into objects to be viewed. In addition, he states that a woman's appearance to a man and actions can determine how she will be treated (Berger 46). It is the woman who is "blamed and punished by being made subservient to the man" (Berger 48). Thus, one can examine Gudrun as under Sigurd's male gaze, which explains her self-punishment for allowing Sigurd's death.

#3:

This theoretical framework can be examined if we adopt the Franks Casket as a case study in which myth serves as both a communicative language and a concept in and of itself. It is generally accepted by scholars, including Leslie Webster and James Lang, that the panels should be read in conjunction, the individual myths intertwining to form overarching themes. In this respect, I agree with the general scholarship. Webster then proposes that in order to achieve this unified reading of the casket, the casket "may" be read as paired scenes in which "a Christian topos offers a commentary on a pagan one" (Webster 230). For instance, she suggests that we read the front panel of the casket from right to left, with the Adoration of the Magi on the right and the myth of Weland on the left. What emerges from this "right-to-left" reading is the interpretation that the casket functions as an object of instruction, used to communicate a lesson.

An Exemplary Model of Source Use

One common interpretation of *L'Étranger*, endorsed by critics such as Patrick Henry and Germaine Brée, contends that Meursault is ultimately an unsparingly honest man whose detached nature stems from his unwillingness to compromise truth in a society predicated on deception, or at least tactful exaggeration and omission (Henry 362; Brée 12). In a sharp break from the traditional reading of *L'Étranger*, however, scholar Robert Solomon contends that the notion of an entirely truthful Meursault is "unconvincing, not just in detail, but in essence" as Meursault "never reaches that (meta-) level of consciousness where truth and falsity can be articulated" (143–44). Solomon uses a Sartrean "distinction between reflection and pre-reflective 'lived experience'" . . . to posit that in Part I of the novel, Meursault is in a *pre-reflective* state and thus lacks the reflective capacity that is prerequisite for honesty (144). In Part II, Meursault's emerging *reflective* self-consciousness prompts him to begin lying, thus refuting the predominant critical interpretation of Meursault as a radically honest character.

Solomon's exegesis of *L'Étranger* is constructive, compelling—and incomplete. To be sure, Solomon's synthesis of existentialist philosophy, as encapsulated by Jean-Paul Sartre's idea that "existence precedes essence," is interesting and serves as a productive starting point to explicate *L'Étranger* and its philosophical underpinnings (Sartre "Being" 20). However, Solomon's analysis of Part II and ensuing conclusion that Meursault is fundamentally dishonest in his embrace of absurdity and impending death is largely unsubstantiated, and appears problematic in light of Camus' stated beliefs on revolt.

Liebman, Jonathan. "A Smile on a Tormented Face: Absurdist Consciousness and Post-Reflective Identity in Camus' *L'Etranger*." *Tortoise: A Journal of Writing Pedagogy* 1 (2014): n.p.

Students Surf Internet in Class! You'll Never Believe How This Instructor Used It to Teach Writing!

Liora Selinger

Turn procrastination into productivity by using clickbait to help students refine motive and structure.

Writing Focus: *motive, structure*
Teacher Preparation: *low*
Student Preparation: *none*
Estimated Time: *80 minutes*
General Disciplines: *humanities, social sciences*

EXERCISE

Prep Work: The instructor should select a few examples of clickbait to share in class. Genuinely intriguing as well as absurdly over-the-top examples work best to engage students and to model how clickbait functions. A few personal favorites, located at ranker.com on a Google search for "examples of clickbait," have been "Here's a Paycheck for a McDonald's Worker. And Here's My Jaw Dropping to the Floor," "Bill Nye Wasn't Always the Science Guy. This Story Makes Me Like Him Even More," and "Baby Ducks See Water for the First Time—Can You BELIEVE What They Do?"—all of which are accompanied by odd and enticing photographs. Students should bring a working draft of their papers. They will also need access to a laptop with screen recording capability, and they should be reminded to bring earbuds or headphones, or to keep their sound off.

Step One: (10 minutes) Invite students to open a browser and start screen-recording. Their task for the first five minutes of class is to get lost on the internet as if they're bored at home. The goal is to find entertaining garbage and click through on impulse to see where it takes them. Have fun with the clickbaitiest of clickbait out there. Obvious caveat: it's a classroom, so they need to maintain some decorum (e.g., no porn). If they're not sure where to start, suggest BuzzFeed or Upworthy.

Step Two: (10 minutes) After five minutes, ask students to go back and watch the screen recording they just made, taking notes on what they observe about their own choices. How does clickbait seem distinct from other internet genres? Which browsing experiences ended up feeling like empty calories and which left them feeling satisfied? What accounts for the difference? What common features do they detect in the clickbait that appealed to them? Ask students to complete their analysis of their own browsing by listing three to five aspects of clickbait that they'll share with the class.

Step Three: (10 minutes) Reconvene the class and invite discussion of what students experienced and observed. Which elements of clickbait grabbed their attention and enticed them to click? Write a list of these elements on the board or a shared Google Doc. In collecting contributions, help students separate out clickbait elements that are pure sensationalism—ALL CAPS, 64-point font, today's celebrity du jour—from those that gesture in the direction of a genuine motive, whether or not they ultimately live up to their promise. Clickbait often works because it combines its hyperbole with a claim to have something genuinely interesting or urgent to say. There's news to impart, a mystery revealed, a debate resolved, a gap in our knowledge that will finally be filled. It usually doesn't turn out to do any of these things—that's why it's disappointing—but underneath the manipulative excess there's often an authentic claim on our curiosity, which is to say motive.

If students get stuck, introduce one or more of your own curated samples and analyze it together to find additional elements of both trash and treasure to round out your list.

Step Four: (20 minutes) Instruct students to take out their own drafts and assign them the task of creating a clickbait version of their essay's motive, using visuals in addition to text if they so choose. Students should feel free to create zany, silly, over-the-top versions of their motive in the style of the most egregious clickbait.

When they've had time to create, ask for a volunteer to share with the class. As a group, analyze how that clickbait sparks a reader's curiosity and brainstorm how the student might write or revise their statement of motive for the actual essay (in a more genre-appropriate way) to reflect what's working in their clickbait.

In pairs or small groups, have students repeat the process for their own essays: share their clickbait and brainstorm how to revise their statement of motive in their introductions to better articulate the puzzle, incongruity, and surprise of their essay to draw in their reader. To preserve a record of the productive silliness, students should post their clickbait and the "before" and "after" of their essays' actual statements of motive in a Google doc to share with the class.

Step Five: (10 minutes) Having clickbaited our way to a stronger statement of motive, we want to make sure our essays do what clickbait articles so rarely do: deliver on their promise. As a full class, have students reflect on times that their browsing experiences *didn't* feel like a dead end or waste of time, but rather when an internet rabbit hole turned out to feel consistently engaging and illuminating. What made those experiences so different from one's typical encounter with clickbait? (Students often note that satisfying browsing experiences are ones that offer a balance of novelty and familiarity, surprise and plausibility, variety and cohesion. Each click connects to or builds upon the last, but also offers new information and presents new gaps.)

Jot students' observations on the board and explain that identifying and applying the qualities of the more compelling rabbit holes will help them refine their essays' structures and paragraph transitions. We want to encourage readers to stick through the unfolding of our argument while making sure they understand the logic behind each twist and turn.

Step Six: (20 minutes) Ask students to choose two body paragraphs from their essay with an awkward or illogical transition between them. Consider how the first paragraph in that sequence might entice a reader to click into the subsequent paragraph and how that subsequent paragraph will live up to the prior paragraph's promise. Then place a couple of spaces between the paragraphs and draft an outrageous clickbait transition sentence to serve as a placeholder hinge between them, enticing the reader with hints about what will come in the second of the two. Reconvene, take a couple of volunteer examples, and ask what they discovered from intentionally, if absurdly, articulating the relationship between their paragraphs in this way, and what revision steps they might imagine. Maybe one or both paragraphs need revision for their call-and-answer dynamic to be clearer. Maybe the transition sentence should stay, but be revised into a less ridiculous register, or maybe it should be deleted altogether. Maybe the clickbait transition unearths more complications than were initially apparent, calling for systematic revision of more than the two original paragraphs.

Students should then share their work and debrief with a partner, discussing their paragraph clickbait sentences and planning their structural revisions. Close by noting that this process can be used for any other troubling transition moment.

REFLECTIONS

During a long revision process, it can be tempting to escape into the pleasures of the internet and avoid the work altogether! Why not turn procrastination into productivity and slackers into scholars? The goal of this exercise is to better understand the concept of motive, to help students state their essays' motives in more explicit and engaging ways, and to harness the principles of curiosity and satisfaction in internet browsing to revise the line of thinking that students are developing in their essays' structures.

Students have fun with the freedom to browse the internet, watch YouTube, or check social media during class, and laugh at the clickbait examples. This is an ideal activity for late-in-the-semester classes when students could use more relaxation. It also works nicely earlier in the semester because it shows how principles of scholarly writing (having and articulating a motive) are not arbitrary but rather fundamental to how we engage with information and communicate—even in our free time and in more familiar contexts.

My students found that creating an over-the-top clickbait version of their motive helped them to understand what a motive is (including its sense of urgency, unexpectedness, and its establishment of partial information, mystery, suspense, and incompletion) and, in turn, to state their motives more clearly and confidently. Some students noticed that their drafts contained no statement of motive at all or had timid or muted statements of their questions or interventions. By having to boldly state the "you'll never BELIEVE . . ." "news" of their paper, they were finally able to recognize and highlight precisely what made their essay so intriguing and worthwhile for their readers. As with other exercises that get students off the page of their draft and into another medium, students were able to return to their revisions with fresh eyes and a bolder voice.

While students laughed at their "really dramatic" statements in their clickbait ("The Cold War is over . . . You'll NEVER believe what these scientists did next!"; "This Library is More Powerful than You!"; "Check out this paper for a NEVER BEFORE SEEN application of a BRAND NEW DATA SET—the results will shock and surprise you!"), they also felt that they had greater license to state their motives more authoritatively in their actual essays afterward.

For example, one student knew that her essay focused on discriminatory policies about Black hairstyles in American schools. But after crafting her clickbait ("According to multiple K-12 schools around the nation, afros, dreadlocks, and durags lead to bad behavior among students. Is this fact or cap? Click here to find out"), she was better able to specify the assumptions held by school policymakers. She then revised her motive in a more specific and engaging form: "It is hard to believe that a hairstyle could be the cause of violence or bad behavior, and yet numerous K-12 schools in the United States have policies that prohibit students from coming to school with afros, dreadlocks, or durags. How, then, did school policymakers arrive at this causal logic and what does it show us about the history of racial discrimination in American schools?"

After analyzing and creating their own clickbait, students reported having a better "intuitive" sense of how to locate the surprise in their argument and entice a reader's interest. Students observed in clickbait a sense of mystery and suspense ("click here to find out . . ."; "you'll never guess . . ."), a promise of novelty, and a challenge to expectations ("most scientists believe that X, but . . ."; "you think you know everything about Y, but . . ."). They noted clickbait's frequent appeals to "belief" (provocations to question one's beliefs and to believe something new) and to emotions (desire, shock, pleasure). They responded to clickbait's direct invitations to a "YOU," in other words, how it asks a reader to be an active participant in the investigation or dispute ("you think you know about X, but . . ."; "which side of this debate will you align with?").

Their browsing experiences also helped students see the effectiveness of sustaining a sense of curiosity and forward movement by means of paragraphs that promise to fill in gaps—and, in turn, illuminate new gaps to fill in. In this way, they were experiencing firsthand George Lowenstein's "information gap theory," in which curiosity is sparked when just enough information is available to allow a person to perceive what's missing. Students' feelings when clicking from one item to the next can help them better understand that motive and structure are interrelated: a strong essay is organized not only as a "line of thinking" or "line of logic," as we so often refer to structure, but also as a "line of curiosity."

Wrecking a Sentence

Sean Cashbaugh

Students learn to improve the clarity of their sentences by first wrecking a perfectly fine one.

Writing Focus: *style, mechanics, conventions*
Teacher Preparation: *low*
Student Preparation: *low*
Estimated Time: *50 minutes*
General Disciplines: *humanities, social sciences, sciences*

EXERCISE

Prep Work: Prepare a four- or five-word sentence that captures your course's theme. For instance, in a class titled American Dissent, I use the following: "Scholars debate dissent's meaning." Ask students to bring an essay draft in progress (or at least a paragraph-long excerpt).

Step One: (10 minutes) Ask students to describe the qualities of sentences that they find effective and appealing. These tend to include qualities like sophisticated word choice or musicality. Generate a list of these traits on the chalkboard and discuss to what extent and in what situations they may lend themselves to academic writing. When students bring up clarity as a value they care about, spend some time trying to elicit what they really mean by the term. This may result in a range of definitions—for example, transparent diction, accessible syntax, and the relationship between an individual sentence and the broader argument. You can reinforce clarity as a cross-disciplinary value, while also emphasizing that "clear writing" is an idea shaped by conventions on a variety of levels (discipline, subject, publication, etc.).

Step Two: (5 minutes) Introduce your prepared sentence. Ask each student to increase its word count to at least one hundred by any means necessary. It must remain a single sentence and make sense. In other words, it must be grammatically sound, and they cannot fill their sentences with nonsense phrases. For example, in the abovementioned class, one student produced the following 142-word sentence:

> Scholars, defined as those who attempt to explore, discover, identify, discuss, and learn about various academic and intellectual topics and pursuits, usually topics or pursuits which are relevant to a defined or given time period or, rather, simply important and impactful historical events that these said scholars may apply to the events and circumstances of the

present day, wherever those scholars may be located or based on this planet, including possibilities such as North America, South America, Europe, Asia, Africa, Australia (which is not only a continent, but impressively also a country and an island), or even Antarctica where the penguins live, tend to consider, debate, and even grapple and struggle with the true and accurate meaning of the term dissent, which can be defined in several complex and multifaceted, albeit difficult, wildly disputed, and possibly even truly oppositional, facets and ways.

Step Three: (15 minutes) Have students share their creations. You can present this as a game: the student with the wordiest sentence wins! As students share, ask them to name the "sentence wrecking" strategies they used. Ask others to identify any "wrecking moves" the writer used but didn't note. List these strategies on the board. These may include repetition; turning to "thesaurus words"; incorporating material that would be better placed in other sentences or omitted entirely (e.g., a list of every theorist of dissent mentioned that semester); resorting to clichés ("Since the dawn of civilization scholars have debated dissent's meaning"); and detouring into digressive details ("Scholars, who are esteemed and deep thinkers, debate dissent's meaning, much like they do many things in life, such as . . .").

Step Four: (10 minutes) Reframe everything on the board into a checklist for sentence-level revision. Have students pair up and exchange the drafts they brought to class. Ask them to find any unintentional instances of the sentence-wrecking strategies the class identified, or other opportunities for sentence-level revision. Students should share their feedback with each other and then take a few minutes to try implementing one or two revisions in their own drafts.

Step Five: (10 minutes) Reconvene the class to have students reflect on the process. What did they learn about the ways they construct sentences? How do they inadvertently "wreck" them? What idiosyncratic tendencies did they discover about themselves? How can they use their style preferences for good instead of evil and wow their audience? Revisit the list of values students generated together in step one. Ask them to reflect on what they might add, remove, or change about it considering the previous discussion. The values list serves as the aspirational counterpart to the revision checklist of pitfalls to avoid.

REFLECTIONS

Students are often skeptical when I ask them to increase a perfectly fine four-word sentence to one hundred or more, rendering its main point unintelligible. Every semester I've done it, at least one student has audibly laughed. The counterintuitive move is essential to the activity: it introduces a generative cognitive dissonance that helps students think about the ways they can, and habitually do, use language to the detriment of their goals. Too often, I've read an otherwise promising essay marred by stylistic affectations that impede its argument. For many, especially first-year students, "strong writing" connotes specific sentence-level stylistic traits. These traits might have some idiosyncratic aesthetic value or reflect stereotypes about academic writing—namely, the idea that a work is scholarly insofar as its sentences are impenetrable. "Wrecking a Sentence" disrupts such ideas. It flips a lesson about mechanics and conventions on its head in an entertaining exercise aimed at developing student understandings of clarity, while also creating a tool they can turn to when revising their prose.

The activity's first step introduces the idea that stylistic elements we find personally appealing may become problematic placeholders in our writing when we ourselves don't yet fully understand what we want to communicate to our readers, or how to do so most appropriately for a given audience. The problem is exacerbated when we feel like we have to fill space or write in an unfamiliar genre. For instance, when I asked students to wreck the sentence "Scholars debate dissent's meaning," one produced a sentence featuring every possible synonym for "dissent" that she could muster, turning to what she called "those fancy SAT words" she liked to use in high school. Another leaned on what he called his "appreciation for lists of three" to produce a sentence with a series of embedded lists, each featuring three examples. As the example reproduced in the previous section demonstrates, students wreck sentences in numerous other ways, many of which align with common causes of wordiness in student writing produced under "normal" circumstances.

The ease (and often glee) with which students take up the task of stretching my short sentences into wordy behemoths suggests, in fact, an intuitive familiarity with what counts as clear writing. The exercise helps them articulate what they know without delving into the minutia of grammar and syntax, or having the instructor dictate what their prose should look like. This empowers students by encouraging them to focus on what their writing is doing in relation to their goals, helping to cultivate their scholarly voices. Step five illustrates the point by asking them to revisit their initial conception of strong sentences, synthesizing the activity's key lessons and ending on a positive note. "Wrecking a Sentence" isn't just about "fixing" sentence-level mechanics: it helps students wield those mechanics to their own ends.

While this activity's primary focus is on mechanics, it also reinforces argument-level concerns by highlighting connections between the local and the global. A student once told me after completing the final phase of the activity, "You can't shoot clearly if you don't know what you're aiming for." I can't endorse the metaphor of writing-as-shooting, but the point is valuable: clarity is impossible if you don't know where you're heading argumentatively. Clear sentences are purposeful sentences, which require paragraphs with defined points, which in turn require an overarching structure and motivated thesis. Students who begin step four thinking they'll just be doing a local revision or two often surprise themselves by refining or reconceptualizing their motive and thesis. The activity can also reinforce students' meta-disciplinary awareness because it's easy to wreck a sentence in a variety of disciplinary-specific ways. For example, a class of mixed majors could be assigned to each wreck a sentence as a parody of their field's most characteristic stylistic quirks.

I use this exercise late in the semester, just before students submit a research paper or are in the latter stages of drafting one. Introducing it after we've already practiced working extensively on global revisions helps assuage one of my fears about the exercise: that the idea that strong writing is reducible to sentence-level issues will sneak in through the back door. Having students bring writing to class pushes them to get started earlier and has the benefit of jump-starting the revision process. Plus, it's a fun exercise. My students have always taken advantage of the creative possibilities it affords, introducing some levity into the always stressful final weeks of the semester. Just try reading the 142-word monstrosity above aloud without grinning—it's impossible.

Disciplining Sentences

Raphael Allison

Teach students to see writing as guided by and embedded in expectations of genre and discipline, even at the sentence level.

Writing Focus: *conventions, style, mechanics*
Teacher Preparation: *medium*
Student Preparation: *low*
Estimated time: *65 minutes*
General Disciplines: *humanities, social sciences, sciences*

EXERCISE

Prep Work: Curate model sentences that highlight stylistic differences across the major academic divisions (sciences, social sciences, humanities). It can be useful to have one model sentence from the field students are working in, but the point is to showcase as much disciplinary contrast as possible. Anywhere from six to nine model sentences will suffice. Ask students to bring two copies of a piece of writing they are working on in your class.

Step One: (15 minutes) Have students read each other's writing in pairs and select one or two sentences they most admire. Intentionally leave the criteria open to allow students to notice whatever strikes them as relevant. Invite a few volunteers to share their partner's sentences with the class and to name what they admire: Do they appreciate the clarity? The rhythm of the syntax? The use of a vivid image? How the writer establishes their own ideas vis-à-vis a quotation? Keep a list of what students say in note form on the board.

Step Two: (15 minutes) Distribute the sample sentences. In their same pairs, have students read the sentences, asking this time what they notice about the differences in sentence style. What exactly sets them apart? Lead a discussion identifying key differences between sentences, mapping them on the board by discipline as you go.

When prompted this way, students often point out that in the sciences sentences are comparatively short and uniform in structure (usually following a subject, verb, predicate format). This simple sentence structure allows for packed, dense lines replete with specialized vocabulary. In the humanities, by contrast, sentences are often longer and display more syntactical variation (dependent clauses, compound sentences) and ideas are often developed through appositive clauses and conditional language ("if this/then that" statements).

Step Three: (15 minutes) Suggest that these differences are not accidental; writing in any field is guided by unspoken principles, and these principles are, in turn, linked to deeper beliefs about how knowledge is produced and communicated. This may be a new idea to many students, but it can be clarified by looking at examples. Ask them to reflect on how the sentences they've just examined might reflect a field's deeper epistemological beliefs. If we can see a sentence not as accidentally but as formally related to its discipline, what is the nature of the relationship? Revisit the map you created on the board in step two and encourage students to field hypotheses that might account for the stylistic differences they observed.

For example, students sometimes claim that the sciences rely on empirical observation to locate facts. Consequently, sentences in the sciences may eschew stylistic ambiguity in favor of stable syntactical patterns; complexity is found in the subject of the sentence, not the sentence itself. The use of passive voice in scientific writing offers another example of the link between field and form, something that students often reference. Passive voice often implies an objective perspective, unbiased and unencumbered by a particular subjectivity. Literary studies, by contrast, tends to prize active voice and the elaboration of nuances of meaning. The field itself demands and honors repeated acts of vigorous analysis and interpretation, and longer, serpentine sentences and conditional language reflect that fundamental preoccupation. Literary texts are often said to have "undecidable" meanings, and critics capture the complexity of their primary object by embracing complex sentences.

You might offer a few caveats. This exercise isn't meant to suggest that sentences must conform to distinct disciplinary styles, or necessarily strive for complex formulations. Nor should we ignore that these are all generalizations (indeed, examples of exceptions abound). The larger point is that all writing is embedded in contexts and responsive to demands that may be invisible to apprentice writers.

Step Four: (20 minutes) Have students locate one or two meaty analytical sentences in their own writing that need revising. Ask students to revise their chosen sentence(s) twice. First, write an over-the-top parody in the style of the discipline in which they are working, exaggerating the field's commitments at the sentence level. What would the caricature of an art historian's style sound like, for example? An economist's? A philosopher's? Draw attention to how silly, and even incomprehensible, the sentences become when we're prioritizing a field's conventional writing style over the substance of what is said. Counterintuitively, using the conventions for evil prepares you to use them for good.

Next, ask students to revise the same sentence(s) from their draft, this time showing an awareness of disciplinary conventions but prioritizing communication of the news the sentence has to share. Ideally the disciplinary style should facilitate clarity and showcase why the conventions are effective. If you have time, invite volunteers to write their (good) before-and-after sentences on the board and as a class reflect on the changes they made. As they continue to revise their essays, encourage students to look for further opportunities to employ disciplinary style to sharpen their claims and analysis, while also watching out for moments where an excess of style inhibits clarity.

Step Five: (Optional) For a fun wrap up that serves double duty as a cautionary tale, ask each student to share a dramatic reading of one of their sentence parodies from the beginning of step four. Offer a prize for the most ridiculous sentence, the one that sounds most like academic writing at its worst.

(For an alternate approach to improving a sentence by first undoing it, see the preceding exercise, "Wrecking a Sentence.")

REFLECTIONS

I developed this activity because I found that students often came to my course certain that there exists a set of universal attributes to good sentence writing. Typically, they have been taught grammar in a way that suggests this universal sentence type. Or they've been schooled in the minimalist style encouraged by writing guides that trace their roots to Strunk and White's *Elements of Style*. This exercise could be the first time your students have made distinctions *within* professional scholarly writing. It will help them see that every genre of writing has demands and constraints, and that writing at the college level requires them to begin considering an unfamiliar variety of styles, tones, diction, and syntax.

Preparing for this exercise requires choosing sample sentences from two or more disciplines. I select three examples that are representative of a field yet also display a range of styles within each field so that students don't imagine that one sentence can stand for an entire field. (If classroom time is tight, I find that even two sentences per discipline can get the job done.) I mostly select good writing as my models but will also include one or two examples that drift toward the professorial absurd. As a model sentence from Ecology and Evolutionary Biology, for example, I have used the following sentence on bacterial diversity in mountain lakes: "Microbial biofilms contain the most reactive component of freshwater systems and thus provide many of the ecosystem services."[1] Students often notice the uniform sentence structure (subject, verb, predicate); the syntactic clarity and relative brevity; and the high ratio of nouns and specialized (but not obscure) language.

I then ask students to consider the radical difference of a sentence from literary studies, this one by Michael Davidson: "On one level, these compositions might seem to propose a kind of aesthetic prosthesis, akin to what David Mitchell and Sharon Snyder see operative in narrative works in which the presence of a one-legged Ahab or a hunchbacked Richard III serves as a 'crutch' in the representation of normalcy."[2] Notable here is the longer sentence length, including dependent clauses and repetition; a wealth of conditional language ("might seem," "could regard"); breezy allusions to canonical texts; and a nuanced tone, established in the opening phrase ("On one level"). In literary studies, you might conclude, there is always at least one other level on its way. The Davidson example not only establishes a contrast between literary studies and Ecology and Evolutionary Biology, but also opens a window into the debates about appropriate style within fields. While many appreciate Davidson's writing as elegant and allusive, others may prefer the calm, clear style of critic David Lehman: "Schuyler's lyric poems, sweet and pungent, offer observations too understated to be called epiphanies and too subtle to be appreciated on one reading."[3]

It will come as no surprise, of course, that comparing sample sentences from Ecology and Evolutionary Biology and English will reveal stark differences. But stark comparisons are helpful since they generate the lesson's deeper motivation: to suggest that different disciplines demand different stylistic emphases that emerge from and that are directly tied to their fundamental beliefs. Helping students make this leap from style to epistemology is the most challenging and rewarding aspect of the lesson. Drawing on the parody exercise, I ask if they could imagine the paragraph from the Ecology and Evolutionary Biology essay composed in the style of a passage of literary analysis. Or vice versa—what would happen if a discussion of a literary text were written according to the demands of a paper from molecular biology? How would these different sentences affect the ideas themselves?

When students turn to their own writing, they often make significant changes. Sometimes their efforts might echo the parodies they composed earlier, the very outcome that writing and discussing the parodies was designed to hedge against. A writer engaged in literary analysis might strive for a long and ambitious sentence structure to indicate that she's understood something about what literary scholars sound like; someone else, writing from a sociological perspective, might try to replicate a more syntactically parsimonious style. It may be that such revision requires further revision. Not to worry. Students will still have taken the first step in learning that all writing isn't written for all readers.

NOTES

1. Mireia Bartrons, Emilio O. Casamayor, and Jordi Catalan, "High Bacterial Diversity in Epilithic Biofilms in Oligotrophic Mountain Lakes." *Microbial Ecology* 64, no. 4 (2012): 860.
2. Michael Davidson, *Concerto for the Left Hand: Disability and the Defamiliar Body* (Ann Arbor: University of Michigan Press, 2008), 2.
3. David Lehman, *The Last Avant-Garde: The Making of the New York School of Poets* (New York: Anchor, 1999), 247.

TRANSFERRING

One of the more unsettling findings of education research is the difficulty students have in taking the skills they've developed and applying them in new contexts: the problem of transfer. This can be especially true for writing courses, which students are sometimes inclined to view as a separate activity from training in their major. Even if they are convinced, in your classroom, that the work they do there will serve them in other courses and beyond the university, that confidence may disappear when a seemingly unfamiliar challenge emerges. As teachers, we are always part of a relay, placing our trust in our students' future instructors to run the next lap with them. But even with the best-laid plans, teaching handoffs are rarely seamless, which further increases the transfer struggle for students. One solution: have students practice transfer in our own classes. Invite them to compare their first and last essays of a semester, for example, so they can see the writerly moves they've already carried forward and applied in new ways. Or share a sample of more advanced writing that might be expected in a later course and help them brainstorm two lists: 1) what seems new and difficult, and 2) what they already know that might come in handy. In teaching writing, you can't give students a recipe for every assignment, discipline, or genre they'll encounter. But you *can* teach them to approach writing's varied landscape with respect for its diverse ecologies and with confidence in the powerful flexibility of the "Lexicon." This final section features exercises in which students learn to imagine their audience for a scholarly abstract, crack the code on technical reports, whitepapers, and slide decks, write a film review, translate their research into an op-ed, and even spot motive in music.

Think Again

Learning to Read Your Readers' Minds

The Accidental Experts

Into the Public Square

The Art of Film Reviewing

Listening to Motive

Think Again

Aaron Colton

Students practice the work of scholarship and flexible thinking by revisiting earlier writing and asking new questions.

Writing Focus: *motive, analysis, method*
Teacher Preparation: *low*
Student Preparation: *low*
Estimated Time: *80 minutes*
General Disciplines: *humanities, social sciences, sciences*

EXERCISE

Prep Work: Instruct students to bring an unmarked copy of their first essay for the course. Essays should be short enough that students can reread and analyze their earlier work relatively quickly. The instructor should bring a copy of the original assignment prompt and a bunch of highlighters, in at least three different colors. (For examples of common types of essay prompts, see John Schulz's "The How and the Why.")

Step One: (15 minutes) Open by inviting a student to reread the first essay prompt aloud for the class. Ask students to recall—without yet looking at the essays they brought in—their perspectives on the topic when they wrote their essays and what they found challenging at the time. What, in particular, did they struggle to do well? After students have shared their responses, place them in small groups and give them five minutes to identify concrete things they've learned since turning in that essay—writing or research skills, key concepts or ideas from later course readings, particular methodologies—which would make them better equipped to respond to that assignment now. (These things don't need to come from your course; "outside" learning qualifies!) When you sense the conversation beginning to lag, reconvene and invite each group to report on what they discovered, jotting down their responses on the board.

Step Two: (15 minutes) Distribute highlighters so that each student has access to three different colors. Have students reread the essays they brought in, now bringing their fresh perspectives to bear. Their task is to identify and highlight key moments in their essays that they now find 1) especially persuasive or cool; 2) confusing or underdeveloped but worth exploring further; and 3) especially unconvincing or ineffective. Each category should get a different color. While students read, they should consider:

- Which ideas or implications have I not examined thoroughly enough?
- What might I rethink, repurpose, or expand?
- What questions can I now see that my essay raises or responds to that I didn't see before?
- Which material, ideas, or lines of inquiry from my essay might help me to get started in exploring one of these new questions?

When they're done, students should select one moment in the essay that they've highlighted. It doesn't matter if it's a persuasive, confusing, or unconvincing moment—only that they find it especially interesting. In the margins, they should write a few sentences explaining why they would be excited to think more about this moment and where it might take their analyses.

Step Three: (20 minutes) Explain that scholarship—and indeed any form of rigorous thinking and writing—often takes one of three forms: 1) building on a success by showing an extension or application of the original finding; 2) identifying and figuring out a puzzle that hasn't been adequately explored; or 3) addressing a mistake or taking on a new perspective. For useful shorthand, you can name these three categories on the board "persuasive," "underdeveloped," and "unconvincing."

Invite three students to share the moments they've selected, one for each category (persuasive, underdeveloped, unconvincing). For each example, ask the students to discuss what it might look like to launch a new project from that moment of curiosity and potential. What new question could they now pose? Why should we want a persuasive answer to that question? How would the work they would need to accomplish be different from what was needed in the original essay?

By the end of this step, you should have three tentative motivating questions that could launch three interesting research projects. Reassure students that you won't actually make them write those papers, but that they will think about them a little. (Optionally, instructors may in fact link this exercise to a required revision or rewrite; see "Reflections.")

Step Four: (15 minutes) Now have students work individually to map out where they would take their new projects. To guide their thinking, write the following brainstorming elements on the board or provide them as a handout.

- Springboard (the moment they highlighted in their original essay)
- Motive (their new question and what makes that question important)
- Method (how would one answer the question successfully and what kind of analysis should be used?)
- Evidence/Sources (what material will be needed to answer the question?)

Step Five: (15 minutes) Put students back into small groups to comment on each other's progress and, using that feedback, to develop their hypothetical projects further. Drawing from each other's writing experiences and intellectual practices, students might consider adopting new methods, researching and examining new sources, or developing new or significantly revised theses. Close by underscoring that we develop new ideas not only in relation to our past work and past thinking, but also in conversation with peers and colleagues and *their* thinking.

REFLECTIONS

Students often think that changing one's mind is a sign of weakness or concession. But, as experienced writers know, one does not make sophisticated arguments simply by improving the same points over and over. Rather, by writing and revising, experienced writers revisit the ideas, assumptions, and analyses that underlie their arguments, oftentimes discovering substantial new questions—and reconstructing their theses—as a result. In this way, changing one's mind can in fact be seen as *necessary* to developing our best and most mature arguments.

The intention behind this exercise is to emphasize the importance of rethinking one's arguments in both intellectual and expository practice. I use this exercise, adaptable for composition courses themed on any subject, later in the academic term when students will have gained critical distance from their first assignment—both in time and in reading and thinking—and are thus prepared to revisit their early work with fresh eyes.

Taking advantage of this timing, the exercise makes reconsidering one's early positions an *explicit* criterion for success. More specifically, the exercise prompts students to see writing as scholars see it: as a recursive process that allows them to determine which kinds of questions are worth asking in the first place. After all, scholars write not just to find out what they think (to borrow from Joan Didion), but also to discover what they might think about—that is, to uncover the most urgent questions about cultural objects, historical events, or critical discourses. So, as students formulate new questions that they could only think to ask *after* the work of their first essays, they also demonstrate the intellectual value in returning to drafts that they might otherwise file away and forget.

In my own courses, students typically revisit a first assignment that asks them to take a position on a complex concept, usually in the form of a definition. For instance, I have asked students in their first assignments to respond to questions such as: What is 'writer's block'? How would you define 'sincerity'? What makes 'an essay' an essay? While students may feel unsure about answering questions like these with only a few weeks of reading under their belts, doing so early on has the dual benefits of 1) encouraging students to take clear positions in response to complicated issues (often the aspect of college-level writing to which first-year students have the greatest difficulty adjusting); and 2) ensuring ample opportunities for students to revisit their contentions over the term. Because students will inevitably read about and discuss the major concepts or issues from their course with increasing breadth and depth, by the time of this exercise, most will already have revised the positions they expressed in their first papers, even if they have not yet articulated those changes in writing.

Perhaps the most difficult aspect of this exercise is getting students over the initial hurdle of taking their previous work seriously. For some students, returning to their first paper for the course (often also their very first college paper) may dredge up feelings of embarrassment or inadequacy. Groans of "What was I thinking?" and "This was so bad," while unhelpful, have been common as I've taught this exercise, and they aren't necessarily impediments to its success. The key is in Step Three of the exercise, where the instructor emphasizes how often our best scholarship grows out of projects that somehow missed the mark. In this moment, I've found it particularly useful to describe the more dramatic of my own writing "failures"—rejected journal articles and essays nixed by editors—and then to demonstrate how the shortcomings of those projects contained the kernels of some of the writing I'm now most proud of.

Depending on the design of their courses, instructors might also tie this exercise to a rewrite or substantial revision of students' early essays. In doing so, instructors not only ensure that students will themselves follow through on the recursive work that this exercise stages, but by requiring a "do-over" that would improve students' standing in the course, they also preempt the negative responses students may have in reconsidering their early work.

One of the most impressive essay improvements I've seen from a student happened in an introductory course I taught on experimental literature. The students' first assignment was to define the genre of "metafiction" (typically understood as fiction that is in some way about fiction) through two short stories. Then, at the end of the term, after reconsidering their first papers, students developed new theses in response to new, self-generated questions about metafiction. During this exercise, a student who had been disappointed by the grade he received on his first essay—and was therefore suspicious of returning to the essay—nonetheless identified the most exciting and persuasive moment in his original essay as his claim that the metafictional narrator acts like an authoritarian. In steps three and four of the exercise, he developed a substantial and intriguing new question out of that claim: "What do metafictional narrators use their authority to do?" In step five, the student found the significance of his question validated almost immediately when his peers responded to it with a plethora of example texts, and even scenes for interpretation, that the student could draw on in his reinvented project.

Later in the course, the student in fact wrote this new essay as his final project, ultimately arguing that the metafictional narrator is an instrument that authors use for teaching readers to recognize the limits of literary interpretation. And where the student's first paper relied on unsubstantiated generalizations, his final essay demonstrated an improved level of specificity motivated by the discovery of a new, targeted question that he analyzed through the textual instances his classmates suggested. In this way, the student experienced one of the most important, if also frustrating, aspects of writing: that sometimes you need to get things wrong so that, when you think again, you can get them right.

Learning to Read Your Readers' Minds

Judy Swan

Introduce a new genre—in this case, the scholarly abstract—by imagining readers' expectations.

Writing Focus: *thesis, motive, conventions, orienting*
Teacher Preparation: *medium*
Student Preparation: *low*
Estimated Time: *50 minutes*
General Discipline: *sciences*

EXERCISE

Prep Work: Prepare a handout of four samples of the genre under analysis, in this case, academic abstracts in science and engineering. One abstract should be an impenetrable example, two others should be effective and persuasive, and the fourth example should both be mediocre—poorly structured and/or missing at least one key element—and yet seemingly accessible. One purpose of the mediocre example is to discover if the group can overlook the disciplinary familiarity and instead analyze rhetorically.

Step One: (5 minutes) Launch the discussion by asking, "What do you know about abstracts? What were you taught?" Get that on the board, then shift the question from form to function and from writing to reading: "As a reader, what are you trying to *do* when you read an abstract?" Because most readers are trying to decide on the basis of the abstract whether to read the entire article, it's possible to assess the quality of an abstract by its effect on readers. A perfect abstract allows its readers to self-segregate accurately and confidently into two groups: those who must read the article, and those who can afford to skip it.

Step Two: (15 minutes) Divide the class into small groups of three or four to answer the following questions: "What information do you as a reader need to have in order to decide confidently and correctly whether to read the article?" Let the groups talk among themselves for a few minutes, then return to a full class discussion, putting their responses on the board. Be sure the discussion includes not only the information needed but also the rationale for needing it, as well as how a reader would recognize the information; the goal is not simply to name the information but to derive it by thinking pragmatically.

Get the key elements (or alternative terms) on the board. My students usually propose terms like the following to describe the information they feel they need from an effective abstract, which I connect to terms from "A Writing Lexicon":

- Orienting information to the field or to previously established knowledge (orienting)
- Problem/unknown/question (motive)
- Purpose (thesis)
- Approach (method)
- Results (evidence/analysis)
- Conclusions/interpretation/implications

Often, students will come up with additional abstract qualities, like "significance" or "novelty." Although such abstractions indeed concern readers, after some discussion we usually decide that these qualities are judgments derived from other information, not the specific elements needed for an informative abstract. Keep these abstractions on the board alongside the elements but separate from them.

Step Three: (15 minutes) Now circulate the handout and test the framework against the four published abstracts. Put students back into groups of three or four, with the following charge: **Read** the abstracts. **Rank** them from best to worst. **Compare** rankings within your group. **Discuss** and analyze your judgments using the terms we've developed. I write on the board "Read, Rank, Compare, Discuss" to keep them focused on their task.

Step Four: (15 minutes) Reconvene the full class and compare the groups' results with one another. *Expect limited consensus*. It is in sorting out the different responses that the group learns to read each other's minds.

Since there's usually near unanimity around the least effective abstract, start the analysis there with these questions:

- Which elements of effective abstracts are present?
- Which elements are missing or incompletely developed?
- How does the analysis above account for your assessment and ranking?

As students respond, ask them to point to specific passages in the abstract and read them aloud so that everyone is able to compare individual interpretations within the context of the group. Make a chart on the board showing which elements are present and which absent or incomplete. By the end of discussing the first, deficient abstract, you will have both validated the group's consensus and analyzed it by reading closely.

Turn next to the opposite pole, asking which abstract was ranked highest.

With every new example, use the same questions above as you analyze and debate the elements of a successful abstract. For each abstract be sure to keep charting the student responses on the board so the class can compare these charts as they go.

REFLECTIONS

Precisely because this exercise leads to productive dissonance and chaos, it works on multiple levels with many kinds of genres and documents. Its explicit goals are to make visible the otherwise tacit expectations of readers and to map those expectations to particular elements of structure and substance. I commonly use scientific abstracts, but the procedure works equally well for abstracts in the social sciences or humanities as well as for other generic forms—introductions, conclusions, figure legends, cover letters, proposals. Because some genres need more work to bring the expectations to the surface, the workshop may need a longer set-up to orient the group to the demands of the situation, especially if participants do not have much experience reading the particular genre.

In parallel with these explicit goals, the exercise models effective writing process *in class*. The class starts with reflection on what we know, then turns to brainstorming to imagine what else might be important. We then shift from the comprehensive and spacious imagining of brainstorming to more focused prioritizing of our criteria. Finally, we test our priorities against both other texts and the responses of other readers to arrive at a deeper and clearer understanding of what makes a strong abstract.

Discussing how to rank the abstracts usually produces common areas of disagreement that are interesting and productive since they can ultimately help us understand how and why readers differ. In particular, the two strongest abstracts in the batch often split the vote. What quickly emerges is that 1) both effective abstracts include all the necessary elements; and 2) readers disagree because they value those elements differently. For example, readers in highly quantitative fields such as geochemistry often prefer an abstract with quantitative data to a more qualitative abstract. Or, readers from outside a field may prefer an abstract with a broader research question, whereas readers from within the field gravitate to more specific but pointed questions. The discussion makes visible the consensus that contributes to genre-level expectations while allowing for the diversity of individual readers and their interpretations. The mediocre abstract in the bunch often also initially has its proponents, but testing it against the criteria tends to reveal its weaknesses and the proponents usually change their rankings. In many cases, they come to see that their familiarity with the field led them to fill in the blanks and assume the abstract was more coherent and informative than it really was.

Most importantly, this iterative process of reflection and discussion allows writers to compare the reactions they imagine from readers with those of actual readers in the room. Because reading is solitary, readers rarely have the opportunity to compare their interpretations of a passage: they easily assume that everyone else reads as they do. This exercise tests that assumption; readers quickly discover that even seemingly straightforward texts elicit a variety of responses. Students compare their analysis and interpretations to those of their peers, and the group as a whole refines its standards for analysis. An added benefit: the instructor becomes simply one reader among many—a more experienced reader, perhaps, or a more skillful reader, but not the authoritative reader.

As a follow-up to this exercise, have students bring drafts of their own abstracts to class. Divide students into groups of three or four to workshop one another's drafts, reminding them to refer back to the criteria for effective abstracts they had generated during the exercise with professional samples. For the final step, reconvene as a full group and ask students which elements of the several abstracts they discussed seemed especially effective, and why. Then ask which elements they are still struggling with and facilitate a troubleshooting discussion. This follow up workshop not only sets students on the path to productive revision, but also makes real for them that the audience for their writing is wider than they may have imagined.

The Accidental Experts

Daniel M. Choi

Through a conference panel simulation, students perform expertise that they *don't* have to identify the critical reading and writing expertise that they *do* have.

Writing Focus: *sources, method, conventions*
Teacher Preparation: *medium*
Student Preparation: *none*
Estimated Time: *80 minutes*
General Disciplines: *social sciences, sciences*

EXERCISE

Prep Work: For this activity, students roleplay being members of a team of professionals presenting on a conference panel. To prepare for class, curate an archive of documents from a number of different professional settings dealing with a common topic or problem. The archive can be a set of links to materials online or printed copies. The aim is to find documents that at first may seem opaque, but where a few minutes of close attention to "Lexicon" elements will allow students to recognize their underlying logic and extract their most important ideas. The final number of documents will depend on the size of the class, but aim for one per three to six students. Ideally, they will be real-life examples of professional writing, such as technical reports, government and NGO whitepapers, or consulting slide decks, written for clients and other external audiences. I have used:

- A cognitive psychology paper presenting a multitasking experiment
- An NGO study of academic outcomes of laptop distribution in schools
- A consulting firm report on the market opportunities of online higher education
- A marketing whitepaper from an education publisher outlining their solutions for the educational technology space

While these documents are dense with charts and tables, they all have clearly marked sections that are functionally equivalent to the sections of an academic paper, even if the overlap isn't perfect.

Step One: (5 minutes) Frame the activity by suggesting that the writing students are practicing in class will directly transfer to different disciplines, industries, and careers. Provide orienting material—or show a short trailer!—for the conference on which you are modeling your simulation. I've used the World Economic Forum at Davos, Aspen Ideas Festival, SXSW, and even Comic-Con! Set the stage: the students are junior members of the organizations that produced their documents, but their busy and disorganized supervisor has been held back and doesn't have a prepared presentation to send ahead. They are responsible for producing a five-minute presentation on their project.

Their presentations should address the following four questions: 1) What is the problem your team wanted to solve? 2) How did your team go about solving it? 3) What were the main things your team found? 4) What are the next steps? The first three questions are designed to elicit motive, methodology, and thesis.

Divide students into teams and indicate which document is theirs.

Step Two: (25 minutes) Allow the students to pore over their documents and begin planning. Many of these documents will be dense, jargon-laden, and long. You'll want to scale the time allowed accordingly, but err on the side of increasing time pressure, both to maintain the pace and focus of the class and to avoid cutting too far into presentation time. The consulting slide deck I use, for example, has over sixty slides of charts and tables. Students can balk at the amount of information they believe they're expected to memorize. I like to give them a gentle reminder that they're not going to be able to master everything, pointing out that while they have twenty-five minutes with the document, their audience will only hear a condensed five minutes' worth of the highlights they select.

Step Three: (40 minutes) Student teams present for about five minutes, followed by a five-minute Q&A. Encourage students to ham it up in performing their expertise during the presentations and similarly indulge the theatrical as the audience asks probing "expert" questions in response to the other team presentations (for example, scientists should ask about methodological and data validity, whereas business experts would probably ask about commercial viability). While I avoid directly timing the presentations, I tell my students beforehand that I will signal when they should be wrapping up.

Step Four: (10 minutes) As you debrief the class, open by congratulating them on tackling difficult documents. Remind them that these documents are real-life examples of writing that they will encounter in the professional world. Take some time to discuss how they can transfer what they learn in the classroom to their professional lives. How are the motives for writing such documents different from academic motive? How do meta-textual and extratextual elements help the reader navigate the document? What kinds of shifts in reading and presentation strategies might be necessary when tackling professional documents? Some of the strategies that come up frequently in my classes include breaking up the reading based on sub-headers, identifying and defining keywords, asking whether the authors have any agendas, and how those agendas shape diction and structure choice. Close by asking, "Were you surprised at how quickly you gained confidence in your expertise?"

REFLECTIONS

"The Accidental Experts" is one of my favorite class exercises because it tackles a persistent challenge in teaching writing: explicitly identifying critical reading and writing skills that students have developed in class so they can transfer them further across disciplines and genres. It also introduces students to the variety of writing that occurs outside of the classroom. This exercise leverages professional writing genres to illustrate the link between the motive of a text on the one hand and its structure and delivery on the other. I find this exercise especially useful toward the latter half of the academic term. By then, students have had the opportunity to engage in different genres of academic writing, and they are more in the mindset of applying the skills they've developed in class to other coursework or other professional settings.

While students can be thrown off by the different formats of the documents they read, reminding them to ask themselves why a given text was composed *and for which audience* can help them apply their reading strategies for academic texts. One student in "Team Education Publisher" noticed that once she was able to understand that her company wanted to *sell* a product, the structure of the whitepaper clicked into place. "Team Consultants" had a similar epiphany—they realized that slide decks were ultimately a visual aid to a verbal talk, and they attempted to reconstruct a "combined text" of both slides and speech to figure out which slides held key arguments and which slides acted as evidentiary support.

"Team Psychologists" and "Team NGO" were presented with a familiar genre (the academic paper), but they had to transform the written paper into a verbal presentation. They did so by building a logical outline of their texts to reduce the articles to essential "talking points." In one instance, the psychology team made a particularly trenchant observation: the traditional order of a scientific research article was uninteresting for a general audience, so they omitted the "experimental methods" section in favor of quickly presenting the top-line experimental results. Only during the Q&A did they refer to experimental methods.

This exercise truly comes alive during the Q&A. It's surprising how quickly students become comfortable inhabiting their expertise. Particularly amusing in my class was the good-natured ribbing of the education publishers, called "corporate shills" by the psychologists. While this activity can certainly be successful without grilling the presenters, encouraging spirited exchanges provides further opportunities for students to explore rhetorical practices in different environments. Students inhabit their expert roles to investigate the professional motives that shape their communications. By encouraging students to be actively skeptical through their expert lenses, they have the opportunity to build a critical awareness of the rhetoric of expertise and compare cutthroat expert cultures with the classroom environment. Of course, it's worth observing that they are only *playing* the role of an expert and have not genuinely acquired professional expertise through this exercise.

The centrality of role-playing in "The Accidental Experts" also provides an opportunity for students to embody real versus performed expertise in three ways. First, they bring their (real) critical reading and writing expertise, accumulated over the academic term, and use it to interpret their assigned document. Second, they gain a sense of the range of professional expertise on display by reading their document with authorial motive in mind. And third, they display their (performed) expertise through their presentation and Q&A, as they are required to digest and communicate knowledge through the frame of their professional roles. Faced with the diverse and immediate demands of the professional world through this simulation, students will experience firsthand how to transfer their skills outside of the classroom. For this class, students' real expertise unlocks the performance of an expertise they don't yet have and also points forward to how critical reading and writing skills will let them grow into future expertise they can wear authentically.

A variant of the exercise employing only academic research articles allows you to draw instead from a variety of disciplines around a topic to emphasize different standards of methodology, evidence, and analysis. I have used this approach in a summer research colloquium with STEM students, tackling the issue of identity with an archive of documents from biochemistry (molecular markers), biophysics (pattern formation, like fingerprints and irises), psychology, and computer science. This approach is a great addition to a research seminar for upper division undergraduates and graduate students who already have mastery over some material but could stand testing their metacognition in other domains of expertise. It's a classroom adventure for the physical chemists to muddle through Deleuze while the classicists right next to them wrestle with Feynman diagrams.

Into the Public Square

Neil J. Young

Teach students to translate their scholarly writing into op-ed form to make persuasive arguments in public spaces.

Writing Focus: *conventions, ethos, motive, thesis, evidence*
Teacher Preparation: *low*
Student Preparation: *medium*
Estimated Time: *50 minutes*
General Disciplines: *humanities, social sciences, sciences*

EXERCISE

Prep Work: This exercise works best when students are working on (or have a first draft of) a research paper. Identify an author who writes for both academic and public audiences, then choose two writings by that author on the same or a similar topic: one academic piece, one op-ed. For example, I like to pair historian Natalia Mehlman Petrzela's 2018 book chapter "Thanks, Gender! An Intellectual History of the Gym" with her *Washington Post* op-ed of the same year, "As Swimsuit Season Ends, Pursuit of the 'Bikini Body' Endures." Since there is value in students scrutinizing their instructor's own work, I sometimes assign my own 2007 journal article, "'The ERA Is a Moral Issue': The Mormon Church, LDS Women, and the Defeat of the Equal Rights Amendment" with my 2012 *New York Times* op-ed, "Equal Rights, Gay Rights and the Mormon Church." Or you can pick a scholar whose academic and public writing works best for your course topic. Before class, ask students to read and annotate both texts carefully, identifying "Lexicon" items, with special attention to motive, thesis, and evidence. You'll also want to prepare the brief worksheet used in step two.

Step One: (25 minutes) Lead a discussion of both pieces with the entire class to tease out the differences in conventions between the two genres. To structure the conversation, draw a grid on the board and use it to identify key "Lexicon" components, while drawing out points of comparison and contrast between how they play out in each text. (You'll want three columns: one for the "Lexicon" terms, and one for each piece of writing.)

Sequence the discussion by taking up one "Lexicon" term at a time. To start, have the class identify the thesis sentence or passage in both texts. Just as with an academic essay, op-eds always have an argument, but they are sometimes implicit or not identifiable as a specific sentence or two as is usually the case with scholarly works. Invite students to talk about how the op-ed's thesis compares to the scholarly thesis and what similarities and differences they see between argumentation in academic and public writing. Encourage them to notice the differences between the size and scope of each thesis, both in how much space they take up in the texts and also in the extent of the claims each is making.

Next move to the varying use of evidence, which should flow directly from your discussion of thesis. Students should see the tight interplay between thesis and evidence in an op-ed as much as they do in the academic essay. Take time to write in the grid the different types of evidence each text uses and to describe their qualities. (For example, when we diagram my two pieces on the Mormon Church and the Equal Rights Amendment, students see that although both use the history of the ERA to build the argument, the scholarly article draws on and cites secondary literature, newspaper articles, and church documents to trace that history closely while the op-ed makes reference to a general knowledge of the amendment's history.)

From evidence, you might discuss both sources and citations with special attention to how an op-ed author indicates where they have found their evidence. (You can do this as a separate line on the grid, or simply while discussing the entries for "evidence.") Scholarly writing cites through formal conventions of footnotes, endnotes, and the like, producing a rich paper trail for readers and colleagues to follow. Op-eds don't have the space to follow the same conventions, and so op-ed writers must identify their key sources in the flow of the prose or via hyperlinking. But it's important to recognize that the ethos and principles remain the same: readers must have confidence that the writer's evidence is reliable and be able to track down the original sources.

While instructors often begin discussion of a piece of writing with a consideration of its primary motive, I suggest for this exercise concluding there. Only after students identify the other "Lexicon" elements can they see clearly the most significant differences between the two types of writing. Op-eds don't have the academic essay's typical motive of making an intervention into the existing scholarly literature. But they almost always intervene in a public debate of some kind, with a motivating move that tends to fall along one of the following lines: alerting the public; advocating for change; changing prevailing perceptions; correcting an erroneous assumption or belief; or shining the spotlight on an ignored or overlooked problem.

Op-eds also have a secondary motive tied to timeliness that answers the question, "Why now?" This is both a question that editors ask themselves when they receive op-ed submissions—"Why should I publish this now?"—and that readers, often unconsciously, ask themselves when they open the newspaper or a website: "Why should I read this now?" In the news business, this element of motive is called the "news hook"—the part of the op-ed, usually in the first or second paragraph, that gives the piece its timely relevance. Close this portion of the exercise by asking the class to identify the op-ed's news hook and how the author connects it to the piece's larger focus. Is there a direct one-to-one connection or is there a pivot from news hook to topic?

Step Two: (25 minutes) Now invite students to practice developing the "why now" for their own writing by searching for a news hook that would allow them to turn the topic of their research essay into an op-ed. Start by modeling one example with the full class, perhaps from a student volunteer. Students with more esoteric or unique research topics may struggle to think how their topic could be tied to current events. For example, a student who is writing about the political implications of aristocratic dress in the eighteenth-century French royal court may think they should look for a news hook about a current museum exhibition of such costumes. But they will face a problem if no such exhibitions are taking place right now. However, something like a recent red-carpet broadcast for the Oscars or Emmys could provide the perfect news hook for a piece that makes an argument about the symbolic power of what we wear and how that is shaped by class and status.

After you've modeled how to find a news hook, turn the students loose on their own research. To help guide the development of their op-ed drafts, distribute a worksheet based on the four prompts below. Once students find their news hooks, the additional questions will help them advance the ball.

1. Write the news hook you have found for your piece.
2. Reviewing your research essay, select three or four pieces of evidence to include in your op-ed.
3. Given the news hook and evidence you have chosen, rework your research essay's thesis into an argument for your op-ed.
4. How would you compare the motive for your research essay to the motive for your op-ed? How do the different intended audiences for each piece shape the motives you have developed?

If there isn't time to complete the full worksheet in class, you can have students finish it before your next session.

REFLECTIONS

This exercise works on multiple levels. It teaches students to read critically, to crystallize the core argument of the research essay that they are either still working on or have recently completed, and to apply what they've learned about motive, thesis, and evidence in order to make persuasive arguments in settings beyond the traditional academic essay—including advocating at a town council, presenting at a board meeting, or speaking at a public rally.

As a former academic who writes op-eds and frequently teaches the craft to students and faculty new to the genre, I care deeply about bringing the best knowledge into the public square. Students often tell me they don't know enough to write for public audiences, but the op-ed forum is a particularly receptive space for the type of expertise they have developed through a research project. When confronted with the task of selecting the most compelling and accessible evidence to include in the typical op-ed of eight hundred words, they realize they know much more than they thought.

Table 10 ("Into the Public Square")

	Academic Piece: **"The ERA Is a Moral Issue"**	**Op-ed:** **"Equal Rights, Gay Rights and the Mormon Church"**
Thesis	Mormon women worked to defeat the ERA in order to serve their church, secure and demonstrate their salvation, and expand their power within the church.	The history of Mormons for E.R.A. provides a warning to the gay rights group Mormons Building Bridges: it may persuade the church to adopt a more friendly stance towards gay Mormons, but the group's members will suffer consequences for their political action.
Evidence	Scholarly literature on anti-ERA movement, New Right, and Mormon history Sonia Johnson autobiography Church teachings from LDS sermons, talks, publications, magazines Mormon doctrine	Mormons Building Bridges story and Facebook page Sonia Johnson's autobiography and public statements about Mormons for ERA Quotations from Church leaders and teachings Examples of LDS Church involvement in gay politics
Motive	Scholarly literature has ignored Mormon Church's role in anti-ERA work. Mormon history holds that women's involvement was driven by the church's hierarchical structure, but does not take into account the influence of Mormon theology regarding eternal life.	News hook of Mormon Building Bridges group participating in Salt Lake City gay pride parade. People think of LDS Church as anti-gay because of its support of Proposition 8, but the case of "Mormon Building Bridges" complicates our understanding.

Students and faculty alike often question the larger relevance of their knowledge, especially those who study more esoteric topics. But this exercise, especially where it deals with motive, should build confidence about how all knowledge can be translated to the public conversation and inform pressing issues. For example, one scholar I worked with, an expert on ancient Greek political theory, believed her knowledge was too specialized to have much contemporary application. But as the talk of "fake news" and "alternative facts" grew in our public discourse, she realized she could use her knowledge of Greek ideas about the connection between truth and democracy to give perspective on political assaults on the free press. Another op-ed workshop participant who had written about how the philosophies of language and gender shaped each other found they could channel their findings to weigh in on the pressing debate over pronouns and gender identity in American society.

Filling in the squares of the grid in the first step of the exercise helps students see concretely how one scholar has accomplished this translation. Table 10 is a sample grid for my two pieces.

My students are sometimes inclined to think the constraints of the op-ed liberate them from onerous academic citation practices. But the inverse is true: the op-ed makes it *harder* rather than easier to be faithful to one's sources because the formal apparatus isn't available to guide one's choices. There are fewer citations but more, and more important, judgment calls. The "common knowledge" exception to citation can be interpreted more broadly in op-eds. Realistically, a writer can't cite *everything* without distracting from his or her argument, and so must carefully decide whether a given piece of evidence will itself prove controversial. I tell my students: if you can imagine a reader pushing back, be sure to include an attribution. If not, this might be an opportunity to buy back some space. Of course, when in doubt a writer should always err in the direction of overciting.

Ideally, this exercise inspires reflection on the civic value of op-eds and public thought leadership. "Why do people write op-eds?" and "Who are the voices we need to hear from?" are worthy questions to consider. Ideally, students will understand that writing op-eds is not just a skill, but also a service to their communities and the wider world. While most students will not become academic scholars, they can all have public voices. The greatest result of this exercise, and indeed this class, is that students realize how its lessons have equipped them for sharing their voices and making the changes they desire. For a follow-up revising workshop, also on the op-ed, see "The Editorial Board."

The Art of Film Reviewing

Diana Fuss

Teach film reviewing by helping students create a do-it-yourself writing guide together.

Writing Focus: *structure, style, analysis, conventions*
Teacher Preparation: *medium*
Student Preparation: *medium*
Estimated Time: *50 minutes*
General Discipline: *humanities*

EXERCISE

Prep Work: For homework, invite students to peruse some film reviews in magazines, newspapers, or blogs, selecting one they particularly like (ideally five hundred to seven hundred words). The review can be glowing, scathing, or just middling. Have them bring enough copies to class for small group workshops, and a copy for you as well. If the conventions of movie reviewing are new to you, take time to familiarize yourself with the standard four-part structure of a six-hundred-word film review: the *lead* (or *lede*), the *plot synopsis*, the *analysis*, and the *conclusion*. A useful resource is Christopher Null's "Putting the Pieces Together," the fifth chapter of his book *Five Stars!*

Step One: (5 minutes) To begin, briefly introduce the four conventional parts of a review (lead, plot synopsis, analysis, conclusion) so you have a shared working vocabulary.

Step Two: (15 minutes) Separate students into small groups (groups of three are ideal) for a deeper discussion of the reviews. Within groups, each student should briefly explain why they chose their review and what in particular appeals to them about it. Then, to guide their discussion, have students work across the reviews in front of them, part by part, focusing first on how the writers individually begin their reviews, second on how and where they introduce plot, third on how and where they provide analysis, and fourth on how they conclude. Instructing groups to move *laterally* across their set of reviews encourages a closer compare-and-contrast approach, highlighting more distinctly reviewers' different writing techniques. As students perform the workshop, you will have time to skim the reviews yourself to get your bearings.

Step Three: (25 minutes) Reconvene as a full group and divide your classroom blackboard or white board into four capacious sections or columns marked "Lead," "Plot Synopsis," "Analysis," and "Conclusion." Explain that the practical goal of this exercise is to build together a do-it-yourself guide to structuring and writing their first review. Pose the same question about strategy for each of the structural parts listed on the board, beginning with "What are some effective strategies for writing a lead?" and eventually working your way across the board to "What are some effective strategies for writing a conclusion?" The board will fill up surprisingly quickly, so try summarizing each strategy in just a few words. (It also works well to have students volunteer to do the board work.) If you like, you can also solicit students' personal thoughts on anything a good film reviewer might do well to avoid (like spoilers!). When students have finished, feel free to survey the board and offer a few tips of your own to fill in any gaps.

Step Four: (5 minutes) End by leading a discussion on what important work film reviewing might culturally perform as you send them off to draft their own reviews.

REFLECTIONS

Even in film studies courses, students are unlikely to have previous experience writing movie reviews for the general public. I have found, however, that the range of professional reviews students discuss in this exercise immediately reassures them that they do not need a sophisticated film theorist's vocabulary to write a serious, interesting, playful, energetic, informative, smart, or useful movie review. They just need a clear claim grounded in evidence and a good sense of audience—in short, the fundamentals of any argument.

At the same time, a film review differs from traditional academic writing in several respects. After completing their reviews, my students were quick to say that they felt more "entitled' to their own personal opinion and less "encumbered" by the need to entertain multiple possible objections. They also stressed that it was "liberating" to write plot synopses, something considered to be a weakness in their academic papers. Some noted that they felt more "confident" about their own analysis without the pressure to integrate secondary research. Others appreciated that the tighter construction of a film review left "no space to waste." The only thing students jokingly complained about was taking notes in the dark.

Perhaps because of the increased freedom writing a film review typically affords, my students seemed even more acutely aware of its chief difficulty: striking the right *tone* for a public audience, a task that involves finding the right *voice* and choosing the right *diction*. They quickly learned that their writing voice needed to be more colloquial and their diction more adventurous. They also took inspiration from their models and began using many more evaluative adjectives (like silly, tepid, dreary, delightful, magical, gutsy, gritty). Tone can be particularly hard to master, so I like to share how Roger Ebert, a serious reviewer who nonetheless wrote like a fan, managed to strike the right tone. His trick? Begin writing every review with a silent "So, anyways . . ." Individual reviewers have distinct writing styles as well as different evaluative criteria. But most, like Ebert, strongly favor a conversational style and highly prize a film's emotional power. It can be helpful to remind students that good criticism begins with the question: did you like it? The "why" of their gut response is where analysis properly begins.

The four-part film review template works exceptionally well to orient students to the genre. The heart of this exercise, building a guide or tip sheet, is an essential step since it distills from successful film reviews concrete and useable writing strategies (some of which, the students discovered, can also be transferred back to their academic writing). Here in abbreviated and cleaned-up form is a student-composed tip sheet (board work from step three) from the first year I taught the exercise in a film blogging course:

The Lead: Begin with a personal anecdote; a joke; a striking statement; an obscure fact; a piece of trivia; a quote; a play on the movie's title; a director's reputation; a film comparison; a broad social context; a key moment in the film; a brief piece of dialogue; an emotional response; a direct address to a specific audience; a comment on the state of the industry; a confession.

The Plot Synopsis: Briefly describe setting, where and when the action takes place; introduce important characters and the names of the actors who play them; identify a main story conflict; highlight a key event; provide historical background; hint at the general plot structure; compare or contrast the type of plot to other films.

The Analysis: Offer your thoughts on the quality of the performances—who was a standout, who was miscast; briefly comment on a scene; describe your emotional responses or note the reactions of the audience around you; place the film within its genre—blockbuster, indie, documentary, fantasy, crime, romance, comedy, suspense, horror, animation; question or defend the director's choices; identify something specific about the film that pleased or irritated you—lighting, camerawork, pacing, dialogue, makeup, costume, editing; identify one of the movie's central themes and share what you think of it.

The Conclusion: Circle back to your lead; complicate an opening question; end on a philosophical note; offer a surprise twist or critical zinger; pose a challenge to your reader; ask a rhetorical question; continue with your analysis; ponder the director's future; add something new; revise your initial opinion; include a warning; describe how you felt when you left the theater; hammer the final nail in the coffin; celebrate the pleasures and possibilities of good cinema; conclude with a meaningful quote.

There is a store of additional practical advice out there for aspiring film review writers: avoid spoilers by limiting your plot synopsis to the film's early action (or "first act"); use the audience-friendly pronouns "we" and "you"; have fun with your leads and conclusions! It is better though to address student questions as they come up: Can you make do with a one-sentence plot synopsis? (Not really, unless the movie lacks a plot.) Should you avoid politics? (Not if that is what the movie is about, or if it speaks directly to the historical moment.) Can you violate the film review's standard structure? (So happy you asked!) Like the academic paper, a film review's structure can be more flexible than it first appears. Analysis and plot synopsis are capable of traveling together, with analysis driving the car and plot synopsis hitching a ride. And analysis in particular can easily move out of its lane, weaving in and out of introductions and conclusions, and even (on occasion) titles. You'll know the exercise has been a success if students start discussing ways to bend the form.

The best titles signal the reviewer's honest opinion of the film in just a handful of words or less, which every review title should try to do. My students had great fun with their titles, particularly for the disappointing films: "Ouija Bored" (*Ouija*); "A Theory of Everything: From Black Holes to Plot Holes" (*The Theory of Everything*); "The Distasteful Eight" (*The Hateful Eight*); "This is the End, of the Good Comedy Film" (*This is the End*); Big Eyes, Blurred Focus (*Big Eyes*); "Over Seasoned and Under Cooked" (*Burnt*); "In Space No One Can Hear You Yawn" (*Interstellar*). Titles provide one more creative opportunity to capture an audience, establish a tone, and begin an argument.

In a subsequent meeting, consider devoting class time to a draft workshop so students can get feedback from their peers on their own reviews. I typically allot ten minutes to workshop a six-hundred-word review, adjusting the size of student groups to the time available (in general, groups of three or four work well). You can prepare a handout that targets specific questions you want students to consider as they read their peers' film reviews, questions at once relevant to most pieces of public writing but also directly pitched to the conventions of a professional film review: What do you enjoy best about the review? How would you describe the review's tone and its consistency? Does the lead grab your attention, and why or why not? Does the amount of plot synopsis seem about right in relation to the analysis, or where might their ratio be adjusted? Do you spy any spoilers that might be removed or infelicitous words in need of revision? What do you think of the conclusion? Having read the whole review, can you imagine alternate titles? For problem spots that need rethinking, encourage everyone to put their heads together to brainstorm possible solutions—for a clearer lead, a stronger conclusion, a necessary reorganization, a sharper analysis, a catchier title, a smoother tone, a pithier word. If there is time remaining, invite students to begin revising their drafts in class, or have volunteers read their titles or leads aloud for full group feedback.

Ultimately the most important conversation you can have with your students takes up an intrinsic question too easily overlooked: what is a film review *for* exactly? It can be especially productive to brainstorm the essential larger functions such reviews might perform—building media literacy, promoting public debate, fostering aesthetic appreciation, raising social awareness. Reviews, after all, have a purpose: "Sure this movie has a great cast and gorgeous cinematography, but should we buy what they're selling?" or "Yes, it's a three-hour long documentary, but it will change your thinking on climate change forever." To help students understand how *motive* applies to writing a film review, I encourage them always to identify why, in their opinion, at least one of the film's themes is significant—personally, politically, historically, aesthetically, culturally. Reviews matter: they help us understand both the mediums and the messages that reflect our world back to us, for better or for worse.

Listening to Motive

Andrea Mazzariello

Show how music can make an argument, and how arguments can sing.

Writing Focus: *motive, ethos, method*
Teacher Preparation: *medium*
Student Preparation: *low*
Estimated Time: *60 minutes*
General Discipline: *humanities*

EXERCISE

Prep Work: Bring two pieces to class: 1) Gordon Harvey's original definition of motive (below), or the definition provided in "A Writing Lexicon"; and 2) Anna Meredith's "Nautilus" sound recording, or any piece of music, film, or story that makes a striking reversal or reframing move. (There are multiple versions of "Nautilus" available online; I use the five minute, thirty second track from Meredith's 2016 debut album *Varmints*.)

Step One: (10 minutes) Begin with a reading, or ideally a rereading, of the definition of motive by student volunteers (see the handout from "Mapping Personal and Scholarly Motive" for a more easily reproducible version of this quote):

> ***Motive***: the intellectual context that you establish for your topic and thesis at the start of your essay, in order to suggest why someone, besides your instructor, might want to read an essay on this topic or need to hear your particular thesis argued—why your thesis isn't just obvious to all, why other people might hold *other* theses (that you think are wrong). Your motive should be aimed at your audience: it won't necessarily be the reason you first got interested in the topic (which could be private and idiosyncratic) or the personal motivation behind your engagement with the topic. Indeed it's where you suggest that your argument *isn't* idiosyncratic, but rather is generally interesting. The motive you set up should be genuine: a misapprehension or puzzle that an intelligent reader (not a straw dummy) would really have, a point that such a reader would really overlook. Defining motive should be the main business of your introductory paragraphs, where it is usually introduced by a form of the complicating word "But."
>
> *From Gordon Harvey's "Elements of the Academic Essay"*

Ask students how this complication, this pivot, might be put into play in works or genres outside of the academic essay. Where else might one find this explicit turning away from a conventional understanding? Give students a few minutes to respond in writing to this question and share with a partner. I like to have students speak for their partners when we regroup because it encourages them to listen to each other attentively and develop their ability to paraphrase, condense, rephrase, and so on. At the beginning of the semester, it also gives them the chance to introduce their colleagues to each other.

Step Two: (20 minutes) Now turn to Meredith's "Nautilus." (If your students haven't offered "music" in the previous step, articulate it as an enticing possibility: What about in sound? In instrumental music? How might that look?). Play the first few moments of the piece and ask students to write down what they hear, represented in whatever form feels comfortable—verbal descriptions are often as valuable as music notation—and then ask for volunteers to offer their observations, recording these on the board as you go. Then continue through the musical text, playing successive segments of the track followed by simple prompts (what do you hear? what seems to be important here?) while continuing to record the students' observations. Make sure to stop the last segment just before the music makes its striking reversal. (For "Nautilus," I use the following segments: 0:00–0:30, 0:30–1:36, 1:36–2:34, and 2:34–3:05.)

Step Three: (20 minutes) Before playing any more of the piece, ask students to describe in writing what they think could/should/will happen next, and then to share their ideas with the rest of the class. Discuss the students' hypotheses both in terms of what work they would do musically, as well as (turning back to motive) what they might look like in argumentative terms—as though the opening of "Nautilus" were the beginning of an essay. With this analogy in mind, encourage them to see how the opening of the piece might represent the "setup" of an essay—the (temporarily) persuasive premise that precedes its necessary complication—such that when the pivot finally happens, the attendant disorientation is argumentatively satisfying. (Or, in the case of "Nautilus," musically profound.)

Step Four: (10 minutes) Now back up and play the full piece, this time from start to finish, allowing the miraculous moment to unfold. Ask students what happens at the pivot, continuing to note their observations on the board.

A hint for beyond the music classroom: Depending on their musical expertise, your students may or may not immediately recognize the pivot. In a music composition seminar, students will reliably hear the move as deeply destabilizing with respect to the old material but deeply satisfying with respect to the way the rhythm slots into a new pulse. Students with less musical training may hear "Nautilus" differently. The initial rhythmic pattern might feel so strong as to override the new material, so to speak, or students might hear chaos rather than coalescence. In cases where the move falls flat, encourage a bodily understanding of the music; clapping along to the initial rhythm and trying to sustain it as the new material enters is one way to feel the rhythms against each other. Or half the class can clap the old rhythm while the other claps the new rhythm.

To conclude the exercise, ask students to return once more to motive, mapping key elements of Harvey's definition onto the unfolding stages of the musical piece: expectations established, hints dropped that this isn't to be taken wholly at face value, signals that a pivot is coming, and then the actual move itself.

REFLECTIONS

Sonification as a practice refers to turning a data system or set into sound. We can hear the data stream, can engage it sensorially; suddenly the flocking behavior of birds or a population's growth over time has a perceptual component, making the data tangible in our ears, as a time-bound aural experience. This exercise aims to sonify in a different way: it takes a core concept in writing pedagogy and asks what it might sound like.

In teaching a music composition seminar, I found myself analyzing what made a certain move in a particular piece of music so compelling and how it might serve as a model technique for students in their own compositions. As a teacher of writing, I suspected that there was a writerly way of understanding the dramatic strategy in question, that it made an offering to the listener in the same way that good writing makes an offering to the reader.

In the writing classroom, I often describe that offer-making, centered on the motivating move, as a kind of redirection or bait-and-switch: here's what we can agree upon, dear reader, or how the relevant literature comes to consensus, or what our shared understanding of this topic might be. Except now I'm going to challenge all of those things; the built frame was only ever provisional, a stepladder that, once used to change the light bulb, dissolves and grants us the power to float around the room.

The metaphor becomes abstract and difficult to manage, as you can see. That's less the case, however, with a sonic experience of motive, one that is perceptually palpable and dramatically powerful. When I conduct this exercise with Meredith's beguiling "Nautilus," I use simple, unpitched musical notations to make concrete my students' observations about the piece. For example, the repetitive opening of "Nautilus" usually prompts them to offer some version of the observation, "an obsessive rhythmic figure." I then present this visually on the board, representing the long-short figure as pictured here.

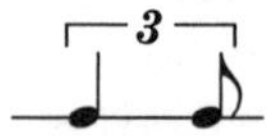

As students respond to the subsequent segments ("The sound-world is primarily synthesized," "The timbres are always shifting," "That rhythm repeats everywhere," or "The line moves from low to high"), I make the development of this rhythmic figure the focal point of discussion, since it most fundamentally contributes to the propulsion that will, in time, set up listeners for the destabilizing moment. I also continue to sketch out the progression of the tune in response to the students offering their own observations, with notations that might look something like this:

The rhythmic cell, repeated

a lot

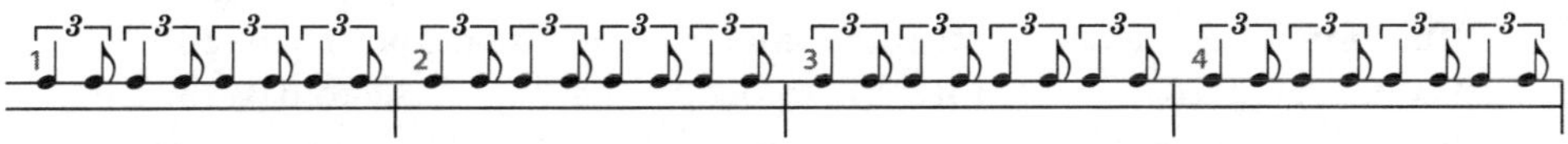

in an ascending contour

By the time we complete step three, my students usually have a clear sense of the work they want the pivot to accomplish musically ("If it keeps repeating this way, I'm going to get frustrated"; "If it fades and ends, I'm going to be bored"), as well as how it might analogize to writing ("The initial premise is going to remain the operating premise throughout, and we won't discover anything; it might actually look like a book report"). And once they finally hear the reversal in step four, I help them annotate the pivot itself:

A straightforward "boom bap" (kick and snare) rhythm

that radically shifts our understanding of the rhythmic figure that's been articulated in so many ways, giving us

in which the top line is that long-short rhythm, but with a completely different rhythmic sense owing to the new material that reframes it. From its original classic shuffle rhythm, four long-shorts per measure (Art Blakey's "Hammerhead" comes to mind as an iconic example), the overarching feel shifts to a classic "boom bap," kick on one and three and snare on two and four, in a slower tempo. This is motive, sonified. (In class, I sometimes also represent the kick-snare rhythm by rocking foot-to-foot *while* clapping the old long-short figure.)

The reframing in "Nautilus" works at the level of pulse and rhythm, but other forms of musical reframing are effective too. To illustrate harmonic reframing, for example, I use a tune that I wrote myself, in which B flat major melodic cells suddenly sound in the relative minor when G enters in the bass. Another exciting reframing move is based on our understanding of music in context. I sometimes play a field recording of Ghanaian postal workers canceling stamps without telling students what they're hearing, asking the same sorts of questions about what seems to be important to the music. Then, after discussion, I reveal that we are listening to people making music to pass the time at work. The important strategy, to my mind, is a radical reframing of the text in question, which can be found in many different media or genres. Think of viewing Salvador Dali's "Gala Contemplating the Mediterranean Sea Which at Twenty Meters Becomes the Portrait of Abraham Lincoln (Homage to Rothko)" at different distances, or the big reveal in films like *The Usual Suspects*, *The Sixth Sense*, or *The Wizard of Oz* (because it was all a dream). It might even be an academic paper, in which one also listens for motive. Or anything, really, with a significant reframing of what we think are its core dramatic or narrative premises.

As important as that dramatic move might be—Dorothy wakes up!—it can't work without first building out the provisional context: the tornado. Or, in the case of "Nautilus," a driving rhythmic figure that says "this is what this music is about." Or, in the case of the academic paper, a belief that we'd actually hold, a premise that is actually persuasive as opposed to a straw man.

In the music classroom, this exercise prepares students for an assignment in which they'll create their own pivot move compositionally. The real goal, though, is to make music that offers listeners a persuasive, compelling premise and then radically shifts their perspective on that premise. The aim is that we hear retroactively—in a sense, re-understand what's come before; we listen backward in time. So too with motive in prose; we pivot around the premise that initially built consensus, and, in that rotation, can't read it the same way anymore. And the impossibility of rereading without the new understanding that motive affords shows us how far we've come, how much we've grown.

PREVENTING PLAGIARISM

Plagiarism is often discussed in terms of mechanics and seemingly arbitrary rules, and students are motivated to avoid it through fear of whatever consequences are inflicted on those convicted of this academic sin at your institution. But this approach misses the point: there are vital ethical and conceptual issues expressed through citation practices, and faithful attention to these values can ease student anxieties *and* make student writing more compelling and persuasive. Engaging and acknowledging the scholarship on which we build our arguments is precisely what makes our *own* arguments possible. In foregrounding the scholarly conversation clearly, it's possible explicitly and concisely to signal the way an original claim is being made. The plagiarism-prevention workshop of this final section helps instructors make the case that academic integrity is about pursuing a positive, and that in doing so students are more likely to avoid the negative.

Bag the Fox: *A Plagiarism-Prevention Workshop*

Shannon K. Winston

Flip the script on teaching plagiarism prevention by introducing faithful source use as the road to stronger, more original arguments.

Writing Focus: *sources, thesis, motive, conventions, ethos*
Teacher Preparation: *medium if using prepared materials*
Student Preparation: *none*
Estimated Time: *80 minutes*
General Disciplines: *humanities, social sciences*

EXERCISE

Prep Work: Bring copies of the three handouts, plus plenty of highlighters (you need five different colors, and enough to supply each small group with one of each color). It pays to invest in a careful review of the handouts in advance so you're prepared to guide a detailed discussion and to field students' myriad questions and hypotheticals. Don't try to wing it from the "Teacher's Edition" included below.

The Handouts: The exercise uses three handouts, which are quite complex and worth previewing here.

Handout 1: "The Princeton Battle Monument, Draft" by "Sloppy Joe" is the primary text for the exercise. You'll present it as a sample introduction to a student essay, though in reality it is a Kafkaesque labyrinth of source misuse and abuse that students will navigate. Some text is bolded: these are Joe's own original words. Everything else is taken, ethically or otherwise, attributed or otherwise, from Joe's sources (including the phrase "bag the fox").

Handout 2: "Joe's Sources" provides excerpts from the sources Joe *actually* uses in his essay, which is quite different from how Joe *claims* to use his sources, as signaled through his citations. Students use highlighters to uncover these differences and think through the conceptual and ethical questions they provoke.

Handout 3: "The Princeton Battle Monument, Revision" by "Neater Joe" is Joe's second crack at his introduction. Here he cleans up his citation practices and, crucially, his more faithful engagement with the sources allows him to arrive at a much more promising, motivated, arguable thesis. It's not perfect, but "Neater Joe" builds credibility as a writer with something important to say.

Step One: (10 minutes) Distribute handout 1 and frame it as the introduction to a sample student draft. Give a brief explanation of the assignment, in which the student was asked to make a researched argument about a monument or memorial. Don't explain the bold text yet. Invite students to read out loud, and then ask what they notice immediately about Joe's introduction. Even without knowing that only the bold text is really Joe's, students should be able to detect that the introduction is overwhelmed by sources and there's not much of the writer here. Nor is there much of an argument; the thesis, if there is one, seems descriptive and unmotivated. Why should we *care* about the subject—in this case the Battle Monument? Despite the assignment's requirement for an arguable rather than a descriptive thesis, Joe may be defaulting to writing a report. He may not understand that he's being asked to do something different and that college-level assignments prioritize argument and originality.

Next explain the meaning of the bold text and ask students how this additional bit of information affects their assessment. (Joe's voice is even less present than we originally thought!) But also, be sure to ask: What's interesting in this draft? What seed or seeds of Joe's own ideas can they find? The point is to help them discern the potential for original argument, even when it appears only in small ways within a report-style paper riddled with citation problems. For example, in Joe's introduction, he wraps up with a sentence that suggests a promising line of inquiry: "It is curious that a monument, however, would be built so much after the fact and it makes one wonder what the role of the monument really might be."

Step Two: (20 minutes) Distribute handout 2 and unleash the highlighters! Explain that all the *un*bolded text comes from Joe's sources, whether or not he explicitly acknowledges that through his citations. Put your students in small groups, where they must don their investigator caps and figure out what Joe really did. For each source listed on handout 2, they should assign a color, and then highlight each *actual*—as opposed to *cited*—use of that source on handout 1 in that same color. All of the unbolded text on handout 1 should end up highlighted in one color or another, as it's all taken from a source on handout 2.

For each use of a source they discover, students should discuss whether that use is appropriate, as expressed through Joe's citation practice, (including those instances where there is *no* citation). If not, why not? What *should* Joe have done, and why? Encourage your students to dig deeply; most of the examples are more complicated than they first appear. These complications are precisely why the instructor needs to spend time closely studying handouts 1 and 2 before using the exercise. To help decode the documents, reference the interpretive "Teacher's Edition" provided below.

Step Three: (30 minutes) Once your students seem satisfied with their discoveries, reconvene and talk through each instance of source use. The discussion will usually uncover more wrinkles than your students found on the first pass. Be ready for a wide range of positions on the propriety of each of Joe's citation decisions. (This will be true even if your students are all scared of plagiarizing and want to avoid it.) It's important not to rush this step. Encountering academic integrity violations that some students thought or assumed were in bounds can inspire anxiety, and you want to steer the discussion toward the ethical and conceptual issues that undergird the mechanical minutia.

In discussing Joe's sloppiness, students will likely disagree about what Joe *should* have done in a given case. It's useful to encourage them to articulate the rationale underlying each solution they propose. Doing so unearths the principles of academic integrity, which is helpful even if they end up being wrong about a particular instance. This is also a good moment to review the three standard modes of introducing evidence from sources: quotation, paraphrase, and summary. You might also have students consider how to choose between the three modes for different purposes. See the "Teacher's Edition" below for some helpful notes to guide this part of the discussion.

Depending on time, there are a couple of other constructive avenues here. If your class employs a style manual, whether in hard copy or through an online resource, you may ask students to reference it to tease out questions of citation mechanics. You could also explore the disciplinary and methodological rationales that underlie the seemingly idiosyncratic differences in convention across citation styles.

Step Four: (10 minutes) Distribute handout 3 and read together as a class. Invite students to identify and discuss the differences between the original and revised versions of Joe's introduction. Good news: he's no longer plagiarizing! But Joe hasn't simply fixed citation problems. The balance between his voice and that of his sources is much better. By engaging with—rather than simply reporting on—his sources' ideas he has found a motive and a promising thesis. There's room for further revision, but Joe has moved a long way in the right direction.

Step Five: (10 minutes) Move to discuss the process by which Joe may have produced his original draft. What are the scenarios or circumstances that may have led there? How could he have avoided these scenarios? This is an opportunity to talk about how to structure the writing process, employ organized and active note-taking strategies, and pace oneself to avoid the hazards of plagiarizing under pressure. You might also discuss the benefits and drawbacks of citation software. While it can be a valuable tool, it must be handled responsibly: students are liable for citation mistakes that are "authored" by their digital allies. By first learning to cite manually, students are then empowered to check competently what the software does.

Conclude by reinforcing the exercise's fundamental message: appropriate source use and citation practices aren't only about avoiding the negative of plagiarism. Academic integrity is a positive that makes us better writers by highlighting our own contributions.

REFLECTIONS

Teaching academic integrity, like teaching writing, is not the work of a single class or a single semester. This lesson will stick most effectively to the extent that the principles of engaging ethically with sources, respecting and citing others' thoughts, and clearly articulating the origins of one's original research according to academic convention are reinforced iteratively throughout your course and the broader curriculum. Depending on your students' familiarity with the basic aims of source use and citation, you may start with "Bag the Fox," or you may build up to it.

The draft in handout 1 is a puzzle. The more closely students look, the more errors they will find and, by extension, the more they will learn about the complexities of proper source use. For this same reason, "Bag the Fox" can be challenging to teach. In their more cynical moments, students suspect this lesson will be a bureaucratic reminder of the rules for avoiding plagiarism. It's easy to see in their slumped body language or the passive way they initially leaf through the material that students may find the topic either boring or daunting or both. Other students become anxious about whether they've accidentally plagiarized before and begin asking hyper-specific questions about comma placement, capitalization, and other mechanics. The method of this exercise, grounded in discovery rather than didacticism, empowers students to uncover problems in the text, which both alleviates their anxiety and better ensures they will retain the lessons. By contrast, a stern lecture on the mechanical minutiae and ethical pitfalls accomplishes neither. Students' work will reveal the often highly nuanced questions at the heart of citation, and some humor along the way, rather than uncovering a black-and-white version of "the rules."

This approach updates an activity originally authored by Kerry Walk for the Princeton Writing Program. Many of the ideas for the current exercise also emerged out of collaborative discussions with my colleagues about how to teach, in dynamic and engaging ways, both plagiarism prevention and original argument. The sample materials were developed from a student paper about the Princeton Battle Monument, which engaged with its sources faithfully to arrive at a compelling, original argument. My job from there was to make it "sloppy" for handout 1. At first, I thought this would be a relatively easy task. After all, how hard is it to be sloppy?

The answer: it's challenging and time-consuming, in part because each source use problem in Joe's draft is designed to illustrate a different kind of plagiarism issue, including the problem of "common knowledge," the pitfalls of misattribution, and multiple incorrect forms of citation, to name but a few. It was vital, too, for the academic integrity of this exercise, that the sources are not fabricated for the sake of illustrating a point. I did my research: I went to the library, checked out all of the sources that the original paper had used, and then cross-checked each sentence with the original source to see how I could tweak the paper in the most pedagogically useful way.

You may also decide to create your own materials for an exercise along the same lines if you'd like to use a piece of student writing from your archives that better suits the themes of your course. Just a heads up that it's a time-consuming proposition. A good sample paper to convert into a "Sloppy Joe" document can come from almost anywhere in the university, and it can address almost any subject.

HANDOUT 1:

"The Princeton Battle Monument, Draft" by "Sloppy Joe"

THE PRINCETON BATTLE MONUMENT

The Princeton Battle Monument, designed by sculptor Frederick MacMonnies to commemorate the Battle of Princeton, fought on January 3, 1777, was dedicated on June 9, 1922, **almost 150 years later. It was** inspired by the engravings on the Arc de Triomphe in Paris, France. **The monument, impressive in its grandeur, was not only built** "in honor of the 'Battle of Princeton,' **but also** in memory of General Hugh Mercer," **as Allan Marquand said.** "Concerning the battle field monuments," **Marquand continues**, the town gave $20,000 for its construction. **That was an impressive sum, especially back then! But although the monument was** "dedicated . . . to heroism" (Kirk 103), monuments also have the function of synthesizing the hero's moral lesson for children of soldiers and their children to follow. **Kirk's point is that a** didactic **monument like this one can teach us something about our past and inform us about our future. But is this monument** a little too much a little too late, **Clark, a scholar of the Princeton Battlefield, questions.**

One hundred and ten years after the Princeton battle, there was a meeting at the Nassau Hotel in order to figure out how to build a proper tribute. Mr. John F. Hageman organized the meeting. He was the Chairman and he was with Mr. Charles S. Robinson who served as secretary (**Marquand 7–8**). **But it was important that this battle was memorialized because it was a dramatic battle in which Washington planned** "to bag the fox" in the morning **with his** "brilliant nocturnal maneuvers," **as Robert Judson Clark so aptly chronicles.** Princeton, like a woman waiting **for a loved one to return home and longingly gazing out the window,** was rewarded with a monument that ranks up there with others. **It is curious that a monument, however, would be built so much after the fact and it makes one wonder what the role of the monument really might be.**

WORKS CITED

Clark, Robert Judson. "Part II: The Princeton Battle Monument: A Documentary Essay." *Record of the Art Museum, Princeton University* 43, no. 2 (1984): 27–59.

Gauss, Christian. "An Account of the Dedication of the Princeton Battle Monument." In *The Princeton Battle Monument: The History of the Monument, a Record of the Ceremonies Attending its Unveiling, and an Account of the Battle of Princeton*, 23–42. Princeton, NJ: Princeton University Press, 1922.

Marquand, Allan. "The History of the Princeton Battle Monument." In *The Princeton Battle Monument: The History of the Monument, a Record of the Ceremonies Attending its Unveiling, and an Account of the Battle of Princeton*, 5–22. Princeton, NJ: Princeton University Press, 1922.

"Princeton Battle Monument." *Wikipedia*. Accessed September 21, 2016. en.wikipedia .org/wiki/Princeton_Battle_Monument.

Savage, Kirk. "Trauma, Healing, and the Therapeutic Monument." In *Terror, Culture, Politics: Rethinking 9/11*, edited by Daniel J. Sherman and Terry Nardin, 103–20. Bloomington: Indiana University Press, 2006.

HANDOUT 2:

"Joe's Sources"

Source #1: Marquand, Allan. "The History of the Princeton Battle Monument." In *The Princeton Battle Monument: The History of the Monument, a Record of the Ceremonies Attending its Unveiling, and an Account of the Battle of Princeton*, 5–22. Princeton, NJ: Princeton University Press, 1922.

#1a) From page 16: By 1907 the moving spirits of the old Battle Monument Association had passed away and new men and other minds took the lead . . . So we selected our sculptor, Mr. Frederick MacMonnies, and left the form of the monument in his hands.

#1b) From pages 7–8: Exactly one hundred and ten years after the battle of Princeton a meeting was called at the Nassau Hotel with a view to procuring a suitable monument. The meeting was called to order by Mr. John F. Hageman as chairman and Mr. Charles S. Robinson as Secretary. After discussion, a long preamble and the following Resolutions were passed:

I. Resolved, That we will proceed to provide and erect a suitable "Monument" in honor of the "Battle of Princeton" and in memory of General Hugh Mercer, and that we will ask our fellow citizens and Legislature of New Jersey for such assistance as will entitle us to demand and receive, under the acts of Congress, "concerning the battle field monuments," the further sum of $20,000.

#1c) From page 7: and now at last Princeton is about to be rewarded for her patient waiting by a monument which in beauty and interest at least will rank with any of the rest.

Source #2: "Princeton Battle Monument." *Wikipedia*. Accessed September 21, 2016. en.wikipedia.org/wiki/Princeton_Battle_Monument.

The Princeton Battle Monument is located in Princeton, New Jersey, adjacent to Morven and Princeton's borough hall. The Monument commemorates the January 3, 1777 Battle of Princeton, and depicts General George Washington leading his troops to victory and the death of General Hugh Mercer. It stands 50 feet (15 m) tall and was inspired by engravings on the Arc de Triomphe in the heart of Paris.

Source #3: Gauss, Christian. "An Account of the Dedication of the Princeton Battle Monument." In *The Princeton Battle Monument: The History of the Monument, a Record of the Ceremonies Attending its Unveiling, and an Account of the Battle of Princeton*, 23–42. Princeton, NJ: Princeton University Press, 1922.

From page 25: It is the part of patriotism to keep alive such associations, and Princeton has been rich in impressive commemorations. The latest and in many ways the most important of these was the dedication, on June 9, 1922, of the Princeton Battle Monument, erected as a lasting memorial to those who participated in Washington's critical campaign of the winter of 1776 and 1777.

Source #4: Savage, Kirk. "Trauma, Healing, and the Therapeutic Monument." In *Terror, Culture, Politics: Rethinking 9/11*, edited by Daniel J. Sherman and Terry Nardin, 103–20. Bloomington: Indiana University Press, 2006.

From page 103: Dedicated as they were to heroism, public monuments were not meant to be therapeutic. They were didactic, condensing the moral lesson of the hero or the event for future generations.

Source #5: Clark, Robert Judson. "Part II: The Princeton Battle Monument: A Documentary Essay." *Record of the Art Museum, Princeton University* 43, no. 2 (1984): 27–59.

#5a) From page 27: Commissioned in 1908 and finally completed fourteen years later, the Princeton Battlefield (Figure 1) has long since been the focus of local arguments and vituperation. It has seldom, however, been the object of scholarly attention. Usually regarded as being too much, too late, the conception is so thoroughly indebted to the arts of the nineteenth century that it has dwelt uneasily in the twentieth.

#5b) From page 27: Lord Cornwallis planned to "bag the fox" in the morning, and thereby end the war. Washington responded with another brilliant nocturnal maneuver.

HANDOUT 3:
"The Princeton Battle Monument, Revision" by "Neater Joe"

The Effect of the Great War on a Monument for the American Revolution

The Princeton Battle Monument was built by American Renaissance sculptor Frederick MacMonnies (Marquand 16). Although MacMonnies was contacted as early as 1907 to begin the project (Marquand 16), the monument was finally finished on June 9, 1922, almost 150 years after the battle was fought (Gauss 25). The monument, "inspired by engravings on the Arc de Triomphe" in Paris, France, and erected to commemorate the Battle of Princeton, is in Princeton, New Jersey ("Princeton Battle Monument" n.d.). Because of the great separation in time between the battle and the construction of the corresponding memorial, one would be hard-pressed to argue that any motivation for its construction stemmed from an emotional need to process the battle's violence and destruction. Allan Marquand, a former art historian of Princeton University, cites the original preamble from one of the first meetings about the monument in his essay "The History of the Princeton Battle Monument," and shows that the organizers intended to erect the monument "in honor of the 'Battle of Princeton' and in memory of General Hugh Mercer" (as cited in Marquand 8). Other than the Preamble's mention of General Mercer, which we see through Marquand's citation, there is no indication that the founders intended the monument to preserve the memory of the soldiers who died in the battle. Thus, the original purpose of the monument was in line with Kirk Savage's definition of a "didactic" monument, in other words, a monument that is "dedicated [. . .] to heroism [. . .] condensing the moral lesson of the hero or the event for future generations" (103). Yet despite these initial impressions, the Princeton Battle Monument in its final form does not function in a solely didactic manner. There is too much pain and too much disorder in the mass of bodies that clogs the bottom of the MacMonnies sculpture. It is impossible for one monument to capture the trauma of this war. Robert Judson Clark, who was an art history professor at Princeton University and is a recognized expert on the Princeton Battle Monument, notes that scholars generally consider the monument "as being too much, too late" (27). The dramatic aspect of the memorial is evidence of the impact of the Great War, which coincided with the development of the memorial, on MacMonnies' design. Thus, the combination of the monument's temporal distance from the event and the effect of the Great War on its development has made the Princeton Battle Monument unique among memorials: it simultaneously serves its intended purpose as a detached didactic monument and effectively conveys the sense of loss that accompanies all wars.

WORKS CITED

Clark, Robert Judson. "Part II: The Princeton Battle Monument: A Documentary Essay." *Record of the Art Museum, Princeton University* 43, no. 2 (1984): 27–59.

Gauss, Christian. "An Account of the Dedication of the Princeton Battle Monument." In *The Princeton Battle Monument: The History of the Monument, a Record of the Ceremonies Attending its Unveiling, and an Account of the Battle of Princeton*, 23–42. Princeton, NJ: Princeton University Press, 1922.

Marquand, Allan. "The History of the Princeton Battle Monument." In *The Princeton Battle Monument: The History of the Monument, a Record of the Ceremonies Attending its Unveiling, and an Account of the Battle of Princeton*, 5–22. Princeton, NJ: Princeton University Press, 1922.

"Princeton Battle Monument." *Wikipedia*. Accessed September 21, 2016. en.wikipedia.org/wiki/Princeton_Battle_Monument.

Savage, Kirk. "Trauma, Healing, and the Therapeutic Monument." *Terror, Culture, Politics: Rethinking 9/11*, edited by Daniel J. Sherman and Terry Nardin, 103–20. Bloomington: Indiana University Press, 2006.

Bag the Fox: The Teacher's Edition

At first glance, this exercise looks far simpler than it really is. A close read of Sloppy Joe's draft introduction reveals intricate citation problems and nuances, with each sentence showcasing at least one academic integrity issue. It is therefore important that the instructor review all the materials carefully beforehand to have an adequate understanding of the examples and their accompanying issues below:

Draft text: The Princeton Battle Monument, designed by sculptor Frederick MacMonnies to commemorate the Battle of Princeton, fought on January 3, 1777, was dedicated on June 9, 1922, almost 150 years later. It was inspired by the engravings on the Arc de Triomphe in Paris, France.

> Issues: These sentences are meant to debunk the myth that you don't have to cite "background information" because that's "common knowledge." This passage is far too detailed to qualify as common knowledge, and background information must be cited in any case. Not citing paraphrased sentences counts as plagiarism, and changing around "a few words" is risky business. You could have students read the *Wikipedia* entry aloud and they will immediately see that the writer lifted many of the same words (e.g., "commemorate") and maintained a similar structure, both of which constitute problematic paraphrase. What is the "tipping point" that makes this sentence *not* count as common knowledge? How do we think about the reliability of nonacademic sources like Wikipedia and the role they play in our research?

Draft text: The monument, impressive in its grandeur, was not only built "in honor of the 'Battle of Princeton,' but also in memory of General Hugh Mercer," as Allan Marquand said. "Concerning the battle field monuments," Marquand continues, the town gave $20,000 for its construction.

> Issues: The student is attributing the quote to Marquand, but the cited phrases actually come from a *"Preamble"* that Marquand himself cites. Thus, the student attributes something to Marquand that he didn't actually say. It's important to acknowledge when you are quoting a source that is embedded in another source. You can't pretend, for example, that you consulted a book or an archive when you read about it in a secondary text. The last part of the sentence is uncited though it is clearly evidence taken from the source. It also misinterprets this evidence: $20,000 appears to

have been requested from Congress, but the student writes that it comes from the town.

Draft text: But although the monument was "dedicated . . . to heroism" (Kirk 103), monuments also have the function of synthesizing the hero's moral lesson for children of soldiers and their children to follow. Kirk's point is that a didactic monument like this one can teach us something about our past and inform us about our future.

Issues: Even though this passage contains a citation, it still has numerous issues. To begin, the student is citing the scholar's first name, "Kirk," and not his *last* name (Savage). Although we want students to feel like they have authority, we are not on a first name basis with our sources. The citation also comes in the middle of the sentence, which suggests that only the quotation comes from Savage. But the rest of the sentence is an awkward attempt at paraphrasing material that *also* comes from Savage. The word "didactic" carries analytical weight for the source, but by not citing it the student is (intentionally or otherwise) passing it off as his or her own. Finally, the writer makes it seem as though Savage is discussing the Princeton Battle Monument in particular, when, in fact, Savage is theorizing about monuments more generally.

Draft text: But is this monument a little too much a little too late, Clark, a scholar of the Princeton Battlefield, questions.

Issues: The original reads "as being too much, too late," so the student has barely changed the phrasing and then doesn't cite it. Naming the source—Clark—in-text is insufficient, so this qualifies as an especially bad uncited paraphrase. More broadly, this is not *Clark's* question, but rather his reflection on the state of the field. *Other scholars* think the monument was too much, too late; Clark doesn't take a position one way or the other.

Draft text: One hundred and ten years after the Princeton battle, there was a meeting at the Nassau Hotel in order to figure out how to build a proper tribute. Mr. John F. Hageman organized the meeting. He was the Chairman and he was with Mr. Charles S. Robinson who served as secretary (Marquand 7–8).

Issues: The student reproduces the information in the exact order in which it appears in the original, making this patch writing rather than paraphrase, though at least it's cited.

Draft text: But it was important that this battle was memorialized because it was a dramatic battle in which Washington planned "to bag the fox" in the morning with his "brilliant nocturnal maneuvers," as Robert Judson Clark so aptly chronicles.

Issues: The student misinterprets the source: it was *Lord Cornwallis* who "who planned to bag the fox in the morning" and Washington who wowed with a *singular* "brilliant nocturnal maneuver." The student only put part of what was being quoted in quotation marks, and there is no citation.

Draft text: Princeton, like a woman waiting for a loved one to return home and longingly gazing out the window, was rewarded with a monument that ranks up there with others.

Issues: This is not only bad paraphrase without citation, but the writer has commandeered the source's central metaphor and run with it to a truly strange place.

ON QUOTATION VS. PARAPHRASE VS. SUMMARY

Instructors may wish to refer to the following when discussing the distinctions introduced in step four.

Quotation: The incorporation of a source's exact text, verbatim, into your document so that readers access that material directly. Quotations must be marked, either in line by " " or indented as block quotes, with a full citation so that readers can find the original location of the text. Writers must not cherry-pick quotes that distort their meaning in the absence of the original context. Visual representations—works of art or presentations of data in graphs, charts, or the like—may be "quoted" as well, and the same citation rules apply.

Paraphrase: A rendering of concepts or evidence from a source wholly in your own words. A good paraphrase is usually similar in length to the material cited because it retains its substance and complexity. Paraphrases should avoid word choice and phrasing that is similar to the original, though they should maintain key terms. Longer paraphrases should also alter the original's structure. A bad paraphrase, which veers too close to quotation or fails to revise structurally, is sometimes called *patch writing*, and is problematic even when cited.

Summary: A distillation of the main ideas of a source wholly in your own words. A good summary is a condensed version of the material cited that draws out its most important elements. Summaries should also avoid unattributed word choice and phrasing that is similar to the original, and take care to cite examples or specific evidence from sources properly.

LIGHTNING STRIKES

What to Do in Fifteen Minutes or Less

Looking for something constructive to do with fifteen minutes (or less) of class time? Some of these speedy interventions are adapted from earlier exercises in the book, (references included below). Others are time-tested writing classroom go-tos.

TITLE WORKSHOP

As students near a revision deadline and need to lock down a title, offer the classic "Intriguing Title: Informative Subtitle" formula as a template. Students individually brainstorm a short list of key terms at play in their paper and then draw two or three from this list to devise a tentative title. The first attempt at a title typically leaves key terms in loose relationship with each other ("x, y, and z") and lands on a generic statement of topic. To show students how to convert a blanket title into a more specific, informative, or engaging one, ask for a volunteer who would like to benefit from the instant feedback of their friendly neighborhood readers. Write the title on the board and lead a miniature, five-minute draft workshop, guiding the class as they ask the writer clarifying questions about their title, pushing for a better understanding of the relationship between the terms and, ideally, at least a hint at the thesis. The results can be dramatic: by honing one line of text, the writer can get a handle on the crux of their argument. For example:

Starting point: "Restoring the Sistine Chapel"
Revision phase 1: "Restoring the Sistine Chapel: Michelangelo, Memory, and Morals"
Revision phase 2: "What's Authentic Anyway?: Patterns of Censorship and Revelation in the Sistine Chapel Fresco Restoration"

REVERSE OUTLINE

Have students distill the main point of each paragraph in a text into one sentence in the margin, whether working with an assigned source or on their own paper drafts. In the former case, the reverse outline helps a student better understand the progression of a potentially confusing or complicated argument.

In the latter case, it helps them identify areas of repetition or logical leaps in their own structure by offering a bird's-eye perspective. A micro version of this tactic also works well for breaking down the role each sentence is playing in a particular paragraph.

HAIKU

Working within creative constraints can produce especially clear or fresh thinking. After asking students to do some analytical work on their own—whether it's evaluation of a primary text, making a constructive suggestion for a peer's draft, or really anything—have them share their work in haiku form (five syllables, seven syllables, five syllables). Give students a few minutes to draft, and reassure them that, for this exercise, bad haikus are the best haikus. Each must be read aloud and as dramatically as possible for full effect. The gimmick can be unleashed for a wide range of classroom purposes:

> Early in your course
> Haikus can break the ice and
> Build community.
>
> Students share their name
> And draft haikus revealing
> Their superpower.

MOTIVE LAYER CAKE

To help students sort out the complexity of motive, serve it up with a delicious slice of metaphor and ask them to imagine each element as one layer of a four-layer cake. Supplement with clip art, an excerpt from *The Great British Baking Show*—or real cake. The students' job is to articulate each layer of their emerging motive in a single, succinct sentence, stacking one on top of the next:

1. The question, problem, puzzle, surprise, or tension they have located within their primary object of study.
2. Scholarly motive, or how they are differentiating their contribution from what has already been said by others.
3. Big-picture motive, or why/how the argument matters in a larger context.
4. Personal motive, or why they specifically are interested or invested in the topic.

Remind students that personal motive is often a layer of the cake they get to keep for themselves—it is not usually made explicit in academic writing. The other three layers, however, should be performed on the page. You might limit students to just a couple of layers at a time, depending on the assignment and the progress they've made. There isn't a prescribed sequence for the layers, but the exercise can spark discussion about the relationships between them and alternatives for effectively structuring an introduction.

IN SEVERAL NUTSHELLS

When introducing a barrage of new scholarly texts, help students hone their at-first-glance evaluation skills with a crowdsourcing exercise. Open a shared document for the class and assign each pair or small group of students a different text to work with. Invite them to sum up the gist of the argument in a nutshell of two or three sentences, relying on key elements of the text (e.g., abstract or introduction). Once summaries have been drafted, have the pairs or small groups shift gears to offer feedback on the nutshell description that appears just below theirs in the document. Guide them to pose questions, note moments that strike them as repetitive or extraneous, or point to important gaps where they would need more information to grasp the argument. The exercise has the added benefit of serving as a DIY overview of upcoming course material.

THE BORING PAPER

Give students a minute to consider the essay assignment they're working on, and then draft the thesis statement of "the boring paper." This thesis is the too-obvious, we've-seen-this-a-thousand-times-before argument that students may unconsciously commit to *before* seriously engaging with the evidence. The boring paper imposes simplicity on complexity, often by taking a preexisting side in an assumed binary—"Affirmative action in university admissions is un/justified" or "Hamlet was/n't in possession of his senses"—when deeper analysis of the evidence will inevitably uncover levels of nuance that should lead to more motivated, and therefore less boring, theses. Have students solemnly read their boring theses aloud, perhaps tearing apart the paper on which they are written in a cleansing ritual to ward against a future in which they turn in "the boring paper."

SAVE THE STRAW MEN

A close relative of the boring paper, this tactic also inverts the exercise "The Principle of Charity" (pg 102). Ask students to begin by identifying two or three main sources or arguments their thesis opposes and then draft *intentionally* weak, straw man versions of each. These might be exaggerated (mis)interpretations that are more vulnerable to criticism, or overtly distorted articulations that the authors themselves wouldn't endorse. But the straw men should be semi-plausible misreads of the originals that an inattentive reader might actually believe the authors intended, and not complete fabrications. Explicitly identifying them early on makes it less likely that writers will succumb to cheap victories in their finished papers—and more likely that they will engage rigorously with their sources at full strength.

THE FALCON ALWAYS SWOOPS TWICE

As a hedge against "the boring paper," redeploy "Project Falcon" (pg 173) and its Four Questions test (arguable, manageable, interesting, important). It works for any assignment where students have a tentative thesis and motive to workshop. As assignments become more complex, "Project Falcon" also invites reflective questions about the four dimensions of an argument under scrutiny. What, for example, counts as "interesting" or "important" when students are required to generate their own research question in a field rather than working within the constraint of assigned course texts?

SYMPATHY FOR THE DEVIL

In draft workshops (pg 156) where students are hesitant to critique a peer's writing, or when you arrive at an unhelpful consensus about a text or claim under discussion, deputize one or more students to play devil's advocate. Make clear that their role is to advance contrary positions and make the best case for them, whether or not they agree. Issue your demonic promotions with care: you want students who will be reasonably comfortable and capable in the role, but beware students who may enjoy it a little too much. As advocates, their cases must be persuasive following the usual draft workshop etiquette and conventions. No fire or brimstone permitted.

FOLLOW THE FOOTNOTES

To make real the idea of scholarship as a conversation across texts, and to teach students to sketch out evolving debates quickly, pick a scholarly source that both draws on several important predecessors and is engaged in turn by later writers. Each author contributing to the meta-conversation should be discussing the same topic, even if they do so in different ways, and this should ideally be obvious by looking at the citation. This means you want writers who are influential but not *so* influential that they go viral across several fields. (Marx, for example, is a very bad choice.) In small groups, have students curate a short list of citations—no more than six—that they would consult to pursue the debate further. They can refer to the footnotes or other bibliographical material in the source text itself, but you can also point students to a database or citation index that allows them to track that conversation forward in time. Debrief about what they included in their short list of citations and why, and what they think the texts they chose probably do. Just as importantly, discuss what they *excluded*, and why they thought some candidates were (probably) less relevant. It's possible, of course, to do a longer version of an exercise along these lines. But the goal in this context is to underscore the importance of quick assessment strategies, as research possibilities are limitless but lifespans are not.

FINDING YOUR KEYS

Whereas "Losing Your Keys" (pg 189) demonstrates key terms' power by taking them away, this tactic shows off their utility by engaging them alone, excluding the rest of the text. When students are struggling with a difficult theoretical or scholarly source, put them in small groups and ask them to identify the three to five key terms they think are most relevant to its argument. Reconvene to crowdsource the options and curate five to seven to write on the board. Ask a volunteer to explain the link the author makes—or *should* make—between any two key terms of the student's choice. Invite other students to offer their own alternative formulations of that link or revise an earlier account. From there, enlist a new volunteer to link one of those terms to a third on the list. Continue with new volunteers until most or all of the permutations have been described. By the end of the discussion, students should have both pieced together the complex meaning of the text, and also identified some potential questions about or weaknesses in the author's claim. This intervention also works well for students' own drafts-in-progress when they're having trouble clarifying the core concepts at stake in their argument and the relationships between them.

INTERPRETIVE IMPROV

Revisit the generative game of composing a rough thesis statement in which you go around the room and have each student contribute one word that builds on the last (see "Thesis Improv" on page 72). This time, rather than using the exercise to transition between discussion and drafting, instead use the improv method to initiate the discussion of a new source. In small groups, have students improvise a provocative but defensible claim about the source and then write them on the board. Use their statements as tentative interpretations to ground your discussion.

NEEDS MORE YELLOW!

To help students discern the relationship between claims, evidence, and analysis in an assigned reading, or to evaluate the balance among these elements in a partner's draft, bring back the highlighters from "Tying Down Your Thought Balloons" (pg 205). Give each student three different highlighters and ask them to color code as much as they can in five minutes before comparing notes with their partner. Especially in early drafts, students tend to under-analyze their evidence when making claims, hence the need for more yellow.

ABOUT THE EDITORS

Amanda Irwin Wilkins began her Writing Center work as an undergraduate peer tutor at Haverford College, received her PhD in comparative literature from Princeton University, and has served as Director of the Princeton Writing Program since 2009. Amanda's interdisciplinary writing seminars for first-year students focus on individual and collective memory, and the landscape of home. She has also co-taught a writing-intensive geosciences course for sophomores on measuring climate change. Together with Princeton's McGraw Center for Teaching and Learning, Amanda facilitates a pedagogy colloquium for faculty designing departmental methods seminars.

Keith Shaw received his PhD in political science from Stanford University and is Director of Transfer and Outreach for the Emma Bloomberg Center for Access and Opportunity. He built and runs Princeton's programs for transfer, veteran, and nontraditional students, and teaches a customized writing seminar for transfer students entitled "Everyone's an Expert," which explores the intersections between authority, knowledge, and democracy. A member of the Warrior Scholar Project's Academic Advisory, Keith co-teaches the writing curriculum of its annual humanities bootcamp at Princeton. He is a former Associate Director of the Princeton Writing Program.

SERIES EDITORS

Diana Fuss is the Louis W. Fairchild Class of '24 Professor of English at Princeton University.

William A. Gleason is the Hughes-Rogers Professor of English and American Studies at Princeton University.

CONTRIBUTORS

Megan Brankley Abbas is Assistant Professor of Religion at Colgate University.

Raphael Allison has taught writing at Princeton, New York University, and Bard College.

Nimisha Barton is a visiting researcher at University of California Irvine.

Fannie Bialek is Assistant Professor of Religion and Politics at Washington University in St. Louis.

Loren B. Byrne is Professor of Biology and Environmental Science at Roger Williams University in Bristol, Rhode Island.

Jacqueline Campbell is a graduate student in English at Princeton University.

Sarah Case is a lecturer in the Princeton Writing Program at Princeton University.

Sean Cashbaugh is a lecturer in the Princeton Writing Program at Princeton University.

Daniel M. Choi has taught writing at Princeton University.

Christopher W. Close is Professor of History at Saint Joseph's University.

Aaron Colton is Associate Teaching Professor and the Director of First Year Writing in the Department of English at Emory University.

Geneviève A. Creedon is Director of the Scholarly Writing Program at Indiana University.

Alexander K. Davis is a senior lecturer in the Princeton Writing Program at Princeton University.

Anne Freeland is a lecturer in Latin American and Iberian Cultures at Columbia University.

Diana Fuss is Professor of English at Princeton University.

Andy Hakim is Director of College Success, Academic Affairs in the Emma Bloomberg Center for Access and Opportunity at Princeton University.

Tim Haupt is Assistant Manager of the Special Projects Division at MedStudy.

Briallen Hopper is Assistant Professor of English at Queens College of the City University of New York.

Amanda Irwin Wilkins is Director of the Princeton Writing Program at Princeton University.

Peter G. Johannessen is Assistant Professor of Public Policy in the Frank Batten School of Leadership and Public Policy at the University of Virginia.

Marcus Johnson is Assistant Professor of Government and Politics at the University of Maryland, College Park.

Soo La Kim is Assistant Dean of Graduate Programs in the School of Professional Studies at Northwestern University.

Leah Klement is an education specialist at the University of California at San Diego.

Christopher M. Kurpiewski is Associate Director for the Writing Seminars in the Princeton Writing Program at Princeton University.

David L. Lindauer is Professor Emeritus of Economics at Wellesley College and director of the Calderwood Seminars in Public Writing Program.

Emma Ljung is a lecturer in the Princeton Writing Program at Princeton University.

Andrea Mazzariello is Assistant Professor of Music at Carleton College.

Roblin Meeks is Senior Associate Dean and Chief Academic Officer of the Macaulay Honors College of the City University of New York.

Patrick Thomas Morgan is Assistant Professor of English and the Dr. William R. Hammond Endowed Professor in Liberal Arts at the University of Louisiana Monroe.

Jonathan Niles-Weed is Assistant Professor of Mathematics and Data at New York University.

Dael A. Norwood is Assistant Professor of History at the University of Delaware.

Rebecca Rainof is a lecturer and associate researcher in English at the University of California, Berkeley.

Linsday Reckson is Associate Professor of English at Haverford College.

Leslie Ribovich is Assistant Professor of Religion in the Religion Program at Transylvania University.

Sajan Saini is an education director in the Initiative for Knowledge and Innovation in Manufacturing at Massachusetts Institute of Technology.

John Schulz teaches English at the Hun School of Princeton.

Liora Selinger is a lecturer in the Princeton Writing Program at Princeton University.

Keith Shaw is Director of Transfer and Outreach, Emma Bloomberg Center for Access and Opportunity, at Princeton University.

Ardon Z. Shorr is a lecturer in the Princeton Writing Program and Writing in Science and Engineering at Princeton University.

Amy L. Shuster is visiting Assistant Professor of Philosophy at Denison University.

Aditi Sriram is Associate Professor of Writing at Shiv Nadar University, Chennai.

Judy Swan is Associate Director for Writing in Science and Engineering in the Princeton Writing Program at Princeton University.

Kerry Walk is President of University of the Arts in Philadelphia.

Benjamin D. Weber is Assistant Professor of English at Wheaton College, Illinois.

Benjamin Widiss is Associate Professor of Literature at Hamilton College.

Shannon K. Winston is a lecturer in the Kelley School of Business at Indiana University.

Marion Wrenn is Executive Director of Writing for the Division of Arts and Humanities at NYU Abu Dhabi.

Neil J. Young is an independent scholar in Los Angeles and an affiliated research scholar with the Schar School of Policy and Government at George Mason University.

FIVE CROSS-INDEXES TO HELP YOU PLAN AHEAD

EXERCISES THAT WORK PARTICULARLY WELL EARLY IN THE TERM

EXERCISES THAT WORK PARTICULARLY WELL LATE IN THE TERM

EXERCISES THAT CAN BE REPEATED OR FOLLOWED UP THROUGHOUT THE TERM

EXERCISES THAT REQUIRE OR RECOMMEND WRITING BEFORE CLASS

EXERCISES THAT REQUIRE OR RECOMMEND READING BEFORE CLASS

INDEX